EBERRON

MAGIC OF EBERRON

BRUCE R. CORDELL

STEPHEN SCHUBERT

CHRIS THOMASSON

Wizards OF THE COAST

EBERRON

MAGIC OF EBERRON™

DESIGN
BRUCE R CORDELL, STEPHEN SCHUBERT,
CHRIS THOMASSON

DEVELOPMENT
ANDY COLLINS, MICHAEL DONAIS, JESSE DECKER

EDITORS
CHRIS THOMASSON, SCOTT FITZGERALD GRAY

EDITING MANAGER
KIM MOHAN

DESIGN MANAGER
CHRISTOPHER PERKINS

DEVELOPMENT MANAGER
JESSE DECKER

DIRECTOR OF RPG R&D
BILL SLAVICSEK

ART DIRECTORS
RYAN SANSAVER

COVER ILLUSTRATION
WAYNE REYNOLDS

INTERIOR ARTISTS
ANNE STOKES
DAVID MICHAEL BECK
DRAXHALL JUMP ENTERTAINMENT
ERIC DESCHAMPS
FRANCIS TSAI
LUCIO PARRILLO
MARK TEDIN
STEVE PRESCOTT
TOMAS GIORELLO

GRAPHIC DESIGNER
LISA HANSON

CARTOGRAPHER
LEE MOYER

GRAPHIC PRODUCTION SPECIALIST
CARMEN CHEUNG, ERIN DORRIES

IMAGE TECHNICIAN
TRAVIS ADAMS

PRODUCTION MANAGERS
JOSHUA C.J. FISCHER
RANDALL CREWS

**U.S., CANADA, ASIA,
PACIFIC, & LATIN AMERICA**
Wizards of the Coast, Inc.
P.O. Box 707
Renton WA 98057–0707
(Questions?) 1–800–324–6496

EUROPEAN HEADQUARTERS
Hasbro UK Ltd
Caswell Way
Newport, Gwent NP9 0YH
GREAT BRITAIN
Please keep this address for your records

Based on the original DUNGEONS & DRAGONS® rules created by E. Gary Gygax and Dave Arneson, and
the new DUNGEONS & DRAGONS game designed by Jonathan Tweet, Monte Cook, Skip Williams, Richard
Baker, and Peter Adkison.
This product uses updated material from the v.3.5 revision.
This WIZARDS OF THE COAST® game product contains no Open Game Content. No portion of this work may
be reproduced in any form without written permission. To learn more about the Open Gaming License
and the d20 System License, please visit www.wizards.com/d20.

DUNGEONS & DRAGONS, D&D, DUNGEON MASTER, d20, d20 System, WIZARDS OF THE COAST, EBERRON, *Player's Handbook, Dungeon Master's Guide, Monster
Manual, Magic of Eberron,* all other Wizards of the Coast product names, and their respective logos are trademarks of Wizards of the Coast in the
U.S.A. and other countries. All Wizards characters, character names, and the distinctive likenesses thereof are property of Wizards of the Coast,
Inc. Distributed to the hobby, toy, and comic trade in the United States and Canada by regional distributors. Distributed in the United States to
the book trade by Holtzbrinck Publishing. Distributed in Canada to the book trade by Fenn Ltd. Distributed worldwide by Wizards of the Coast,
Inc. and regional distributors.
This material is protected under the copyright laws of the United States of America. Any reproduction or unauthorized use of the material or
artwork contained herein is prohibited without the express written permission of Wizards of the Coast, Inc. This product is a work of fiction. Any
similarity to actual people, organizations, places, or events is purely coincidental. Printed in the U.S.A. ©2005 Wizards of the Coast, Inc.

Visit our website at
www.wizards.com/dnd

620-88291720-001-EN   9 8 7 6 5 4 3 2 1   First Printing: October 2005   ISBN-10: 0-7869-3696-7   ISBN-13: 978-0-7869-3696-0

CONTENTS

Aldred slipped from the yellow grass, silent as a still breeze. The hunt was nearing its climax, and soon these daelkyr horrors would be erased from this world. . . .

The halfling abomination hunter glanced at the symbiont curled around his forearm. It was somehow fitting that Aldred used the daelkyr's own creation against them. As the daelkyr approached the corrupt mound, Aldred made his move. . . .

INTRODUCTION

Aldred flinched when he heard the scream.

The halfling paused, holding himself as still as a board. But his symbiont, the damned thing, kept twining and twisting on his arm.

"Quiet," he hissed. He doubted it would do any good. The stormstalk had a mind of its own.

Ahead, beyond the high, swaying grass that hid him, Aldred saw something move. Something . . . large? Is that what had screamed? Or . . . He'd have to risk moving closer. If Aldred had glimpsed his quarry, then he had no choice. He fitted an arrow to his composite longbow and pressed forward, almost to the edge of the tall grass.

A rude track stamped through the waving plain of yellow grass, under the damp gray sky. The track was used just often enough to keep it mostly clear of the crowding yellow blades. To Aldred's right, the path wandered away to hide around a grassy bend. To his left, the way ascended a bald hill. A dull gray obelisk squatted there.

"Gotcha," whispered Aldred. He recognized the style. It was like the Moon Portal.

Despite his zeal and dedication to his life's work, he knew he wasn't yet strong enough to brave the corrupt gates of the Moon Portal, where horrors unimaginable were pulled up from Khyber. Upon the hill was but a small temple, by its looks. It was in his power to slink in and see what his enemies were up to.

The horrors of the daelkyr were unmitigated nightmares to the average citizen of the Five Nations. But Aldred knew the enemy better than most. In fact, the halfling's fight against corruption had been infused with new strength after he had . . . co-opted some of the daelkyr's progeny for his own use. The symbiont squirmed on his arm again, as if reacting to his thoughts and seeking to lunge free.

Aldred stroked the wriggling snakelike creature, and looked into a single staring white eye, where static danced with impotent fury.

"Soon," crooned the halfling, "I'll let you discharge. The dolgrim trail ends here."

Indeed, he thought, what am I waiting for?

The impure prince stepped from the grass and ascended the hill.

WHAT IS MAGIC OF EBERRON?

When one speaks of magic in Eberron, one is also speaking of weather, or philosophy, or life itself. Magic is as varied, changing, and as little understood as all these, and it suffuses everything. It is part of the fabric of existence, dancing in the Ring of Siberys and echoing in the vaults of Khyber. Magic, whether it comes from some external but hidden source, or whether it seeps from the land itself as one more renewable resource that can be tapped and utilized, is without question the single most important aspect of the world.

But the word "magic" hides myriad categories of thaumaturgical workings, from essentially pedestrian alchemical marvels to the true miracles of artifice, elemental binding, and the magic of dragons. Beyond even that, the term "magic" can cover the corruptive influence of the daelkyr and their aberrational progeny, psionic power of the quori, and even more esoteric arts.

For instance, the homunculi employed by artificers can provide far more options for the experimenter than is generally understood. Indeed, enterprising artificers can choose not only different types of homunculi, but also to enhance homunculi they already own, increasing their constructs' armor, strength, and other qualities.

Just how are elementals bound into items or vessels? The process developed by the Zil is extensive and exacting, but if followed can lead to the perfect binding every time. Adventurous binders have gone so far as to develop elemental grafts, which function similarly to magic items, but which tie the essence of a living elemental to another creature's body.

What of the elves of Aerenal? They are little understood, and often feared because of their obsession with death. Solitary, mysterious, and disturbing, these elves form the basis of any number of rumors throughout Khorvaire. This tome promises to dispel some of those mysteries.

More truly diabolical are the necromantic arts of Karrnath. While Kaius III, current ruler of Karrnath, has publicly made plain that his nation no longer supports the creation of undead for military purposes, the truth is more nuanced.

In sum, the magic of Eberron is a vast field encompassing far more than can easily be identified in a single tome. It is a world in itself, filled with islands of thought and use that can be identified, clarified, and described in greater depth.

WHAT YOU NEED TO PLAY

Magic of Eberron is intended for use in any DUNGEONS & DRAGONS game. You will need the *Player's Handbook*, *Dungeon Master's Guide*, and *Monster Manual* to make use of the material in this book, and the EBERRON *Campaign Setting* is also a requirement to get the most out of the information described herein. In addition, you will find it useful to have the *Epic Level Handbook* and the *Expanded Psionics Handbook*, since this book includes references that utilize rules found in those books.

Vamirese strained to keep the fire elemental from slipping free of the damaged airship, but the Karrnathi skeleton wasn't making her work any easier. . . .

The airship, its fiery ring shattered, spiraled toward the fast-approaching ground, as the fire elemental shrugged off the magic that bound it. . . .

Lord ir'Krast sennndz hizzz regarrrdz . . ." the skeleton said, its voice like ragged nails dragged across dry stone, ". . . and hopes you diiiie painfulllly . . ."

CHAPTER ONE

MAGIC IN EBERRON

Magic is as prevalent among Eberron's many cultures as it is on nearly any other world. But Eberron's magic is not static—it constantly evolves, like a species of living creature (or, more accurately, several species in delicate balance—or open warfare). As some types of magic are used, they are refined, combined, and improved. Other magic lends itself well to the application of simple technological synergies. One approach to magic might be lost and fall out of usage for thousands of years, only to be later rediscovered and either embraced or banned. Sometimes disparate forms of magic come to influence each other, creating entirely new strains of power that can realize tasks that neither magical antecedent could have accomplished. In many cases, magic is harnessed to build the infrastructure of society itself.

The fabric of the Five Nations is built upon magic—it pervades and infuses the life of each and every creature on Khorvaire. The utilization of magic provides comforts and conveniences whose mere nature is undreamt of in less developed worlds, or in the more savage regions of Eberron. The castles and towers whose heights scrape the skies would not reach so tall without a magical foundation. Quick and efficient transport to all corners of the Five Nations, and even across continents, is aided or depends entirely upon the utilization of special applications of magic.

Eberron is awash in arcane, divine, and psionic energy, and it has developed not through the studious application of science, but through the mastery of various mystic secrets. Magic is so important, in fact, that a working class of minor mages, called magewrights, provides the services that keep society moving forward.

In a broader sense, it must be recalled that magic has no single face. While it would be accurate to say that the world of the Five Nations is drowning in magic, it takes so many different forms, is called into existence in so many ways, and requires such a myriad of sacrifices from those who would work it, that no one mortal can hope to master more than one or two types. Those who wish to stretch their minds beyond their chosen field in an attempt to encompass more magical styles can only be called dabblers. While some magic practitioners are happy to be considered jacks-of-all-trades, masters of none, those who specialize discover that the heights of a particular type of magic have much to offer.

This chapter touches on various approaches to the magic and psionics practiced across Eberron, from the most common to those less popular (although not necessarily less powerful). This chapter provides new hints, secrets, rituals, a few sites, and even a racial legend or two to supplement each sort of magic presented. All the philosophies of magic described and framed in this introductory chapter thread into other chapters of this book, spawning specific prestige classes, feats, spells, creatures, races, or items, depending on the magic involved. Pointers to related material in later chapters are given in sidebars.

ARTIFICE

The great towers of Sharn, the flying ships of House Lyrandar, and the warforged that fought for the Five Nations during the Last War owe their existence, in part, to artificers. The more prominent the artificers' role in the world, the more necessary they have become to the day-to-day existence of the average Eberron inhabitant. Artificers also become mighty adventurers, exploring the wilds and performing mighty deeds alongside other heroes.

No discussion about artifice could really be complete without mention of House Cannith. Those who sport the Mark of Making do not have a monopoly on all artifice magic done in Khorvaire, despite what some of that family believe. Like any family, Cannith has its saints and black sheep, and like any power, artifice can be used for good or ill. Of those who practice artifice in the name of House Cannith in the city of Sharn, Baron Merrix is suspected of doing more ill than good—a man with an unhealthy obsession for obtaining ancient schemas, at any price.

MERRIX'S FORGE

No artificer in the country of Breland receives training without hearing a few rumors about a secret creation forge that Baron Merrix supposedly hides in the bowels of one of Sharn's many towers. But not only does Merrix continue to produce more warforged, the artifice-mad maker is relentless in his research concerning the disposition of any and all schemas. While not a few schemas might yet lie in the blowing wastes of the Mournland, Merrix also seeks schemas from the lands that originally birthed them: Xen'drik. To this end, he sometimes dispatches groups to that southern continent (usually by proxy) to stir up schemas or news of the same.

Any artificer would give her left hand to be able to spend but one day in Merrix's forge and subsidiary study, library, and laboratory. His understanding of artifice magic is a generation ahead of that of any other master who now studies in the field, and the tools and infusions he employs on a daily basis are said to surpass (or at least equal) those lost when Cyre was destroyed and the premier Cannith facility, Whitehearth, was lost.

At the most basic level, Baron Merrix uses infusions that are not widely known, and artificers who gain access to his resources might gain access to new sources of power.

Adventure Idea

—A rival of Merrix wants to discover what he's really up to in his creation forge. The PCs are challenged with penetrating the most legendary laboratory in Eberron.

WHITEHEARTH

Whitehearth was the facility where House Cannith created magic weapons to sell to each of the five great nations during the Last War. Prior to the war's end, Whitehearth was situated in the nation of Cyre. Spells and items considered too dangerous or volatile to test near civilization were developed at the facility as well. While no one is sure whether the magewrights, artificers, and wizards present in the facility were responsible for the Day of Mourning, the energies from that terrible event certainly penetrated the facility's confines. Most of the Cannith family members and staff perished instantly, while others quickly followed when the destabilized magical experiments cycled beyond control. Now chaos rules the halls of Whitehearth.

Word has spread that a recent expedition, commissioned by Baron Merrix, has successfully returned from Whitehearth. If true, it might mean that the wider facility is now open to exploration, beyond the mere top-level laboratories that the Merrix-sponsored expedition visited in its short foray. Perhaps new schemas wait inside Whitehearth's halls to transform the magic of artifice.

Adventure Idea

—Reports indicate that daelkyr agents have infested Whitehearth. Worse, they have penetrated the deeper, hidden levels that House Cannith thought had been permanently sealed on the Day of Mourning. If the secrets of making and the relics important to House Cannith are to remain sacrosanct, someone must be sent to sanitize and reseal the lower levels of Whitehearth.

LEARNING NEW INFUSIONS

Infusions are neither arcane nor divine, but these spell-like rites are central to artifice magic. Using infusions, an artificer can imbue an item or construct with special qualities and abilities.

Many artificers throughout Eberron have continued to evolve their infusions. They might create entirely new infusions or find an ancient schema with instructions on a new magical technique. The infusions in this book represent a small portion of the widely varying infusions in use.

When incorporating new infusions into a campaign, two primary options exist. A DM could simply allow an artificer to use any infusion she is of an appropriate level to cast. This option provides a character with a small upgrade to her existing list of infusions, but only a few at each level. The second option is to require an artificer to learn new infusions. These infusions could be found in ancient ruins or provided by an exclusive guild or organization.

To learn a new infusion and add it to her list, an artificer must make a Spellcraft check (DC 20 + infusion level). If she fails the check, she can try again when she gains another rank in Spellcraft, assuming she still has access to the new infusion.

ELEMENTAL BINDING

Spellcasters across Khorvaire began experimenting with the process of binding elementals to their service long ago. However, the gnomes of Zilargo, with the aid of House Cannith, have been the most successful at turning the esoteric theories of elemental binding to a profit. Magical knowledge of any sort is difficult to keep entirely under wraps, and some small groups across Khorvaire have begun duplicating the experiments that result in elemental items. The gnomes remain on the forefront of elemental binding magical research, though, and some in Zilargo have recently begun taking their experiments with elementals to the next level (see the Power of Purity organization description on page 34).

In the modern era, the Zil were the first to master the process of elemental binding, and by and large, the gnomes retain their secrets. Thus, gnomes from Zilargo are responsible for the majority of elemental-bound items and vehicles seen in and around the Five Nations today. House Cannith runs the workshops in Zilargo and helps design and craft the items to which the elementals are bound, but the gnomes

---

ARTIFICE IN THIS BOOK

Chapter 3 introduces two new prestige classes that enhance an artificer's ability: the alchemist savant on page 53 and the renegade mastermaker on page 81.

In Chapter 2, new feats that enhance the unique skills of the artificer are presented, including Etch Schema, Improved Homunculus, and Rapid Infusion, among others. The feats focus on creating items, using those items in more effective ways, and improving the artificer's infusions and other class features.

Several new infusions are presented in Chapter 4, providing the artificer with new ways to use his magic. These

infusions include *concurrent infusions*, *reinforce construct*, *metamagic scroll*, *censure elements*, *ablative armor*, and more.

Chapter 5 includes some new artificer items, as well as many other magic items and services artificers can find useful. The *Cannith goggles*, *wand bracelet*, and *spare hand* are but a few samples of artificer ingenuity at its best.

Chapter 6 portrays a few new varieties of an artificer's most faithful servant: the homunculus. In addition to new types of homunculi, additional advancement options are provided.

keep the secrets of the binding process to themselves . . . for a reason that no one else in Khorvaire is privy to.

STOLEN MAGIC

Contrary to current belief (and gnome assertions), the gnomes of Zilargo did not invent the process now used to bind elementals into items and vehicles. Certainly, the gnomes introduced the arcane techniques of elemental binding to the modern age, and they remain the undisputed masters of the process. (Indeed, they jealously guard the secrets of the process from others, sharing only what they must with the crafters of House Cannith to make the partnership that has developed between them succeed.)

While the techniques behind elemental binding are ancient (as the gnomes claim), the gnomes have only had the process since 793 YK (a date that is in direct conflict with the fanciful tales of gnome elementalists who supposedly appeared 1,200 years ago). Here is the story of how the gnomes stole magic. It is a story that remains hidden from most of those living on the continent of Khorvaire, and the handful of gnomes who know the truth guard it with their lives (and with all the resources of the Trust).

While seeking to increase his knowledge (a gnome passion if ever there was one) and his standing in House Sivis, Byrnid Dojurn, a minor functionary, uncovered the journals of a Xen'drik explorer from the previous century in a forgotten corner of the Korranberg Library. Within these journals, Byrnid found hints of a new form of arcane magic never before seen in Khorvaire—a form that seemed to control the very power of the elements. To learn more, Byrnid knew that he had to travel to the Continent of Secrets and visit the wielders of this new magic. He had to go to the mysterious dark elves of Xen'drik. He had to meet the drow.

Byrnid Dojurn brought his discovery to his superiors in the house. News quickly made its way to the doyenne of the High Council, Aliwas Lyrriman d'Sivis. The doyenne recognized an opportunity and funded a secret mission to Xen'drik. Along with the usual warriors and scouts, Byrnid would take a number of wizards and artificers to help with the "information gathering." In the end, Byrnid led a gnome assault force into the jungles of Xen'drik for the express purpose of discovering and attaining the secret to elemental binding.

Byrnid retraced the path described in the old journals, and eventually his expedition encountered Merranzabad and a drow clan living within the ruins of an ancient giant complex. With flowery words of friendship and a lavishing of exotic gifts from the Five Nations, Byrnid won the trust of the leader. Over the course of many weeks, the gnomes

and the drow exchanged knowledge and information. The gnomes shared some small wonders with the drow, and the dark elves showed the visitors amazing weapons and armor enhanced by bound elementals. At last, in a gesture of friendship, Merranzabad opened a sacred chamber to Byrnid's view. There, amid jewels and other treasures from the age of giants, were the stone tablets of arcane knowledge that were passed from the dragons to the giants in a time before memory.

Byrnid returned and started to copy the ancient texts that explained the process. Just as he was finishing and deciding what other wonders to copy, Merranzabad discovered the gnomish treachery. Byrnid and a small number of his expedition managed to escape while the rest died fighting the drow.

Sick with fever from a wound that became infected over the course of the return trip, Byrnid was near death when he handed the copied manuscripts to doyenne Aliwas. The gnome never lived to see what wonders were created thanks to his efforts; instead, he was haunted by Merranzabad's curse as he slipped from this mortal life.

"We will kill all those who stole our magic," the drow leader proclaimed as Byrnid ran. "Every gnome is cursed this day, for now and until our magic is returned!"

Those few gnomes who know the truth of the origin of elemental binding magic harbor secret fears that someday the drow and their scorpion-clad assassins will find a way to reach Zilargo. And then the gnomes will have to answer for their crime.

BINDING AN ELEMENTAL

The process of binding an elemental to an inanimate object requires a great deal of care and expertise. House Orien (for its lightning rail) and House Lyrandar (for airships and galleons) hire the foremost experts on the subject of binding elementals, but other groups and individuals have recently begun attempts at unraveling the gnome mysteries of binding elementals into items using Khyber dragonshards. (More information on Khyber dragonshards can be found on page 265 of the EBERRON *Campaign Setting*.) In addition, some makers of magic items in Zilargo have found new ways to bind elementals to their service, as described later in this chapter.

The process of creating elemental items is similar to the process for creating elemental vessels, but binding an elemental to a vessel is more difficult. In both types of binding, an elemental must be called using powerful magic, then bound within an arcane matrix. The focus of the matrix is a Khyber dragonshard, usually one of the

ELEMENTAL BINDING IN THIS BOOK

Chapter 3 introduces a new prestige class closely affiliated with elemental binding: the elemental scion of Zilargo.

Chapter 4 features several new spells and infusions useful when dealing with elementals, including *censure elementals*, *control elementals*, and *elemental prod*.

Chapter 5: Magic Items introduces several elemental-bound items, including the *water whip* and *fiery tunic*. Chapter

5 also introduces new elemental-bound vessels: the tumbler and the earth sled.

At the end of this chapter, an organization known as the Power of Purity is presented. This group specializes in binding elementals.

Binding an elemental to an item is nearly routine, to those with the proper know-how

finest quality, although the matrix itself is mostly composed of magical energy, indiscernible to the eye. Should a dragonshard ever be shattered, the elemental is immediately freed—and is often quite enraged. Khyber shards have hardness 10 and 15 hit points per inch of thickness, although most of those used to bind elementals have been magically strengthened with a *hardening* spell (see page 112 of the EBERRON Campaign Setting).

Calling the Elemental

Elementals must be called to be bound; elementals summoned simply return to their native planes when the duration of the summoning is up, even if they have since been transferred to an item. If the summoned elemental is trapped within a magic circle and an attempt is made to transfer it directly to an arcane matrix, it escapes to its home plane in transit. The most common spells used to bind elementals are the *planar binding* spells.

To bind an elemental to an item requires a spellcaster capable of casting a *planar binding* spell of the appropriate strength. The particular version of the spell varies depending on the purpose and strength of the intended item. Wizards and artificers most commonly perform the binding service, because they most often possess the requisite item creation knowledge, as well as the focus necessary to keep an elemental from escaping before it is transferred to an item. However, clerics, sorcerers, and even a few druids and bards number among the creators of these items.

Transferring an Elemental

Once an elemental has been successfully called and bound, the process becomes slightly more complex. The elemental must be now transferred to the item. Doing this requires the participation of at least two spellcasters. The item must be physically complete to receive the elemental, and it must have been created with space allowed for the Khyber shard.

Binding an elemental is a three-step process, as outlined here.

Step One—Gather the Shard: Without a Khyber dragonshard, an elemental binding is not possible. The shard provides a structure that accomplishes two key goals. The first is that it forms the focal point for a lattice of energy—an arcane matrix—that traps the elemental in the elemental item. The ordered structure of the crystal essentially forms a maze with no exit, which the elemental follows endlessly as long as it remains within the item. The second is that by providing this structure, the shard acts as a conduit for the elemental's raw energy. As the elemental is forced through the crystalline lattice of the arcane matrix, it gives off energy, which is then transferred to the item. The concept is similar to the *conductor stones* used to allow lightning rails to move, except in this case, one *conductor stone* is the elemental, and the other is the matrix, with the Khyber shard at its heart. Instead of motion as a by-product, the elemental's "chase" through the arcane matrix provides a magical effect, as determined by the item's creator.

The size of a shard is not necessarily in proportion to the size of the elemental within it. However, larger elementals are more easily bound into larger shards (see Step Three, below, for details). The average Khyber shard used to create an elemental weapon, suit of armor, or similar item is roughly 6 inches in circumference, or about 1 to 3 inches thick, and no more than 6 inches long. Larger shards, or greater Khyber shards, are more suitable for use in elemental vessels for several reasons, not the least of which is that larger shards require more space when mounted (see Elemental Vessels, below, for more details on the shards used in the construction of those items). Greater shards are typically 6 inches in diameter, and anywhere from 8 to 14 inches long.

Transferring an elemental of a particular size has no effect on the final powers of the item, which are determined by the creator of the item (and thus determine the final cost, as well as the cost in materials). While binding a larger elemental does not add power or extra abilities to the item, it does reduce the cost to create the item. When determining the gold piece cost in raw materials needed to craft the item, the elemental item's creator reduces the base price by 5% per size category of the elemental above Medium (an elemental to be bound must have at least 4 Hit Dice). Thus, binding a Medium elemental to an item provides the same effect as binding a Huge one, but the former item costs normal price, while the latter item costs 10% less to create. This discount does not impact the market price of the item; savings on elemental item creation go directly back into the pocket of the creator—or the organization that employs the creator.

This cost saving is why dragonmarked houses and other organizations with wealth create most bound items. These organizations must pay the spellcasters in their employ who create the items. But while such houses and governments might pay more in salaries or fees to the higher-level spellcasters on their payrolls, the money saved by binding larger elementals translates directly to a larger profit.

Step Two—Gather the Flow: Two spellcasters are required to bind an elemental to a nonvessel item. The first of the spellcasters, called the shak'krek (a Gnome word that means "flow gatherer") is responsible for releasing the elemental from its binding and holding it, through force of will alone, for just a few seconds. The shak'krek must be of sufficient level to cast a *planar binding* spell capable of calling an elemental of identical power to that which she is holding. However, the shak'krek need not have the requisite spell prepared or available for the day, nor does she need to call the elemental herself that she plans to help bind. Thus, if a Large elemental is being bound, the shak'krek must be able to cast *planar binding*, while if a Medium elemental is being bound, the shak'krek need only able to cast *lesser planar binding*.

Being able to cast the spell is only part of the picture, however. The shak'krek must make a Concentration check to hold the elemental (DC 10 + the elemental's HD). A shak'krek can hold an elemental for 5 minutes per caster level. All shak'krek are at least 9th-level sorcerers or wizards, but most are at least 10th level in case a hevrae fails to bind an elemental on the first attempt (see Step Three, below). Holding an elemental in this fashion requires continuous concentration. If a shak'krek's focus is disrupted in any way (see page 170 of the *Player's Handbook* for details on

disrupting concentration), she might lose control of the elemental. If this happens, the elemental is immediately freed, and is likely to turn on the shak'krek and anyone else in the vicinity.

Step Three—Tie the Knot: The second caster, called a hevrae (Gnome for "one who ties knots"), must then bind the elemental into the armor, transferring it from the grasp of the first caster into its receptacle. The shak'krek is necessary in this process because the hevrae cannot break the wards of the binding and simultaneously transfer the elemental to its new home. Doing so requires too much concentration, and to falter even a bit in the transfer would release the elemental. In some cases, the creature might simply cause some small amount of property damage, but at worst, the furious creature might decide to stay on the Material Plane long enough to punish those insolent enough to capture it in the first place. Of the two spellcasters making the transfer, the hevrae is the one who must possess the Bind Elemental feat (see page 51 of the *EBERRON Campaign Setting*).

Transferring an elemental into an item takes 20 minutes, and once the process is begun, it cannot be halted. To complete the transfer, the hevrae must make a Charisma check opposed by the elemental's Charisma check, as described in the *lesser planar binding* spell description (see page 262 of the *Player's Handbook*). The check is more difficult if the hevrae is trying to force an especially large elemental into the matrix of a smaller Khyber shard. The table below provides the size of elemental (in number of Hit Dice) that is appropriate for binding into a shard of the indicated diameter.

Shard Diameter	Elemental HD
Up to 2 inches	4 to 7
More than 2 inches, up to 4 inches	8 to 15
More than 4 inches, up to 6 inches	16 to 20
More than 6 inches	21 or more

A shard of a given size can be used to bind an elemental of the appropriate number of Hit Dice or less without any extra difficulty. Attempting to bind an elemental with more Hit Dice than the number recommended for a shard becomes more difficult. An elemental with more than the maximum size for a given shard can still be bound into the item, but it is more difficult to "fit" the creature inside the arcane matrix. The DC of the Charisma check made by the hevrae binding the elemental increases by 5 for each increment of size beyond the maximum. For example, a shard 3 inches in diameter can be used to contain an elemental of 15 or fewer Hit Dice without increasing the difficulty of the hevrae's Charisma check. If the same hevrae tried to use the same shard to bind an elemental of 16 Hit Dice, the DC of his Charisma check would be the result of the elemental's Charisma check + 5. If he tried to use the same shard to bind an elemental of 25 Hit Dice, the DC would increase by 10.

If the hevrae has helpers, who must also be present for the entire transfer, the helpers can each make a DC 10 Charisma check using the aid another action, much like combining a skill attempt (see page 65 of the *Player's Handbook*). Success on this check provides the primary hevrae a +2 bonus on his Charisma check. If the hevrae fails his check by less than 5, the transfer attempt fails—but the hevrae can try again after 10 minutes, although the DC increases by 2. Failure by 5 or more means the ritual is interrupted and the elemental breaks free. If the transfer is interrupted, for this or any reason, the hevrae (and each of the hevrae's helpers) takes 4d6 points of damage from a release of pent-up magical energy, and the materials used in the transfer are lost. Helpers must each also have the Bind Elemental feat.

This step in the process is where binding an elemental to a vessel differs from binding it into any other item. See Elemental Vessel Binding for the key differences between the two processes.

Elemental Vessel Binding

Binding an elemental to a vessel is in some ways similar to, and in some key ways different from, binding one to another type of item. The sheer size of a vessel requires that the process be approached differently, but the early stages share some similarities.

The elemental to be bound must still be called and trapped within a magic circle, and again, *planar binding* spells are most commonly used to accomplish this goal. Also as with items, a Khyber shard is required to bind the elemental, but in this case, the arcane matrix to bind the elemental is built into the hull of the vessel. The dragonshard is housed in a special containment chamber in a vessel's engine room. Once activated, the energy of the bound elemental travels from the core of the ship, through its binding struts, and then through the matrix along the hull.

The first stage in the matrix is the binding struts that force the elemental into a ring shape and give every elemental vessel its distinctive appearance. From there, the elemental continues to flow through the ship's hull, appearing as jagged, snaking lines of living energy that pulse and shift.

These living conduits of elemental energy take on an appearance related to the type of elemental bound into the vessel. A fire elemental, for example, sends tendrils of flame along the hull of its ship, while flowing veins of rock and crystal indicate the presence of an earth elemental. *Explorer's Handbook* features a great deal more information on elemental vessels, focusing on piloting and negotiating with the elemental bound within a vessel.

Again, as with items, more powerful elementals are not necessarily required for larger items; they simply result in a reduction in the cost of the vessel's creation. This means that most elemental vessels feature more powerful elementals by default. Greater Khyber shards are nearly always used when constructing elemental vessels. Impractical for nearly all nonvessel elemental items, greater Khyber shards require more room to house, which elemental vessels have in abundance. Vessel builders also like greater Khyber shards because they are thicker and more difficult to break, making sabotage that much more difficult. Vessel builders also have an easier time binding larger elementals into the larger shards, as described in Step Three (see above), further increasing the value of greater Khyber shards—a larger elemental bound into a vessel results in a wider profit margin for the vessel's seller.

More spellcasters are required to transfer the elemental from its prison inside the magic circle to the vessel. As with other items, only one shak'krek is necessary to temporarily hold the elemental between the circle and its final destination, but the hevrae must have assistants. All told, the hevrae and assistants must have a combined caster level equal to twice the elemental's Hit Dice. Usually, a master crafter acts as the lead hevrae, accompanied in the process by several acolytes or apprentices. Unlike with the transfer of an elemental to an item, this transfer takes 1 hour per HD of the elemental, minus 1 hour per caster level of the hevrae and assistants that exceeds the elemental's HD (minimum 1 hour). The hevrae's assistants still use the aid another action to help the hevrae with the Charisma check, as described above. Any disruption of this process results in the immediate release of the elemental, and each hevrae takes 4d6 points of damage from a release of magical feedback. Again, failure also means the materials used in the ritual are wasted. Once the elemental is safely ensconced in its new home, the process of creating the energy used to power the vessel is identical to that described in the process above.

The checks required by both the shak'krek and the hevrae in this binding process are the same as described above (including the more difficult checks if the binders use a smaller shard than appropriate for the elemental to be bound). Vessels are subject to the same discounts for binding more powerful elementals, but, of course, doing so has its own risks.

Adventure Idea

—The PCs are hired by a representative of House Lyrandar to travel to Zilargo and act as guards on a recently purchased airship that is to be delivered to the house. However, many other organizations would love to get their hands on a newly built airship, including pirates from the Lhazaar Principalities and warforged loyal to the Lord of Blades. The PCs must contend with a number of these abnormal threats during this "routine" mission, leading them down a trail of clues to evidence of a conspiracy of corruption and betrayal within House Lyrandar.

DRAGONSHARDS

Much of the great magic of the Five Nations would not be possible without the existence of dragonshards, and the economies of Khorvaire demand a steady supply of all three dragonshard varieties. The Siberys shards that fall from the sky, the Eberron shards dug from the earth, and the Khyber shards mined from the caverns deep beneath the surface are all vital elements of magic in the world. Some believe dragonshards to be the physical remnants of the ancient progenitor wyrms, though many concern themselves more with the harvesting and selling of the peculiar crystal shards. The following section presents not only insight into the nature of each of the types of dragonshards, but also discusses how and where dragonshards are found, the methods of harvesting the shards, and the general market for each type of shard.

EBERRON DRAGONSHARDS

Eberron dragonshards, also called bloodstones, are found encased in geodelike stone shells—egg-shaped rocks perhaps a foot across. These stone shells usually lie just below the surface of the ground, covered by 2 to 10 feet of dirt and sediment, but always above the bedrock layer. Since Eberron dragonshards are not found buried within rock, most shard fields are in lowlands, as opposed to mountains or rocky barrens.

Some of the most productive Eberron dragonshard fields are in the swamps of the Shadow Marches. In such places, the water of the swamps has transformed much of the dirt covering the shards into mud, and in some cases washed the dirt away completely. Dragonshard geodes thus sit hidden underneath standing water or muck.

In some fields, House Tharashk workers wade through the fetid waters, picking up individual dragonshards that have broken free of their casings. Other orc and human tribal members use extra-long divining rods, letting the forces of nature guide their hands while plunging the 10-foot poles into the mire in search of the solid resistance a dragonshard shell might offer.

Many of the most lucrative Eberron dragonshard fields have already been claimed by House Tharashk—nearly all of them within the Shadow Marches, as well as those fields within Droaam.

Of course, Eberron shards might be a few feet under the surface of most of the lands in Khorvaire, but the task of digging up most of the continent is daunting, so a prospector usually won't dig indiscriminately unless an area is expected to have a high concentration of Eberron shards.

Harvesting

Many Eberron dragonshard fields are discovered by accident; perhaps land was being excavated to raise a keep and shards were removed as part of the excavation, or maybe the shells were discovered when digging a mass grave for the fallen of the Last War. Once a single dragonshard-bearing geode is found, a safe assumption is that more will be discovered nearby.

More often than not, however, the best dragonshard fields are found using magic. Dragonmarked members of House Tharashk and magewrights in their service employ *locate object* judiciously in their search for more Eberron dragonshard fields.

The excavation of Eberron dragonshard shells is a time-consuming but relatively straightforward process. A prospector simply digs or plumbs an area until he finds the telltale egg-shaped geode that houses the dragonshards. Once unearthed, the shell is usually transported to a secure work area, where a skilled expert can crack the rock and extract the dragonshards.

Removing dragonshards from a geode requires careful hands and some knowledge of how the shells are formed. A

Telltale egg-shaped rocks often house Eberron dragonshards

DC 15 Profession (miner) check is required to open the shell. If this check fails by 10 or more, the shell is cracked open, but half of the dragonshards within are shattered and ruined.

When a shell is carefully opened, a number of dragonshards can be extracted from it. The largest dragonshard shell on record was over 4 feet in diameter—so large that the dragonshards had to be extracted on site. A typical shell yields 1d6 large dragonshards or 5d8 small shards.

Availability

Eberron shards are the easiest dragonshards to obtain, at least on the continent of Khorvaire. House Tharashk provides Eberron dragonshards to markets in all major cities of the Five Nations. The larger cities of the eastern reaches, including Regalport in the Lhazaar Principalities, usually have a few Eberron dragonshards available at a given time, and the cities of Q'barra are surprisingly well stocked with bloodstones, most likely due to the rich shard fields scattered throughout that frontier land. Less of a market exists for Eberron shards in western Khorvaire, even though it is the source of most Eberron shard production.

Eberron shards are the most plentiful of the dragonshards, and the smaller shards are so inexpensive as to be commonly found for sale in most towns and cities. The

DRAGONSHARDS IN THIS BOOK

Dragonshard-related feats are described in Chapter 3, and dragonshard-related spells and infusions can be found in Chapter 4.

Individual dragonshard prices, based on type and size, are provided with each dragonshard's description in this chapter.

The Finders Guild, an organization that specializes in harvesting dragonshards, is presented at the end of this chapter.

smallest of Eberron shards have a market value of 1d8 gp each. Some Eberron shards have a greater affinity for magic, and these greater Eberron dragonshards fetch prices in the neighborhood of 4d4×10 gp.

Other Sources

The Aereni have limited Eberron shard harvesting operations, and they sell the shards in their trade town of Pylas Talaear. Untapped fields also exist in Q'barra, though House Tharashk is working hard to bring them into its monopoly.

SIBERYS DRAGONSHARDS

Siberys dragonshards fall from the Ring of Siberys, littering much of equatorial Eberron. Nearly all Siberys shards came from Xen'drik, harvested from the jungles around Stormreach as that city grew. Eventually, the relatively civilized region around the city was picked clean of most dragonshards, and now most shards are primarily found deep within the wilds of Xen'drik.

Prospectors spend weeks perched atop cyclopean ruins, looking out over the teeming jungle in a vigilant watch for a Siberys shower. Such showers occur infrequently, and the mists of the Xen'drik jungle can sometimes make spotting the showers somewhat difficult. Usually, a shower drops Siberys dragonshards over an area perhaps 100 feet wide but over a mile long.

Even if a Siberys shower is detected, it might take many days for a mining expedition to reach the fall zone, and a few days to gather those shards that survived the fall. The prospectors must be on their guard, and they usually expect attacks from drow bands, renegade giants, and all manner of other creatures that make their homes in the wild, not to mention other groups of prospectors heading to the same fall zone.

A typical prospector troupe plans a month-long expedition for dragonshard recovery. The plan usually includes no longer than two weeks waiting for a Siberys shower, a

A shower of Siberys dragonshards can be dangerous to those caught within it

week to find the fall zone and gather as many shards as possible, and finally a week to return to Stormreach. An average of only one in three expeditions is successful, and such an expedition usually yields ten to fifteen Siberys dragonshards.

Some prospectors sift through the silt of the rivers, staying closer to what counts for civilization while panning for dragonshards washed downstream. Every few years a Siberys shower rains shards in the vicinity of Stormreach, usually resulting in a drop in shard prices as the market becomes temporarily flooded with easy-to-acquire shards.

Once located, Siberys shards are the easiest to collect. They fall with great velocity from the Ring of Siberys, embedding themselves in the underbrush and soil, usually to a depth of no more than a foot or two. In the Xen'drik jungles, shards might be slowed as they pass through the thick canopy of branches and leaves, and they can sometimes be found barely buried by fallen foliage. Only a fraction of these shards survive the fall through the trees, though, making searching for these dragonshards a time-consuming venture. Some shards have also been found in the trunks of jungle trees, though many shards that impact trees are rarely recovered, because trees seep sap over the wounded wood and eventually envelop the dragonshard.

Harvesting

Siberys shard prospectors might simply wander into the jungle hoping to stumble onto a fall zone or witness a Siberys shower firsthand, but those brave and foolhardy souls are only sometimes successful. Most experienced teams employ magic to increase the success rate of their expedition. The frequency of Siberys showers can be predicted with a certain degree of accuracy by various magical means, and teams might employ magewrights, or sometimes even priests, to cast *augury* or other divination magics. Some sages also purport to have studied the movement of the Ring of Siberys and claim to be able to predict with some precision when a shardfall might occur. In most cases, however, even the most accurate of forecasts can only narrow down a Siberys shower to within a week of its actual occurrence, and the fall zone itself can only be isolated to within a twenty-mile radius.

When a fall is imminent, teams are sent to vantage points near the expected fall zone. There they wait, on mountain crests or atop ancient ruins, ever vigilant for the rain of dragonshards. Usually, a team guided near a shard fall by magic ends up 2d10 miles from the actual fall zone. A Siberys shower is potentially visible for miles around. A DC 10 Spot check will notice a shower while it is active at a distance of a mile or less, and the DC increases by 2 for every additional mile between the fall zone and the vantage point. Environmental conditions, such as rain or fog, can also impact the Spot DC.

If a shower is spotted, the team can then mark its direction and begin moving toward the fall zone. A DC 15 Survival check each day keeps the team moving in the right direction; through trackless jungle, most parties can cover four to six miles per day. Even direction is not enough, however, since only the most experienced shard hunter can find signs of a Siberys shower once it is over. A DC 25 Knowledge (nature) or Survival check can correctly identify a fall zone, and team members can also search as they move (see below), but doing so halves their movement. The dragonmarked of House Tharashk are particularly useful here, since those with the greater Mark of Finding can use *find the path* to locate the fall zone directly.

Once a fall zone is identified, the area can be canvassed for fallen dragonshards. A typical fall zone yields a dozen or so (4d6) usable Siberys shards. A successful DC 20 Profession (miner) check results in a 20% chance of finding a single intact Siberys shard after an hour's work, or a 5% chance of finding two shards that hour. A character with at least 5 ranks in Profession (miner) can instead make a DC 20 Search check to find fallen Siberys shards with the same rate of success. A team usually employs four or five searchers, while the rest of the team keeps an eye out for native creatures. Most of the time, teams search for only two or three days before leaving the site, because every moment that passes in the jungle only increases the chance of an eventual hostile encounter.

Siberys shards vary in size, and the markings within have varying levels of complexity, much like the differences between least, lesser, and greater dragonmarks.

Availability

Siberys shards can be found in quantity only in the Xen'drik trade town of Stormreach and the metropolis of Sharn. Nearly all Siberys shard trade passes through these cities. Other major cities of Khorvaire and Aerenal might occasionally have a limited supply for sale, but the market is anything but steady.

The majority of Siberys dragonshards fetch 4d4×25 gp on the open market, an average of 250 gp. About one in ten Siberys dragonshards found after a shower has more complex markings, and can bring 4d4×200 gp each (2,000 gp on average). One in a hundred Siberys shards is considered a greater Siberys dragonshard, containing much more complex marks. These greater shards can be sold for 2d4×1,000 gp each.

Other Sources

While the Finders Guild employs prospectors in Xen'drik and controls much of the trade in dragonshards, some groups have found other means of acquiring Siberys shards.

Some shards can be purchased from the Aereni in the trade city of Pylas Talaear. The exact locations of the elves' shard harvesting operations have not been discovered, although many speculate that the shards are gathered in

the Blackwood Jungle and Thal Taluna, in the southern regions of Aerenal. Another possibility is that the elves are also scouring Xen'drik for shards, and not passing through Stormreach to do so.

Other Siberys shards have been traced to the Lhazaar Principalities. Those shards almost certainly did not fall in that coastal region, and the popular rumor is that the pirate princes plunder the dragonshards from the Seren tribes off the coast of Argonnessen. This has spurred the endeavors of many diplomats and explorers who hope to gain access to the lands of the Seren barbarians, or perhaps even enlist the savage people to gather shards from Argonnessen.

Adventure Idea

—A ship bearing a cargo of Siberys dragonshards set sail from Stormreach bound for Regalport in the Lhazaar Principalities, but barbarian raiders from the island of Seren waylaid the vessel. The dragonshards must be recovered before the Seren tribe reaches Totem Beach and sacrifices them in a totem ritual (see Dragon Totem Rituals, page 43, for details).

KHYBER DRAGONSHARDS

While Siberys shards are the most rare variety of dragonshard, Khyber shards are the most hazardous to obtain. Nevertheless, prospectors and members of the Finders Guild (see page 32) send expedition after expedition to find the Khyber shards that fuel so much of Khorvaire's industry. Lightning rails and airships have transformed the economy of the Five Nations, and elemental forges increase the output of many of Khorvaire's smiths and craftsmen. As a result, many organizations pay handsomely for these dragonshards, making the expeditions profitable—provided shard hunters make it back alive.

Khyber shards are found only in the depths of Khyber, growing in clusters on cavern walls and floors near pools of magma. The dragonshards reflect the orange-red glow of the molten rock, and the silhouette of a swirling dragonmark is barely visible within the smoky crystal.

Well before an expedition reaches the caverns and tunnels of Khyber, it must first determine its route. The most expedient paths to the depths are found in the Demon Wastes and Droaam, and both regions offer their own obstacles. Some miners try to find their own way into Khyber, searching for lost ruins in Q'barra, plumbing the depths of the Black Pit in Breland, or exploring vast caverns in the ruined and fallen giant cities of Xen'drik. These attempts don't entirely circumvent the hazards;

SIBERYS STORMS

A shower of Siberys dragonshards can be dangerous to those caught within it. All creatures in the fall zone during a Siberys shower have a 10% chance each round of taking 2d8 points of damage from a falling shard (Reflex DC 15 negates). A Siberys shower lasts for 4d4 rounds (an average of 1 minute). Once a shower has started, characters can take cover behind large trees or other obstacles to avoid further damage.

Characters caught in a shower are more likely to find dragonshards once the shower is over. Any character who spends an hour looking and then makes a DC 20 Profession (miner) check or a DC 20 Search check (provided that character has 5 ranks in Profession [miner]) has a 50% chance of finding an intact dragonshard, or a 10% chance of finding two shards.

Newly mined, unattuned Khyber dragonshards can be sold on the open market

I.P

they merely delay it, or replace it with an entirely different danger.

The deeper one delves into Khyber, the greater the chances of finding a Khyber dragonshard cavern, but so is the likelihood of encountering some of Eberron's more hostile underground denizens. If a prospector band is lucky, it might only have to fight off small groups of dolgrims or the occasional minor aberration, such as a grick. If a group tarries too long, however, it is likely to encounter dolgaunt patrols, mind flayers, beholders, or other denizens of the darkness below.

Once discovered, extracting raw Khyber shards from the igneous rock in which they are embedded is a time-consuming and arduous process. Great care must be taken not to damage a crystal as it is removed, and extracting a cluster of crystals might take a day or more of tedious work. The largest Khyber shards, called greater Khyber shards, are often used in lightning rail coaches or other elemental vessels, where their size is less of an issue in an item's construction. Such dragonshards might require nearly a week of careful digging to free.

Even after freeing a dragonshard from its rocky resting place, the danger is not yet over, for days of travel back up from the depths await the prospectors. Some shard hunters report an increase in resistance on the journey back to the surface, as if the denizens of Khyber were waiting until the shards were mined before ambushing the expedition. Others recalled attacks by fiendish forces, such as rakshasas or demons, shortly after the Khyber shards were cut from the rock.

Harvesting

Khyber shards are relatively easy to find, compared to Eberron shards. The shards grow openly from rock walls, and are therefore easy to spot once a Khyber shard cavern is located. However, the crystal clusters grow not only out of, but into the granite or basalt of the cavern walls. A miner must carefully dig the rock from around the base of the dragonshards, being careful not to break the shard itself. In addition, not all crystals in the cluster make effective dragonshards; the crystals mature as they grow, and only fully mature crystals are able to manifest their magical binding properties. A typical Khyber cluster has only one mature dragonshard.

Finding a new Khyber shard cavern might require days or weeks of searching. First, an appropriate region must be located in the Dragon Below, usually near lava pools or magma rivers. A DC 30 Knowledge (dungeoneering) check in such a region will discover a Khyber cave. A character gains a +1 bonus on this check for each day spent searching the depths, to a maximum bonus of +10 after ten days of searching (provided the expedition's members are alive that long). A newly found Khyber shard cave typically has 5–10 (1d6+4) small Khyber shards and 0–2 (1d6–4) greater Khyber shards.

Extracting a small Khyber shard requires a DC 20 Profession (miner) check and about 1 hour of uninterrupted work. A failed check means no significant progress was made in the extraction, and a failure by 10 or more accidentally breaks the dragonshard.

Extracting a greater Khyber shard can be much more time-consuming. At a minimum, mining a large shard takes 8 hours. At the end of this time, the miner can attempt a DC 25 Profession (miner) check. If successful, he has extracted the dragonshard. If the check fails by 10 or more, the miner has damaged the shard. If the check fails by 20 or more, not only is the shard ruined, but the miner falls victim to some other hazard, such as a lavaburst (see the sidebar) or a cave-in.

Location: Khyber Cavern

Deep underground, near red-hot pools of lava, Khyber dragonshards are found. A fiery glow illuminates the walls and enhances the deep orange glow that emanates from the dragonshard crystals growing in clusters on the walls. In many cases, the walls are covered with glyphs and symbols that suggest dragonmarks, and yet rarely do these writings ever match one of the twelve recognized dragonmarks. Occasionally these marks disappear or appear when dragonshards are brought into the cave or taken from the walls.

A Khyber cave seems a strange mix of the natural and the manufactured. A river of lava might flow through the

LAVABURST

One of the dangers of extracting Khyber shards is the possibility of releasing trapped magma in a lavaburst. A lavaburst showers the area around the dragonshard with molten rock, dealing 6d6 points of fire damage to creatures within 20 feet (Reflex DC 15 half). In addition, a creature adjacent to the source of a lavaburst that fails its saving throw is immersed in lava and takes 20d6 points of fire damage on the following round.

cavern, yet other features seem too conveniently placed to have occurred naturally, such as an arcing stone bridge that provides passage over the molten rock. Floors are relatively smooth, if uneven, and the cavern walls rise over the heads of most human-sized creatures before leaning inward toward the ceiling. No signs of stonework or modification are visible. Some scholars speculate that the daelkyr modified the underground passages to their liking, or that some connection to the dragonshards forces the caverns to form in a specific way. These mysteries might never be revealed.

Khyber dragonshard-prospecting adventurers will eventually find themselves in a Khyber cavern, at least if they hope to be successful in their mission. Even PCs not specifically looking for Khyber shards might stumble upon such a cavern while journeying through the dark underground of Khyber.

The open caverns make ideal places for combat with the denizens of Khyber, as lava and rock formations help to create a unique battlefield. Dolgaunt monks with dolgrim enforcers might defend the dragonshards from those who would take them, or the PCs might stumble onto a group of prospectors who have already set up a mining operation.

Newly mined, unattuned Khyber dragonshards can be sold on the open market, though nearly all shards not sold on the black market are sold to the Finders Guild.

Availability

The entrances into the Khyber depths from which these dragonshards are drawn are spread across Khorvaire, so no single location or region can provide a consistent supply of Khyber shards. House Tharashk, through the Finders Guild, supplies Khyber shards to the major markets of Khorvaire: Sharn, Flamekeep, Fairhaven, Wroat, and Trolanport. While most of this supply is ordered and rationed to specific artisans or Houses based on a carefully regulated priority list, House Tharashk does supply small amounts of Khyber dragonshards to the general markets in those cities.

The price of a small Khyber shard varies based on size and quality; a small shard is typically worth $4d4 \times 75$ gp, or an average of 750 gp each. Larger shards, known as greater Khyber shards, are in even greater demand, fetching $4d4 \times 500$ gp, or an average of 5,000 gp each.

Other Sources

Rumors suggest that the gnomes of Zilargo maintain secret caverns beneath Zolanberg where Khyber shards are grown. After all, the gnomes were the first in the modern era to master elemental binding, and Khyber shards are an integral part of the process. These rumors conclude that the gnomes must have had a source of such shards before a market for them existed. More likely, the gnomes used their diplomatic skills to trade with agents of the daelkyr, gaining Khyber shards without endangering themselves.

The Cannith Forgehold, House Cannith's mighty fortress in the Cogs of Undersharn, is built near the lava beds underneath the city. Some speculate that House Cannith maintains secure Khyber caverns, but only those in the confidence of the masters of making would know for sure.

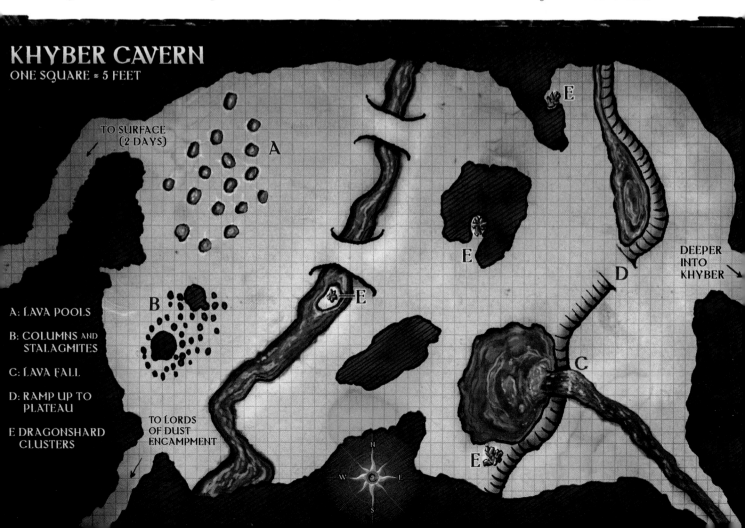

KHYBER CAVERN

ONE SQUARE ≈ 5 FEET

TO SURFACE (2 DAYS)

A

E

E

E

D

DEEPER INTO KHYBER

C

A: LAVA POOLS

B: COLUMNS AND STALAGMITES

C: LAVA FALL

D: RAMP UP TO PLATEAU

E DRAGONSHARD CLUSTERS

B

E

TO LORDS OF DUST ENCAMPMENT

THE DRACONIC PROPHECY

Few outside the dragon lands of Argonnessen know of the draconic Prophecy. Most common folk of Khorvaire view the long-lived dragons with fear and mistrust, when forced to think of them at all. However, the dragons shepherd vast and intricate plans toward fulfillment, plans that have at their heart the sacred Prophecy. Some enlightened individuals among the "lesser races" have gained an understanding of the Prophecy, or at least of its existence. A rare few scholars have even attempted to study the Prophecy. Such research is typically short-lived, however, because dragons do not tend to look kindly on those seeking to meddle in any fashion with the Prophecy. Some of these researchers simply disappear, while others develop a sudden interest in some other project.

A few members of the lesser races have learned something of the Prophecy. After the emergence of dragonmarks, the dragons realized that, just perhaps, humanoids have some important role to play in the unfolding Prophecy. Many dragons believe that observation of the bearers of dragonmarks, especially those that find some greater purpose in life, is enough. But a few dragons decided several hundred years ago that they desired an insider's perspective.

INCEPTION OF THE DRAGON PROPHETS

Overtures were made to specific individuals the dragons had observed for some time. Some bore dragonmarks themselves, but most did not. The individuals in question were all of an arcane bent, much like dragons themselves, and they were tasked with being the eyes and ears of their draconic masters, seeking signs of the Prophecy and occasionally acting on behalf of the dragons in causes in which the dragons were interested. In every case, these individuals acted to further the dragons' understanding of the Prophecy. In the process, they gained some insight into its mysteries themselves and began to manifest strange new abilities reminiscent of the great dragon deities. These individuals collectively came to be known as dragon prophets (see page 63 for information on the dragon prophet prestige class).

The dragon prophets have learned much from their draconic mentors (or masters, depending on the specific relationship involved), many dealing directly with a greater understanding of the draconic Prophecy. These abilities focus on the insight of the complex Prophecy, as well as a greater understanding of the world at large. As a prophet gains more of a grasp on the Prophecy, she begins to see everything around her in a different light. Many find themselves able to predict the future, while others simply become more aware of their surroundings.

Adventure Idea

—On a trip through Khyber, the PCs stumble across a mysterious chamber. Dragonmarklike sigils adorn the walls in continually shifting patterns. While there, they encounter a dragon prophet, who came to the cavern to research the odd marks and their connection to the Prophecy, just as he is ambushed by cultists of the Dragon Below. The PCs have the opportunity to be exposed to the mysterious draconic Prophecy for the first time, as well as uncover the motivations of the lunatic cultists in attacking the prophet. Is some portion of his research pertinent to Khyber?

DRAGONSHARDS AND THE PROPHECY

The dragons of Argonnessen are convinced that dragonshards are essential to understanding the Prophecy. The dragons read the true meaning of the marks within the shards, and realize that some marks are only truly understood when combined with or exposed to other marks.

Eberron shards, in particular, seem responsible for the manifestation of dragonmarks on the humans, elves, and other races of Khorvaire. Many sages believe that the dragonmarks were brought about due to long exposure, over many generations, to the Eberron dragonshards that lie just beneath the ground. Of course, those sages are unable to explain why no dragonmarks manifested among the orcs of the Eldeen Reaches or the goblinoids of the great Empire of Dhakaan during the millennia that passed before human, elf, and dwarf colonization.

Many dragons spend every night for centuries looking up at the Ring of Siberys. The ring shifts subtly over time, as some of the dragonshards that comprise the ring fall to Eberron as Siberys showers. The dragons feel that signs and portents from the ring represent omens from the spirit of Siberys, guiding the dragons so that they can be prepared if the spawn of Khyber once again emerge to dominate the world.

Tales are told of great Khyber caverns, whose walls are covered in markings of all sorts, and yet those markings shift and fluctuate if a strongly attuned dragonshard is carried through the cavern. Some of the markings seem to shirk away from Eberron shards, yet they crowd toward a powerful Khyber shard. The effect is subtle, however, and only those possessing the great patience and attention of

THE DRACONIC PROPHECY IN THIS BOOK

Certain dragon prophet abilities are represented by feats, including Dragon Prophesier, Prophecy's Artifex, Prophecy's Shaper, and Prophecy's Hero, all found in Chapter 2: Character Options.

The dragon prophet prestige class is described in Chapter 3, on page 63.

Spells useful for interpreting the draconic Prophecy (or lesser forms of detection) are sometimes used by those who know of them, including *scry trap*, *glimpse of the Prophecy*, *overwhelming revelations*, *sense weakness*, and *ancient knowledge*. Spells inspired by the draconic Prophecy are presented in Chapter 4: Spells and Powers.

the dragons can truly appreciate these mark manifestations. Only the dragons and those versed in the Prophecy, such as dragon prophets, can gain any insight from the sigils deep within Khyber.

A few nondragons have been exposed to slivers of the Prophecy. Some deranged Dragon Below cultists who worship Khyber, the progenitor wyrm, believe that Khyber dragonshards bind the ancient dragon within the depths of the world. These cultists strive to remove or destroy Khyber shards through magical rituals designed to break the binding forces. Still another cult faction believes that the dragonshards represent the physical form of the dragon itself. These cultists are convinced that if a large enough concentration of Khyber dragonshards were collected, Khyber could find the strength to rise again. These cultists have amassed secret caches consisting of tens or hundreds of Khyber shards.

Other, more scholarly types have suggested that the dragonmarks represent the dragon Eberron expressing its will through the dragonmarked races—races Eberron has chosen. What the races have been chosen for is unclear. Perhaps a cataclysmic showdown is inevitable, with the dragonmarked races battling the aberrations, fiends, and other forces of Khyber, as well as the dragons, the chosen of Siberys. This theory is but one of many regarding the relationship of dragonshards with the Prophecy.

DAELKYR MAGIC

Eberron is a world awash in magic, but like everything, magic is not a seamless whole. Instead, it is composed of many strands—beauty, savagery, power, grace, evil, desperation, hope, and corruptions that can (and do) shiver the soul.

While the saying "Without darkness, what of light?" might be true, civilizations have proved through the eons that the price paid for effulgence is sometimes a void so limitless that only the truly mad can hope to withstand and channel its depredations. The taints of Eberron are many, but few reach the excretory virulence of the magic of Karrnath, or the corruptions of the Khyber-dwelling daelkyr.

Plane-wrecked in Eberron, the daelkyr were once lords of a realm where madness stalked the skies, burrowed in the earth, and blasted the minds of any nonnative it touched. Cut off from that plane, called Xoriat, the Far Realm of Madness, the surviving daelkyr are sealed

FT

Corruptions are force-bred by those versed in the magic of the daelkyr

in Khyber—sealed, but not powerless. The power of each remaining daelkyr is hard to encompass—it rivals the strength of demigods, and some believe that when their home plane once again comes into proper alignment, the surviving daelkyr will ascend into true godhood, raining down insane abominations on the world that kept them imprisoned for so many ages.

Xoriat's return is a frightening possibility, but most sages believe that such a concordance is yet thousands of years in the future. For the daelkyr, the time is not time wasted. They spend their centuries in darkness, plotting, experimenting, breeding new strains of corruption, and releasing their abominations into the world through intermediaries. Indeed, the daelkyr are not even content to wait out the centuries until the celestial alignment

DAELKYR MAGIC IN THIS BOOK

One of the most effective tools of corruption in a daelkyr's arsenal is the husk of infinite worlds described on page 123. In addition to the relatively "recent" creations of dolgaunts and dolgrims, daelkyr projects have produced a variety of new servitor creatures, including the dolghast and several symbionts, which are described in Chapter 6.

One unforeseen result of the daelkyr's push into the world is the miscegenation-turned-evolution of a new race, called daelkyr half-bloods. This race is described in Chapter 2, on page 37.

Daelkyr workings—such a dread threat against Eberron's continued survival—are intolerable to those who understand their true depth. Such understanding comes at a price; those who join the ranks of the impure princes do so to force back corruption and keep the daelkyr and their servitors bottled up in Khyber. The impure prince prestige class is described in Chapter 3, on page 73.

next favors their ascension—why wait when their powerful experiments could open the way sooner? Why wait when their aberrant and insane minds are willing to pursue any means to achieve their world-ending goals?

The daelkyr do not wait. Terrible plots and machinations are in motion, directed by the corrupt scions of Xoriat ensconced below the earth.

MASTERS OF CORRUPTION

Are the daelkyr masters of creation, or corruption? Do their symbionts and servitor creatures represent the truly new, or are they corruptions of what was once healthy and pure?

Most sane creatures argue the latter, for it is clear that dolgaunts, dolgrims, and many symbionts are essentially other organisms that have been either devolved, combined, modified, or distilled down to a nearly unrecognizable biological mass. Beholders and illithids, at least, seem to be almost too different from any regular being to be considered mere corruptions; however, it is possible that illithids, at least, accompanied the daelkyr into the realm of Eberron from Xoriat, and that they represent a corruption of a creature from another reality ruined ages before they encountered Eberron.

The daelkyr employ a subtle arcanoscience in their ongoing corruptions. Because of their enforced imprisonment at the center of their various fortresses, the science of corruption has been left in the hands of daelkyr servitors. Even with the proper instruction, the necessary tools are insanely difficult to use. But in the thousands of years since the daelkyr's physical imprisonment, some few new corruptions have been successfully generated.

The tools used by the daelkyr are mad in their reach and disregard for the natural order of the multiverse. Each time a daelkyr, or its minion, attempts to create a new symbiont, minion, or other corruption, it essentially "spins up" a series of miniature realities from unstable astral material, then rapidly screens for anything that even remotely resembles some sort of specified ideal, typically a unique ability or trait that the daelkyr would find useful in a new creation. These created minirealities are born and die in mere minutes, and most of what occurs within their boundaries is sick nightmare.

CORRUPTION IN THE SHADOW MARCHES

The extent and reach of daelkyr-spawned abominations and their nightmarish influence has spread far and wide across Eberron. However, that influence is felt even more strongly in a few places. In the Shadow Marches, bizarre cults keep alive the worship of those entities better left unremembered. A region, not a nation, the Shadow Marches is widely regarded as a dank land of degenerate people, where mixed-race locals observe obscene rituals by the cloak of night, only to retire by day to sodden huts and unkempt villages to sleep.

If not for a House Sivis expedition that discovered dragonshard deposits, the Shadow Marches would probably be entirely unregarded. However, the mining of the shards makes certain that contact with the wider world is maintained. As a result, the corruption of the Cults of the Dragon Below continues to influence Khorvaire and beyond.

Of course, no matter the travails of life, some people can rise above their means and build a better situation for themselves. Witness the establishment of House Tharashk, a house populated by what were once natives of the Marches. Still, the swamps remain one of the dark places of Khorvaire, hiding ancient secrets and deadly creatures.

One such secret is rotten with daelkyr corruption. Called the Gate of Corruption by those outside the Marches, and the Moon Portal by the half-orc cults that revere the ancient ruin from nearby villages, the structure is something that will have to be dealt with, because its influence has begun to threaten the prospecting of nearby dragonshard fields.

Gate of Corruption

Deep in the Crawling Swamp of the Shadow Marches are vestiges of ancient daelkyr warfare. Strange structures, obelisks, and land formations are ascribed to that ancient event. One ruin in particular is a close-kept secret of the cults of the Dragon Below, since it serves as an active center of cultist and aberration plotting.

Also called the Moon Portal, the Gate of Corruption sometimes releases horrors during the dark of the moons. These horrors are brought up from Khyber by prolonged cult rites and chants by those that live in the structure year round.

The main structure is built into the face of a cliff, and it presents a gaping entrance between towering granite walls, empty of valves or other fortifications to keep out weather or visitors.

Two separate cult encampments reside within the main hall, one made up of orcs and half-orcs, the other mostly humans. See the standard cult statistics on page 231 of the EBERRON *Campaign Setting*. However, more powerful cult leaders are sprinkled in among the others, though these tend to claim spaces in the various empty ruined chambers that lead off the main hall. The cultists, over a hundred total, defend the entrance to the structure by their constant presence. Every third night, they engage in an hour-long ritual involving chanting, candles, and various obscene observances, but the rest of the time they go about a permanent-camp lifestyle, including hunting, gathering, and other activities necessary for habitation.

Once every month, the ritual is more elaborate, and coincides with the dark of one of Eberron's twelve moons. Sometimes a dolgaunt, dolgrim, or dolghast emerges from the inner chamber, past the spell-enruned doors that lead to a sacrosanct shaft to Khyber.

Once every year, on the Night of Trammel, more and more potent creatures are sent up the shaft. Gatekeepers and impure princes living in the Shadow Marches have come to expect a yearly exodus, but they so far have been unable to locate the Moon Portal and deal with it in any meaningful way.

CORRUPTION IN KHYBER

The unguarded tunnels of the neverlight, called Khyber, sometimes serve as a conduit for creatures sealed deep

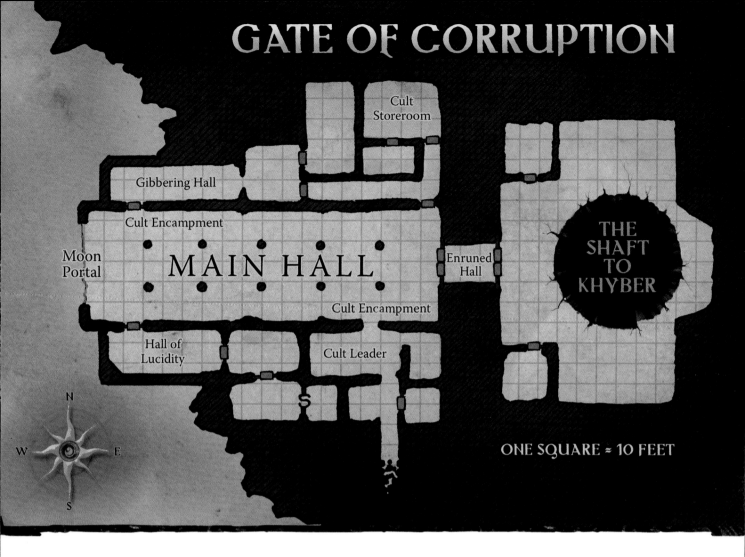

Cult
Storeroom

Gibbering Hall

Cult Encampment

THE
SHAFT
TO
KHYBER

Moon
Portal

MAIN HALL

Enruned
Hall

Cult Encampment

Hall of
Lucidity

Cult Leader

ONE SQUARE ≈ 10 FEET

N
W E
S

below to find the surface (and as a path for creatures of the surface to delve too deeply). Underlying Eberron, Khyber is a vast network of tunnels, caverns, vaults, rifts, and ancient spaces. This vast expanse of subterranean darkness is home to a multitude of creatures, including goblinoids and magical beasts, monstrous humanoids and renegade dragons, undead, and more. Of all these evils, the influence of the daelkyr is the most terrible, and the source from which the greatest horrors flow.

Thankfully, the daelkyr number fewer than ten, but even in so few numbers, the effects of their constant workings are felt throughout Khyber and even onto the surface world. While the daelkyr are mostly sealed into immobility, aberrations of their creation roam through the dark tunnels below the earth. Sometimes by mere chance, but more often through insidious calculation and planning, these aberrations ascend to the surface and begin rampaging until destroyed or forced to return to the world below, where abominations rule.

Fortress of the Stained

The whispered conjectures and worst guesses are all true. The daelkyr persist yet under Eberron, encysted in great fortresses where, despite their physical inability to act, they possess a malign psychic influence so strong that reality itself is warped in proximity to their isolation pods.

The Fortress of the Stained is but one daelkyr fortress in Khyber, and for all its many levels, vaults, armories, galleries, labs, and barracks, is accounted the least of those fortresses that have daelkyr ensconced at their heart. This daelkyr, referred to as the Stained One by the illithids, daelkyr half-bloods, beholders, dolgrims, and other aberrations that serve it, is determined to put its mark on the world, and thus has devoted much of its energy to churning out armies of aberrations.

The Fortress of the Stained is built within a vast cavern and actually encompasses several structures. Many of them are built on the floor of the cavern, but the tallest buildings reach up toward the ceiling of the cavern, connected by a stone column to the underbelly of "The Cyst." These chambers are reserved for the high-ranking illithids, beholders, and daelkyr half-bloods that are allowed within a particular radius of the daelkyr itself, which is sealed within a shimmering translucent sphere that no magic has yet been able to penetrate. The daelkyr was originally buried in solid stone, but its followers found it, and hollowed out or built the structures around it.

Most living creatures that enter the chamber directly surrounding the Stained One's isolation pod are instantly slain (Fortitude DC 19 negates) by reality run riot. In this area, called the corruption zone, only aberrations can withstand the pull, weft, alteration, and madness of such close proximity to the daelkyr. However, sacrifices (prisoners from surface raids) are regularly thrown directly into the corruption zone to appease the

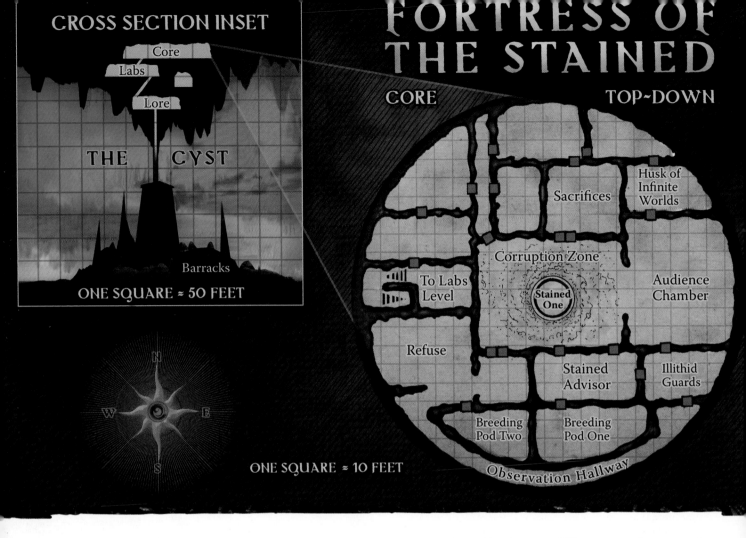

Core
Labs
Lore

THE CYST

Barracks

ONE SQUARE ≈ 50 FEET

ONE SQUARE ≈ 10 FEET

Sacrifices

Husk of Infinite Worlds

Corruption Zone

Stained One

To Labs Level

Audience Chamber

Refuse

Stained Advisor

Illithid Guards

Breeding Pod Two

Breeding Pod One

Observation Hallway

daelkyr within. Creatures the aberrations wish to subject to the otherworldly radiations without immediate lethal results are secured into body stocks in the audience chamber.

Because the Stained One cannot directly communicate with its followers, the fortress is under the command of an illithid telepath referred to simply as the Stained Advisor. All that occurs in and around the fortress is due to the wishes of this supremely powerful illithid lord.

DRAGON TOTEM RITUALS

The dragons control Argonnessen, and they suffer no trespass into their land by any of the "lesser races." While their seclusion gives the dragons a low profile within the Five Nations, the dragons are still revered by their closest neighbors, the barbarians of the island of Seren.

The Seren tribes truly worship the dragons, and traveling across the Dragonreach by longboat to the shores of Totem Beach is a spiritual journey for the barbarian warriors. Of all the societies in Khorvaire, even those who have seen the Silver Flame in Flamekeep, the Seren barbarians are the only ones who can see up close the majesty of their chosen deities.

Seren warriors view dragons as their patrons and protectors, and they often claim dragons as totems. Dragon totem warriors have been seen abroad in many of the Five Nations, but still unknown in Khorvaire are the secrets of dragon totem magic.

The spiritual leaders of the Seren tribes are the dragon disciples, tribe members who have so dedicated themselves to their dragon totems that they slowly transform into half-dragons. They hold the secrets of ancient rituals, passed down through the generations, that more fully embrace their draconic heritage, allowing them to experience brief glimpses of dragonhood.

These dragon totem rituals involve the sacrifice of Siberys dragonshards, collected from the shores of Argonnessen. The greater the number of dragonshards included in the ritual, the longer the benefits of the ritual will last. The dragon disciples perform rituals for a variety of occasions, such as preparing the tribe for a raid, as a rite of passage or coming of age ceremony, or to demonstrate their dedication to their inattentive dragon masters.

Few visitors have ventured beyond the shores of Seren, and fewer still have witnessed the totem magic rituals. A recent expedition from Khorvaire included a professor from Morgrave University, who managed to convince a group of Seren warriors to take him to Totem Beach on the coast of Argonnessen. There he bore witness to this secret rite. Later, he would write about his experiences, and discuss whether the totem magic came from within the Seren barbarians, was granted by the magic of ancient dragons, or perhaps was the result of magic harnessed as the dragonshards were destroyed. No subsequent expeditions have provided further information on the topic, however.

No Seren tribal members capable of performing dragon totem rituals are known to exist beyond the shores of Argonnessen. However, a PC with the right background can learn the Dragon Totem Lorekeeper feat in order to perform such rituals. Alternatively, a DM who wishes to introduce dragon totem rituals in his campaign without lengthy trips to Argonnessen can create an adventure that introduces the PCs to a tribal leader capable of performing such rituals. The characters should not take this benefit lightly; they should work hard to earn the trust and friendship of such an NPC, and they might have to prove themselves worthy again and again to continue to benefit from the NPC's rituals.

Dragon totem rituals are further explained on page 43.

Adventure Idea

—Some Seren Dragon Totem warriors have decided to reignite the ancient feud between elves and dragons. With the help of dragon totem magic, the warriors have been making raids on Aerenal and Valenar. Can they be stopped? More important, what motivates them to reawaken a millennia-old war?

PSIONICS

Psionics is one thread of power in the tapestry of forces at work in Eberron. Psionic ability taps the mind's potential. A psionic character is blessed with innate mental abilities that grant access to realms of personal power beyond the mundane, or even the magical. Knowing this path, the psionic character walks it, and takes on the mantle of psionic might.

Various psionic races are known (and feared) in Eberron, including the quori-possessed Inspired and the true-breeding kalashtar. Both the Inspired and the kalashtar appear similar to humans, especially at a distance.

Besides the occasional wild psionic talent that any sentient race exhibits now and again, the Five Nations harbor additional instances of psionics that go largely unsuspected.

PSIFORGED

After the Last War, warforged with crystal integuments and carapaces emerged from the Mournland. Similar, but strangely unlike the other warforged with which the world was familiar, these were a new variety of warforged: the psiforged (see page 39).

But the question remains—whence came the first progenitor psiforged? House Cannith swears that none of its facilities in Cyre had anything to do with merging warforged technology with the fruits of psionic minds.

The only creatures that might know the truth are the Five Progenitor psiforged. But all knowledge of their current whereabouts has been wiped from the minds of any who previously knew them—even Baron Merrix himself, who was instrumental in the creation of the psiforged that followed after.

Seren warriors view dragons as their patrons and protectors, and often claim dragons as totems

Five Progenitors

The mysterious Five Progenitors are generally believed to no longer exist; however, a dangerous magical ceremony (the Rite of Inverted Daggers), conducted by a Cannith "witch" named Celia d'Cannith, revealed that the Five still walk Eberron. Moreover, Celia learned that they had used their psionic mastery to wipe the knowledge of their existence from the minds of many who knew of them. If not for the Rite of Inverted Daggers (a ritual designed specifically to counter charms, compulsions, and manipulations of the mind) occurring when it did, all knowledge of their existence might have been permanently obliterated from every mind in the Five Nations. As it was, only Celia and a few of her confidants discovered the truth.

Celia learned that the Five were called Aliana, Arden, Brielle, Grayson, and Ramla. Furthermore, she learned that Aliana and Ramla were no longer in the world (dead or fled, she couldn't determine), while Arden, Brielle, and Grayson remained, but had retreated north to a small island lost in the storm-wracked Bitter Sea.

Inspired by her success, and interested in the origin of the psiforged, Celia determined to track down the surviving Progenitors for herself. To this end she prepared an expedition that numbered thirty souls, including a kalashtar mercenary named Keeganatash. She hoped that Keeganatash's psychic repertoire would aid her in tracking down the vanished Progenitors. Strangely, she couldn't seem to interest any second-generation psiforged to accompany her on the expedition. It was as if they forgot the request mere minutes after it was put to them—one more mystery to chalk up to the Five Progenitors, Celia decided.

Celia chartered an airship for her northward voyage, and put out of Sharn on a beautiful spring morning. Neither Celia d'Cannith, Keeganatash, or any other member of the expedition was ever seen again.

A year after the expedition's loss, a journal fragment purporting to tell the story of the expedition's passage into the Bitter Sea turned up in a rare books auction in Sharn. No one seemed to know how it had come to be part of the lot. The story told in the journal was generally dismissed as a hoax.

Excerpts from Celia d'Cannith's Journal

Day 3

Keeganatash woke this morning with another terrible headache and a nosebleed. He passed it off as nothing, but I saw a look of fear in his eyes that has quite unsettled me.

Day 7

The crew took the loss of the captain as an ill omen, and pushed to turn back. I only managed to retain their services by promising to double their commissions upon successful completion of the expedition. The odd thing is, we never found the captain's head.

Day 13

More ice flows than normal—the navigator seems to think we've gotten off track somehow. But I can't see how that could be possible. How could we be farther north than we've traveled? Keeganatash has taken to his chamber and only glowers at me when I ask him questions. What's wrong with him?

Day 15

We reached the island today. But first I need to report the dream I had last night. Truth to tell, it is the same dream I've had every night since we put out, but last night it seemed particularly—realistic. In my dream, a voice warns me of something, but I can never remember what upon waking. Last night, I finally remembered what the voice told me. It says, "The Contamination is contained—but only because of our enforced sequestration! Just thinking about us puts you at risk—we are immune, but we are carriers of the Contamination. Proximity could destroy your minds—cry off!"

Final Entry

Keeganatash slaughtered half the crew. His eyes glow a terrible green. He raves, he laughs—I can hear him in my mind. And, by Galifar . . . I think I like what I hear!

Psiforged Adventures

Psiforged typically focus on solving mysteries and discovering the unknown, themes that underlie many

---

PSIONICS IN THIS BOOK

Magic of Eberron presents additional rules for use in a campaign that features psionics. A new race, the psiforged (see page 39), provides a psionic-themed living construct. Players interested in a psionic twist on the magic of artificers should consult the psionic artificer class variation on page 42. Chapter 2 also includes new psionic feats, including some that give psionic characters new ways to spend their action points.

The Inspired and their vessels have evolved additional psionic powers (presented in Chapter 4) to facilitate their control over Riedra, and to help pave the way to an eventual quori invasion. Other powers were discovered by the kalashtar mystics. Any powers the mystics are willing to teach can be learned in the monasteries of Adar. The kalashtar refugees hope that these new powers might be used to counter the Inspired's growing influence in Eberron.

The quori, and their Inspired vessels, are introduced in the EBERRON Campaign Setting. New quori spirits are described in Chapter 6. For characters who truly want to involve themselves in the growing conflict against the quori, the quori mindhunter prestige class (see page 77) is tailor-made for such a quest.

A few psionic items, including the *galvanic crysteel blade* (see page 125), are described in Chapter 5.

AERENAL HALL OF THE DEAD

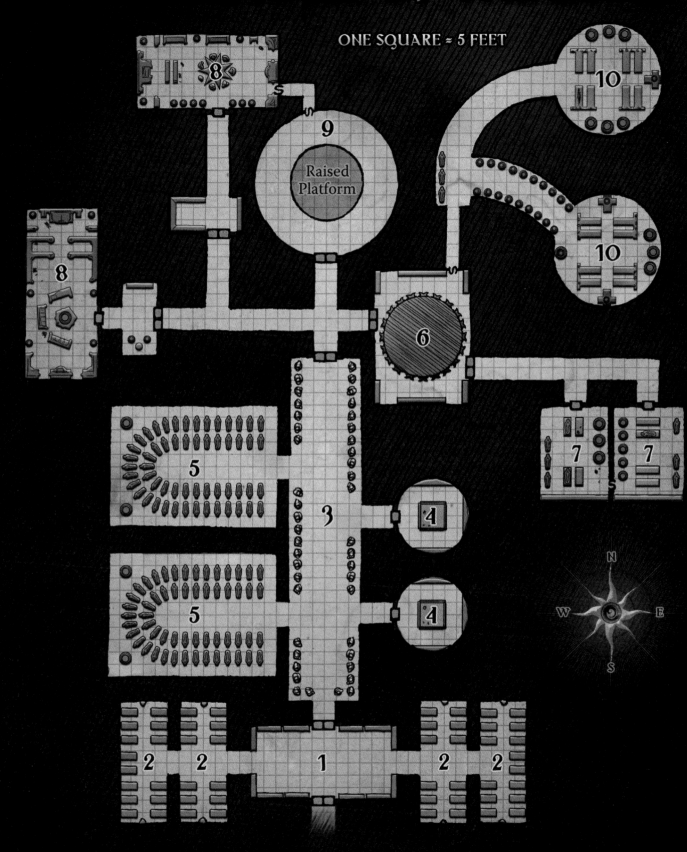

ONE SQUARE ≈ 5 FEET

1: ENTRY FOYER
2: UNDYING SOLDIER BARRACKS
3: HALL OF THE HONORED DEAD
4: PREPARATION CHAMBERS
5: MAUSOLEUMS

6: MEETING CHAMBER
7: FALSE LABORATORIES
8: UNDYING COUNCILORS' QUARTERS
9: CHAMBER OF THE UNDYING
10: TRUE LABORATORIES

adventures. Adventures featuring psiforged are likely to involve powerful groups such as House Cannith or the Lord of Blades, or might instead focus on the psiforged's psionic heritage.

House Cannith knows that some psiforged must have been constructed from within the Mournland, and the house will pay handsomely for information regarding the location and disposition of any creation forge operating within the ruins of Cyre.

MAGIC OF AERENAL

Of all the varied cultures and races in Eberron, few are as misunderstood—and subsequently condemned—as the elves of the continent of Aerenal. Solitary, mysterious, and obsessed with death, these elves are the basis of several rumors throughout Khorvaire.

The elves of Aerenal pursue many paths to power. Common choices include the path of the arcane archer, archmage, and loremaster. However, Aerenal is not a nation entirely devoted to the arcane arts. Some among the elves keep a constant watch for threats to their island nation. Chief among these defenders of the realm are the vigilant sentinels of Aerenal.

The elves of Aerenal have spent many generations perfecting the rituals that transform their most honored warriors and wisest advisors into the undying. In the course of those studies, they learned much about the nature of positive energy and how to harness it. This knowledge has proved increasingly useful over the years with the insidious incursions of the Blood of Vol and their ilk into Aerenal. The church has developed many new spells to combat these and other threats, many of which are also useful to arcane casters.

The elves of Aerenal have also begun creating grafts in the few years since the Last War ended. In homage to their deathless leaders, grafts constructed by the elves use donated flesh and tissues of the undying. Only the most noble and worthy Aereni are afforded this honor, although rumors of dark cabals that grow deathless flesh and bone for their own grafting purposes have begun to circulate, especially in areas where the Stillborn hold some amount of power. The grafts of Aerenal are known as deathless grafts (see page 127).

AERENAL HISTORY

The elves of Aerenal have a compelling obsession with death, which originated millennia before humans came to the continent of Khorvaire, back in the days of the elves' origins as slaves of the giants of Xen'drik.

In the dark days of the Aereni, they served the empires of Xen'drik. At that time, the elves hardly resembled the proud, powerful race they have become, but they carried the spark of magic within them. As the decades passed, the elf slaves concealed their magical gifts from their giant masters, nurturing them with each passing generation.

Contemporary Aereni know little of this time. The histories reliably begin tracking the elves' history—magical or otherwise—with their escape from Xen'drik. But the legend of the elves' grand, race defining escape is still told to all Aereni, forming the foundation of their acceptance of death and reverence for their ancestors in the form of the undying.

THE LEGEND: ESCAPE FROM XEN'DRIK

As all good legends do, the Aereni story begins with a hero, an elf slave named Aeren Kriaddal. Aeren served a powerful giant shaman for the greater part of his life. Eventually earning the mighty creature's trust, Aeren was allowed to observe and even aid in the giant's most potent rituals. Through this participation, he learned to cast simple spells.

One day, Aeren was ordered by his master to retrieve the day's sacrifices for the ritual. Kept in a small pen near the giant's house, these sacrifices typically consisted of livestock or captured wild animals. This day, however, Aeren opened the door to the large pen and found that it contained only a single small figure: an unconscious female elf. In a numb daze, Aeren took the elf slowly back to his master's abode. His conditioning was too thorough for him to do anything else, and on some level, he doubted his master meant to slaughter his fellow elf simply for his magic.

Aeren's assumption was wrong.

The giant shaman plunged a knife—a weapon the size of a large sword in an elf's hands—into the elf, spilling her blood to power a potent magical ritual. Horror struck Aeren just as cruelly.

The magic released by the sacrificial ritual was more potent than any Aeren had seen his master perform before. Despite his shock at the death of the sacrifice, the portion of his mind fascinated with magic took note of the power released by the sacrifice of an elf (as opposed to that of a mere beast). But the betrayal of his trust in the giant seeded a new thought into Aeren's mind: revolt.

Aeren began to carefully and slowly build a secret contingent of like-minded slaves, including a few who

THE PROPHECY OF AERENAL

Some say Aeren's journal contains more than the secrets to the Ritual of Undying. These whispers imply that the elf was inspired with the gift of prophecy just before the first ritual and sacrifice, and laid out a plan for the elves to follow once they were free. Supposedly the undying now work to fulfill this prophecy in their own patient way, and this pursuit is what drives a faction of dragons on Argonnessen mad with rage. This prophecy, these same scholars believe, is what has led to the dragon assaults on Aerenal over the course of so many years. These dragons seem to believe that the prophecy of the Aereni conflicts in some way with the pursuit of their own draconic Prophecy.

Giants of ancient Xen'drik performed rituals to unlock the power of blood

were eager pupils of the magic Aeren could teach. From these unpromising beginnings, the revolution nurtured the seeds of magical lore, and slowly expanded it with each passing year. Eventually, the elves began magical experiments of their own. The slaves at first recorded their trials and successes on pilfered scraps of parchment and leather, but the thefts were too risky—the giants might find them out. Instead, they found that their own blood was an ideal ink, and the bones of their own dead served as a perfect record of their findings. The giants suspected nothing.

Aeren never forgot the power unleashed by the sacrifice of one of their own race, and he conducted his own secret experiments apart from those of his conspirators, always seeking to unleash the power of blood. He had no desire to sacrifice his own people for any reason, but he felt that he was close to recognizing some key element.

Aeren's giant master felt the same way. Many more elves passed across the giant shaman's sacrificial altar, but to no greater effect. Those who were sacrificed wailed in their chains if conscious, asking for release, or fought wildly to avoid the drugs that would render them mutely accepting of the giant shaman's sacrificial knife.

With a flash of intuition, Aeren finally recognized the missing element one day after a particularly vicious sacrifice. Each victim was unwilling. Even when unconscious or drugged, the slaves' souls cried out for life, not death.

Aeren's insight fired him with steely determination. In the wake of his hard-won knowledge, it was finally time to initiate the elves' escape from Xen'drik.

Aeren shared his theories on the power of sacrifice with the trusted core of his secret movement. With this precious knowledge, they hatched a daring plan for the elves to escape the captivity of the giants. But secrecy, even among the elf slaves, was vital, lest betrayal ruin all their years of hidden labor. Of all the thousands of elves held in captivity, Aeren selected only one hundred others to share the magical knowledge necessary to free the elves, as well as the exact time of the escape.

When the appointed day of freedom came, Aeren walked into his master's chambers. All across Xen'drik, his cohort of conspirators did the same. They all spoke the final words of a terrible ritual, prepared in advance over many months. The ritual was powered by the sacrifice of all the collected elf heroes. In that instant, all these participating elves, scattered across the continent in key locations, gave up their lives.

Mighty detonations of power were born flaming into the world. Giant citadels fell, towns were expunged of their giant populations—and elves everywhere saw the signal. Led

MAGIC OF AERENAL IN THIS BOOK

The vigilant sentinel of Aerenal is a prestige class native to Aerenal that is described on page 85.

Spells developed by the Aereni include *glimpse of eternity*, *mindburn*, and others. These spells can be found in Chapter 4.

Deathless grafts, including *bone plating*, *deathless visage*, and *deathless flesh*, are described in Chapter 5.

by agents of Aeren and his inner circle, the elf slaves slipped away in the tumult.

During the Flight of the Slaves, as the elves call their exodus, a powerful, mysterious elf cleared the way for the fleeing elves of Xen'drik, diverting giant patrols, guiding lost groups of elves, and even obliterating obstacles (giant or otherwise) in displays of blazing power. Upon arriving at the coast, the freed slaves discovered a journal, prepared by Aeren and placed within a platinum urn. Carried to the shore by an unwitting messenger, the journal documented the ritual that resulted in the great sacrifice of the elf heroes, as well as Aeren's notes on the rite the elves eventually came to call the Ritual of Undying.

Aeren, unlike the other heroes, did not perish. The influx of magical energy sustained his existence even as it ended his biological life. He was transformed into the first of the undying.

MAGIC OF KARRNATH

Karrnath: The name alone summons images of necromancy and deadly spells of life-sapping potency. Karrnath is famous for its powerful necromancers and its willingness to use undead to supplement its military forces.

While Kaius III, ruler of Karrnath, has publicly declared that his nation no longer supports the creation of undead for military purposes in the aftermath of the Last War, the truth is somewhat more vague.

Karrnath's lead necromancer, Count Vedim ir'Omik, still maintains secret laboratories throughout the countryside for the express purpose of creating new types of undead to protect the borders of Karrnath—or perhaps to expand those borders should the opportunity arise. These workshops adjoin hidden, often underground, chambers of vast size, where rank upon rank of Karrnathi zombies and skeletons wait silently in utter stillness for the call to arms.

Not all Karrns indulge in this quest for power through necromancy. Some Karrns, in fact, despise the undead, seeking to end any influence the dark creatures might have on their beloved nation. One such group, the Red Watchers, actively seeks out and destroys undead wherever they can be found. They focus especially on enclaves of the Blood of Vol, despite their tolerated status in portions of Karrnath. The Watchers believe that only by entirely purging their homeland of the foul undead will it ever return to its former, pre-War glory.

Meanwhile, the common folk of Karrnath continue to remain ignorant of either secret faction. They certainly are aware of their nation's connection to the undead, and many worship at Blood of Vol temples without any thought for the church's darker connections. This blind tolerance allows the Blood of Vol to operate more freely in Karrnath than nearly any other part of Khorvaire, and the researches and plots of the Queen of the Dead advance rapidly beneath the dark streets of Atur, the City of Night.

Adventure Idea

—The PCs encounter a group of Order of the Emerald Claw agents attacking a half-orc. The half-orc is badly wounded and seems in danger of falling. This is Taarak Half-Ear, a member of the Red Watchers and a deadgrim. He was discovered poking around a secret Blood of Vol archaeological dig site nearby, and was set upon by the Emerald Claw agents on his way to report his findings. If the PCs aid him, they have the opportunity to help him figure out what the Blood of Vol is doing at the dig site—what appears to be an ancient crypt complex of some sort—and how best to stop it.

NECROGENESIS

Count Vedim ir'Omik has plans of his own. While still ostensibly loyal to King Kaius III, he misses the glory days of the Last War, when he could stride openly through court, enjoying the nervous glances of fear and respect (or loathing) from his noble peers. Relegated now to underground, underfunded laboratories, he has begun to seek ways to hurry the onset of the next chapter in the war that he never believes ended. Rather than create simply more Karrnathi zombies and skeletons, as per his orders from his liege, he has recently turned his research in new directions. The results have been more than he dreamed, and now, while seeking to create still more powerful, potent undead, he also looks for ways to use his new creations to seed the start of a new war.

So far, the creatures created by Vedim's necrogenesis program are few. The count is far from stupid, and he knows that should the king discover his program, he might be the next victim on the altar of the Blood of Vol. The fashioned undead (urdarks and vours) are carefully controlled by Vedim, answering only to him or those he provides with specific arcane pass phrases.

BLOOD OF VOL

The Blood of Vol has established quite a foothold in the lands of Karrnath. Its leaders continue to seek new ways to expand their power base at the behest of their organization's powerful lich leader. The cult continually recruits new undead, as well as exploring the creation of new types of undead, much as Count Vedim ir'Omik does. It also looks to create new spells that focus on undead and their abilities.

MAGIC OF KARRNATH IN THIS BOOK

The elite deadgrim form the potent core of the Red Watchers' organization. These stalwart undead hunters have learned to borrow some of the power of their hated foes, using the ancient philosophy that only when you truly, thoroughly know your enemy can you defeat it. Deadgrim are described in Chapter 3, on page 57.

Two new Karrnathi-created undead are presented in Chapter 6: the vour and the urdark.

Some of the spells described in Chapter 4, including *suffer the flesh*, *orb of dancing death*, and *leech undeath*, are just a few created by the Blood of Vol in Karrnath.

KARRNATHI UNDEAD RESEARCH FACILITY

ONE SQUARE ≈ 5 FEET

Teleportation Circle

1: HIDDEN ENTRANCE
2: LIVING HUB
3: RESEARCH HUB
4: UNDEAD HUB
5a: DINING HALL AND MEETING ROOM
5b: KITCHEN

6: SENIOR RESEARCHER QUARTERS
7: LIVING QUARTERS
8: SENIOR APPRENTICE QUARTERS
9a: COUNT OMIK'S QUARTERS
9b: COUNT OMIK'S LABORATORY

10: ALCHEMICAL LABORATORIES
11: SUMMONING CHAMBERS
12: ZOMBIE AND SKELETON STORAGE
13: HOLDING CELLS
14: UNDEAD CREATION ROOMS

Adventure Idea

—The PCs encounter a pack of vours while visiting the city of Atur, the City of Night. After defeating the creatures, they spot another a short while later disappearing into a side entrance of a building owned by the king himself. Further investigation leads the PCs into the depths of the city to a research laboratory operated by a wicked gnome wizard named Yeksir Unday Dark, a lackey and lead researcher into new types of undead for Count Vedim ir'Omik. He is currently working on developing several new undead variants, making this a great time to use supplements such as *Libris Mortis* to spring new undead on your PCs that they have not already encountered.

EBERRON ORGANIZATIONS

In an EBERRON campaign, the PCs might have the opportunity to join with one of several groups, each with different motivations and means to achieve their ends. Two such organizations include the Finders Guild and the Power of Purity.

FINDERS GUILD

"What is lost will inevitably be found, and we will find it."
—Kaarvis d'Tharashk of the Finders Guild

House Tharashk, the bearer of the Mark of Finding, founded the Finders Guild. Centuries ago, the dragonmarked members of the house decided to market their unique services to tribes and nations that neighbored their native Shadow Marches. While the dragonmarked inquisitives and explorers of House Tharashk were quite adept at their trade, they discovered many other individuals offering similar services. To capitalize on the entire market, the house created the Finders Guild, inviting others to join so they could benefit from each other's knowledge and provide a network of resources across the continent.

Now, the Finders Guild is still primarily composed of House Tharashk members, but it also includes many independent inquisitives, bounty hunters, explorers, and prospectors. House Tharashk manages the operations of the guild from its enclaves in major cities across Khorvaire. If something needs to be found, the first place to turn is the Finders Guild.

Dragonshards and the Finders Guild

Dragonshard prospecting isn't the only function of the Finders Guild, but a significant part of the income produced by the guild comes from the acquisition of dragonshards of all varieties. The Mark of Finding gives Tharashk prospectors a leg up on the competition, since they can use their dragonmark magic to more quickly locate dragonshard deposits. Through the Finders Guild, House Tharashk has control of, or at least prospecting rights for, most Eberron dragonshard fields in western Khorvaire, including the most lucrative fields in the Shadow Marches and Droaam. The guild maintains a presence in Stormreach, organizing expeditions into the wilds of Xen'drik to acquire Eberron or Siberys dragonshards.

Even expeditions into the depths of Khyber usually involve the Finders Guild in some way. Either the expedition is following a map provided by the guild, is led by a guildmember guide, or will sell unearthed Khyber shards to the guild, provided it returns to the surface.

Even if the Finders Guild isn't directly involved with a dragonshard prospecting expedition, it is likely that the guild soon learns of its existence. The guild pays competitive prices for unattuned dragonshards, with a premium if the origin of the shards is also provided. Of course, with the inquisitives and bounty hunters at the guild's disposal, a new Khyber cave or Siberys fall zone won't stay secret for long, at least within the guild.

The Finders Guild in the World

"Looking for somethin'?"
—Braak'akka, Finders Guild mercenary

The Finders Guild sponsors a number of activities that draw the interest of adventurers. Exploration, investigation, bounty hunting, and the search for wealth are all fine endeavors for a PC. Add to this the fact that House Tharashk maintains enclaves throughout Khorvaire, and characters would always have a source of potential employment and adventure.

The Finders Guild is operated by House Tharashk, and the leaders of the guild are humans and half-orcs that bear the Mark of Finding. The headquarters of the guild is located with the house headquarters in the city of Zarash'ak, in the Shadow Marches. There, a council convenes to discuss all aspects of the guild's business: mining, prospecting, bounty hunting and tracking, investigation, and the new mercenary enterprise.

The head of dragonshard acquisition, which includes mining and prospecting regarding dragonshards, is Vurlaak d'Tharashk (N male half-orc rogue 4/dragonmark heir 3). Vurlaak has a particular knack for judging market conditions, and he has kept the dragonshard business profitable since before the end of the Last War. He is keenly interested in expanding guild operations into Q'barra and Xen'drik, because he fears that the Eberron shard fields in the Shadow Marches will eventually be depleted, and looks to those locations as new sources of revenue.

Vurlaak is well respected by other members of the guild and the house. He proved his dedication to the success of the Finders Guild by once personally leading a team of prospectors on a Khyber shard reclamation mission. Only half the team returned, but the spoils of that mission alone funded the operations of the guild for many months. When not in the Shadow Marches, Vurlaak attends to guild business throughout Khorvaire, flying from city to city on an airship on loan from House Lyrandar.

Most members of the Finders Guild are happy to be a part of it. The guild provides consistent leads for work that the members would have a difficult time arranging independently, due to the capricious nature of the professions that the guild represents. With the Finders Guild, a bounty hunter can start off after a new mark, a prospector can get a new lead on a lode, and an investigator can start the trail of a new mystery.

NPC Reactions

The citizens of most of Khorvaire's nations treat the Finders Guild with the same measure of respect they have for the other dragonmarked houses. Even though many members of the Finders Guild are independent contractors, when on guild business they are afforded a higher level of cooperation, and membership in the guild confers some validity and authority to a guildmember's position. The common people of the Five Nations are generally indifferent to the guild, and they do not go out of their way to work against the guild's aims.

Finders Guild Lore

Characters with Knowledge (history) can research the Finders Guild to learn more about it. When a character makes a skill check, read or paraphrase the following, including the information from lower DCs.

DC 10: "The Finders Guild is a bunch of bounty hunters and trackers, and orcs, too."

DC 15: "House Tharashk runs the Finders Guild. It supplies most of the dragonshards in the Five Nations."

DC 20: "The Finders Guild pays handsomely for dragonshards, and sometimes contracts independent adventurers to investigate rumored dragonshard locations."

Because the Finders Guild is active in most major cities, a DC 15 Gather Information check in any town or city will get a character information regarding the nearest contact for the guild, and in most major cities will also gain the information above for a DC 15 check result.

The Finders Guild in the Game

The Finders Guild provides a perfect means to start an adventure for PCs of nearly any level. Low-level PCs could register with the guild to gain information on adventuring opportunities, such as locating a missing person or escorting Eberron shard shipments. At mid-levels, PCs might be contracted to lead a Khyber shard mining expedition. Even high-level PCs might be contacted by the Finders Guild to assist in artifact retrieval or to track down a particularly dangerous fugitive.

As members of the guild, the PCs not only would have to deal with the missions they are assigned, but would need to make positive impressions on other, more senior guildmembers. Completing missions not only successfully, but also in a timely fashion, is important to ensure future work.

The Finders Guild could also represent competitors of the PCs' group, racing toward the same goal, which could be a dragonshard deposit deep within Khyber or a fugitive marked for death whom the PCs know to be innocent. In these cases, conflict need not be deadly, but can still be suspenseful.

Any character who bears the Mark of Finding is eligible to join the Finders Guild. All others must pass a cursory background check before the guild will provide anything more than menial tasks, such as guarding caravans or finding lost pets. The guild doesn't pay any bounties directly, but acts as an intermediary between those who have lost someone or something and those who find that same person or object. In the case of dragonshard acquisition, the Finders Guild collects and purchases the shards at the behest of House Tharashk, which then sells the dragonshards to other interested parties.

In nearly all instances of business arranged by the Finders Guild, the guild assumes a commission on every bounty and sale equal to 15% of the bounty's writ or the sale price of the item in question. Since any money exchanging hands for these services passes through the guild, this fee is automatically deducted from the payment.

Dragonshards are a different matter. The Finders Guild pays the market prices given earlier in this chapter for unattuned dragonshards of all kinds. In addition, if the selling party also indicates the source of the dragonshards, a 10% premium will be paid upon confirmation of the source. In a well-defended location deep within the House Tharashk compound in Zarash'ak, the Finders Guild keeps records of all known dragonshard harvesting locations, including Khyber caves, Siberys fall zones, Eberron fields, and ancient ruins of the daelkyr and the giants in Khorvaire and Xen'drik, respectively.

Sample Finders Guild Member

Vurlaak d'Tharashk, the head of dragonmark acquisition for the Finders Guild, is a dedicated member of the organization who adopted the dragonmark heir prestige class at his earliest opportunity, so as to maximize the benefits of his Least Mark of Finding and Lesser Mark of Finding.

VURLAAK D'THARASHK   CR 7

Male half-orc rogue 4/dragonmark heir 3
N Medium humanoid
Init +3; **Senses** darkvision 60 ft.; Listen +6, Spot +6
Languages Common, Orc, Giant

AC 20, touch 13, flat-footed 20; uncanny dodge
hp 33 (7 HD)
Resist evasion
Fort +5, **Ref** +10, **Will** +5

Speed 30 ft. (6 squares)
Melee +2 short sword +9 (1d6+4) or
Ranged +1 longbow +9 (1d8+1)
Base Atk +5; **Grp** +7
Atk Options sneak attack +2d6
Combat Gear potion of invisibility, 3 potions of cure light wounds
Spell-Like Abilities
 2/day (CL 9th)—locate creature
 1/day (CL 4th)—identify, locate object

Abilities Str 14, Dex 16, Con 13, Int 14, Wis 8, Cha 8
SQ trapfinding, trap sense +1, house status, improved least dragonmark, improved lesser dragonmark
Feats Favored in House (Tharashk), Iron Will, Least Mark of Finding, Lesser Mark of Finding
Skills Appraise +11, Bluff +6, Climb +6, Disable Device +9, Gather Information +10, Hide +10, Jump +4, Listen +6, Move Silently +10, Open Lock +10, Spot +6, Search +9, Sense Motive +9
Possessions combat gear plus +2 short sword, +1 longbow with 20 arrows, +1 mithral chain shirt, +1 buckler

House Status (Ex) +3 bonus on all interaction checks with others of House Tharashk

Hook "Aye, I lost half m' team in Khyber . . . but the shards! Gods, the shards we brought back were enough t' make a mother disown her son, I swear it!"

POWER OF PURITY

"I'll not stand oppression."

—Harkra Loivaerl Lonadar

Many years ago, while the Last War raged on, a revolution of sorts took place quietly behind the closed borders of Zilargo. For years, gnome spellcasters of all sorts believed that elementals were merely manifestations of the raw elements of which they were composed. Certainly they had languages and exhibited behaviors that indicated some amount of intelligence, but most thought the creatures were mindless drones capable only of receiving orders or serving in some other capability. Only after researchers had observed the creatures on their native planes directly did anyone suspect that elementals were as sentient as any human. None of Zilargo's casters dared suggest that their exploitation of elementals cease, however, but one wizard made a daring suggestion.

This wizard, a gnome named Harkra Loivaerl Lonadar, felt that more could be accomplished with the art of elemental binding by negotiating with the elementals. Her theories, which began to gain strength only toward the end of the Last War, were not popular.

Most of the nation's spellcasters and elemental experts felt that the system in place was fine. They saw no need to tamper with something that worked, and especially felt no compassion for the creatures they were binding to service in their airships and weapons. Harkra managed to convince a small coalition of merchants in positions of influence within Zilargo that her ideas had merit, however, and the Power of Purity was founded.

The Power of Purity in the World

"You attract more flame with tinder than ash."

—Power of Purity saying

The group exists today as part of the elemental binding industry in Zilargo. The initial skepticism of their ideas has since been overcome by their results. In 991 YK, an elite group within the faction, called the Inmost, was founded by Harkra Loivaerl Lonadar, who had grown tired of the increasing bureaucracy required for running a rapidly growing business, which is what the Power of Purity had become. Harkra gave up control of the larger organization's interests to more fully dedicate herself to her ideas on binding research. The Inmost is primarily composed of elemental scions (see the elemental scion of Zilargo prestige class, page 68) and other eccentric individuals. Combined with the knowledge of the Power of Purity, which includes some of the foremost experts on elemental binding in all Khorvaire, the Inmost's members have made the organization quite powerful. These individuals act as agents, guards, and even repositories of elemental knowledge. Many elemental savants (a prestige class found in the *Complete Arcane* supplement) also number among both the Power of Purity and the Inmost, and the group has gradually become responsible for filling a large number of Zilargo's elemental vessel contracts.

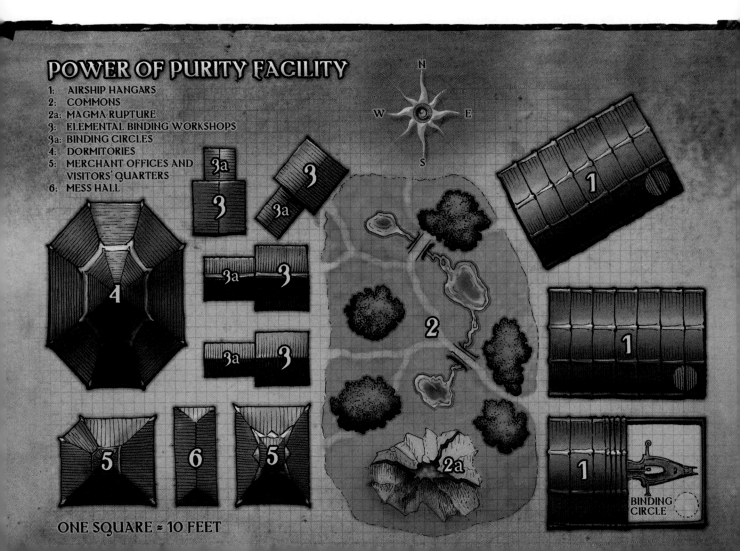

POWER OF PURITY FACILITY

1: AIRSHIP HANGARS
2: COMMONS
2a: MAGMA RUPTURE
3: ELEMENTAL BINDING WORKSHOPS
3a: BINDING CIRCLES
4: DORMITORIES
5: MERCHANT OFFICES AND
   VISITORS' QUARTERS
6: MESS HALL

BINDING CIRCLE

ONE SQUARE ≈ 10 FEET

Power of Purity Lore

Characters with Knowledge (history) can research the Power of Purity organization to learn more about it. When a character makes a skill check, read or paraphrase the following, including the information from lower DCs.

DC 15: The Power of Purity has two basic goals: to more fully understand elementals and their power, and make that power their own.

DC 20: The Power of Purity believes that it will find more success in dealing with elementals through parley than through brute force. It frequently negotiates with the elementals it binds into vessels and other items before the binding process begins, gaining permission, or at least acceptance, from the creatures.

DC 25: Some say that some members of the Power of Purity bind elementals to more than items—they bind elementals, or parts of them, to their own flesh.

The Power of Purity in the Game

The Power of Purity's goals make an interesting foil to the traditional role of good and evil in the game, and NPC "purists" can add color and interest to what could otherwise be uninteresting encounters.

Purists who take too much interest in PCs who call or bind elementals might even attempt to interfere with the party's goals, perhaps going so far as to kidnap a "guilty" party member and keep him or her captive in a Power of Purity research facility.

Power of Purity Facility

The Swiftwind facility lies in the northwest corner of Zilargo, at the foot of the Howling Peaks, and has long been in the forefront of elemental binding research. Its massive airship hangars churn out an airship a year each, and the crews in each have friendly competitions to see which can fulfill its order before the others.

The massive commons area in the center of the facility (area 2) is an equally remarkable feature. Because the Power of Purity believes in willingly negotiating with elementals, many of these rare extraplanar creatures wander the commons at all times. The water elementals find the commons' three large ponds quite interesting, the air elementals enjoy the trees, the earth elementals roam beneath the natural vegetation, and the fire elementals particularly enjoy the magically created rupture in the earth (area 2a) at the south end of the area. Here a miniature volcano has formed. It does not erupt because this is not a volcanically active region. The leadership of the installation decided to create a fissure in the earth for the comfort of its fire elemental visitors here by bringing a steady, but slow, stream of magma to the surface. The compound also features several grafting workshops (area 3), each complete with a summoning and binding chamber (area 3a). Area 4 is the dormitory, where members of the organization can find comfortable quarters, whether they are visiting or engaging in research themselves.

This installation was founded ten years ago as one of the first created by the Power of Purity. Other than adding a second and then a third airship hangar, it hasn't grown much in that time. The compound suffers frequent raids from bandits out of the Howling Peaks, and PCs might be hired to root them out of the mountains once and for all. The characters might also arrive here on behalf of a powerful merchant or noble to retrieve a newly purchased airship, or they might come on their own to purchase elemental grafts (see page 129).

Sample Power of Purity Member

Roywin Garrick, a wizard who has taken up the elemental savant prestige class (described in Complete Arcane), is fast becoming an accomplished wielder of cold-based magic.

ROYWIN GARRICK   CR 8

Female gnome wizard 5/elemental savant (cold) 3
N Small humanoid
Init +2; **Senses** low-light vision; Listen +3, Spot +1
Languages Common, Gnome, Draconic, Dwarven, Elven

AC 18, touch 16, flat-footed 16; +4 AC against giants
hp 44 (8 HD)
Immune sleep
Resist cold 5; +2 against illusions
Fort +5, **Ref** +4, **Will** +8

Speed 20 ft. (4 squares)
Melee quarterstaff +2 (1d4–1) or
Ranged mwk light crossbow +6 (1d6)
Base Atk +3; **Grp** +2
Atk Options +1 on attacks against kobolds and goblinoids
Special Actions +2 bonus on caster level checks to overcome spell resistance when casting cold spells
Combat Gear scroll of *teleport*
Wizard Spells Prepared (CL 8th):
    4th—*ice storm* (2) (DC 19), *stoneskin*
    3rd—*fireball* (cold) (2) (DC 18), *lightning bolt* (cold) (2) (DC 18)
    2nd—*Melf's acid arrow* (cold) (2) (DC 17), *scorching ray* (cold) (2), (DC 17)
    1st—*charm person* (DC 15), *mage armor†*, *magic missile*, *shield*, *sleep*
    0—*arcane mark*, *message*, *ray of frost* (3) (DC 15)
    †Already cast
Spell-Like Abilities (CL 1st):
    1/day—*dancing lights*, *ghost sound* (DC 10), *prestidigitation*, *speak with animals* (burrowing mammal only, duration 1 minute)

Abilities Str 8, Dex 14, Con 16, Int 19, Wis 13, Cha 8
SQ elemental specialty, familiar (none at present)
Feats Empower Spell[B], Energy Substitution (cold), Scribe Scroll[B], Spell Focus (evocation), Toughness
Skills Alchemy +7, Concentration +14, Knowledge (arcana) +15, Knowledge (the planes) +8, Listen +3, Search +9, Spellcraft +15, Spot +1
Possessions combat gear plus masterwork light crossbow, quarterstaff, *headband of intellect +2*, *+1 mithral buckler*, *bracers of health +2*, diamond dust worth 250 gp (material component for *stoneskin*)

Spellbook spells prepared plus 0—all others; 1st—*chill touch*, *expeditious retreat*, *identify*; 2nd—*levitate*, *misdirection*; 3rd—*fly*; 4th—*wall of ice*

Elemental Specialty (Ex) Whenever Roywin casts a spell with an energy descriptor, the spell becomes a cold spell if not already so.

Hook "When they pulled me from the wreckage, I made a promise to myself. So you see, I've embraced the cold. What a difference ice can make."

The warforged titan was large and slow, but it only had to hit Halkhad once to end this battle. The soulknife focused all his will and danced around the huge construct, striking multiple times with his whirling mind blades while avoiding the titan's crushing maul and slicing axe. . . .

CHAPTER TWO

CHARACTER OPTIONS

This chapter presents a variety of new options for EBERRON characters, including a new character race (the daelkyr half-blood), a new offshoot of the warforged race (the psiforged), a variant artificer, rituals to imbue yourself with magic powers, and a host of new feats.

DAELKYR HALF-BLOOD

"It's hard being me."

—Faran Coolworm

Despite being sealed away under the earth, a daelkyr can reproduce, after a fashion. A daelkyr's corporeal incarceration constantly leaks the virulence of its corrupting spirit. The unborn are especially vulnerable to this influence, and those innocents growing in the wombs of their mothers within the sphere of this beastly influence are born as daelkyr half-bloods.

DAELKYR HALF-BLOOD RACIAL TRAITS

Anguish burns in the eyes of daelkyr half-bloods, because their spirits are always in conflict. The most obvious outward sign that a creature has been "womb-warped" is the natural symbiont that is first birthed with a daelkyr half-blood (the symbiont is sometimes mistaken for a disfigured twin or gruesome afterbirth), then later befriended, worn, and utilized by the adult half-blood.

Daelkyr half-bloods are most often born of human mothers, and as such share almost all physical features in common with humans. A daelkyr half-blood stands between 5 and 6 feet tall and rarely weighs more than 170 pounds.

- Aberration Type: Daelkyr half-bloods are creatures with the aberration type. As aberrations, daelkyr half-bloods have darkvision out to 60 feet. They are proficient with all simple weapons and any weaponlike symbionts they use, as well as with whatever types of armor (light, medium, or heavy) that their classes allow. Daelkyr half-bloods eat, sleep, and breathe.
- Medium: As Medium creatures, daelkyr half-bloods have no special bonuses or penalties due to size.
- Daelkyr half-blood base land speed is 30 feet.
- Personal Symbiont (Ex): All half-bloods begin play with one personal symbiont that they can pick from the following list: breed leech, crawling gauntlet,

or throwing scarab. If a personal symbiont is lost, a daelkyr half-blood can grow a replacement from his own flesh over a period of 2d4 days. A daelkyr half-blood can't grow or regrow symbionts that he has gained in any other manner, nor can a daelkyr half-blood grow a replacement for a symbiont if the original symbiont yet lives.

As a daelkyr half-blood advances in level, he can grow a new personal symbiont as indicated on the table below. Any new personal symbiont grown replaces the old symbiont. A daelkyr half-blood can choose additional symbionts from the list provided above, as well as from new choices as they become available, as indicated on the table.

Level	Choices[1]
1st	Breed leech, crawling gauntlet, throwing scarab
5th	Stormstalk, winter cyst
10th	Spellwurm, tentacle whip
15th	Tongue worm

1 All choices from an earlier level are also available to a higher-level daelkyr half-blood.

- Symbiont Mastery: A daelkyr half-blood gains the Symbiont Mastery feat (see page 51) as a bonus feat.
- Symbiont Dependency (Ex): Daelkyr half-bloods' facility with symbiont usage comes at a price. Without daily contact with at least one symbiont, a daelkyr half-blood begins to die. If a daelkyr half-blood has no contact with a symbiont for 24 hours, he takes 1 point of Constitution damage. He takes this damage every 24 hours until contact is restored, and Constitution damage sustained in this fashion cannot be restored by any means as long as the daelkyr half-blood remains separated from symbionts.
- Unbalanced Mind (Ex): The minds of daelkyr half-bloods are in constant self revolt, reflecting their daelkyr "parents" mixed with the more standard mindset of their biological mothers. Any creature that attempts to read the thoughts of a daelkyr half-blood, or otherwise study his mind, must make a Will save (DC 10 + 1/2 half-blood's level + Cha modifier) or be dazed for 1 round.
- Automatic Language: Common. Bonus Language: Daelkyr.
- Favored Class: Rogue.

SQ naturally psionic, psicrystal body (3 power points), warforged traits

Feats Narrow Mind*, Overchannel*, Psionic Body*, Psionic Meditation* *See the *Expanded Psionics Handbook*.

Skills Concentration +8 (+12 to become focused), Diplomacy +8, Gather Information +8, Sense Motive +9, Psicraft* +11 *See the *Expanded Psionics Handbook*.

Possessions combat gear plus masterwork light crossbow with 20 bolts, +1 *cloak of resistance*, +1 *ring of protection*

PSIONIC ARTIFICER

The industries of magic pervade Khorvaire. The prevalence of House Cannith, and the predominance of magewrights and other artisans, resulted in the perfection of the creation process for all manner of magic devices and items.

Artificers endeavor to understand and replicate the magic around them. In recent years, many artificers have been exposed to psionics through a variety of sources: Kalashtar are not unknown now in many parts of Khorvaire, and the Inspired have an increasing presence in Q'barra and other nations. Eventually, some artificers developed a knack for crafting psionic items.

Psionic artificers are similar to standard artificers, but they craft psionic items instead of magic items. Many of these artificers are kalashtar, but innate psionic talent isn't absolutely necessary to advance as a psionic artificer. A few psionic artificers work in Q'barra, supplying their crafts to the larger concentrations of psionic people in those regions. They might choose to set up shop in Stormreach, selling their wares to psionic characters who travel to Xen'drik looking for dragonshards. They might also be kalashtar secluded in the mountains of Adar, applying the skills of artifice to psionic creations they can use to defend themselves against the Inspired. Few psionic artificers are found in Riedra, however, because the Inspired maintain tight control over the production of any magic or psionic items.

Some artificers wield the power of the mind, rather than magic

GAME RULE INFORMATION

A psionic artificer is identical to the artificer presented in the EBERRON *Campaign Setting*, with the modifications below.

A psionic artificer is treated as a standard artificer for purposes of meeting feat or prestige class prerequisites. A character cannot have levels in both artificer and psionic artificer.

Class Skills

A psionic artificer gains Knowledge (psionics), Psicraft, and Use Psionic Device (all described in *Expanded Psionics Handbook*) as class skills in place of Knowledge (arcana), Spellcraft, and Use Magic Device.

Class Features

The psionic artificer's class features function identically to the normal artificer class features excepted as noted here.

Artisan Bonus: A psionic artificer gains a +2 bonus on Use Psionic Device checks to activate an item of a kind for which he has the prerequisite item creation feat.

Infusions: A psionic artificer's infusion list remains the same, but references to spells are replaced with references to powers. For example, *spell storing item* becomes *power storing item*, and *metamagic item* becomes *metapsionic item*, and affects a power trigger item.

Item Creation: A psionic artificer cannot emulate spells to create magic items.

When a psionic artificer emulates a power for item creation, he uses his Use Psionic Device skill (rather than Use Magic Device).

Feats: A psionic artificer does not gain the standard artificer item creation feats. He instead gains psionic item creation feats, as indicated by the following table.

PSIONIC ARTIFICER FEATS

Level	Artificer Feat	Psionic Artificer Feat
1st	Scribe Scroll	Imprint Stone
2nd	Brew Potion	Scribe Tattoo
3rd	Craft Wondrous Item	Craft Universal Item
4th	Bonus feat	Bonus feat*
5th	Craft Magic Arms and Armor	Craft Psionic Arms and Armor
6th	Craft Wand	Craft Dorje
8th	Bonus feat	Bonus feat*
9th	Craft Rod	Craft Cognizance Crystal
12th	Craft Staff	Craft Psicrown
13th	Bonus feat	Bonus feat*
14th	Forge Ring	Craft Psionic Construct
16th	Bonus feat	Bonus feat*
20th	Bonus feat	Bonus feat*

*Bonus feats are selected from a restricted list.

A psionic artificer gains a bonus feat at 4th level and every four levels thereafter (8th, 12th, 16th, and 20th). For each of these bonus feats, the psionic artificer must choose a metapsionic feat or a feat from the following list: Attune Magic Weapon, Craft Construct, Exceptional Artisan, Extra Rings, Extraordinary Artisan, Legendary Artisan, Dorje Mastery (see page 46).

Metapsionic Power Trigger (Su): At 6th level, a psionic artificer gains this ability in place of metamagic spell trigger. A character can apply a metapsionic feat he knows to a power trigger device, such as a dorje. Using this ability expends additional charges from the item equal to 1 + 1/2 the number of additional power points normally required to employ the metapsionic power.

Metapsionic Power Completion (Su): At 11th level, a psionic artificer gains this ability in place of metamagic spell completion. The character can apply a metapsionic feat he knows to a power completion device, such as a power stone. He must succeed on a Use Psionic Device check with a DC equal to 20 + twice the total number of power points required to manifest the metapsionic power normally. For example, applying the Empower Power feat to a *power stone of ego whip* has a DC of 20 + (2 × 5), or 40. A psionic artificer can use this ability a number of times per day equal to 3 + his Int modifier.

Skill Mastery: At 13th level, a psionic artificer can take 10 when making Psicraft or Use Psionic Device checks, even if stress and distractions would normally prevent him from doing so. This ability circumvents the normal rule that a character cannot take 10 on a Use Psionic Device check, and replaces the skill mastery ability of a standard artificer.

DRAGON TOTEM RITUALS

Any character can take part in a dragon totem ritual, though the ritual itself can only be performed by a character with the Dragon Totem Lorekeeper feat (see the feats portion of this chapter). This feat requires a character to have the Dragon Totem feat, which can be found on page 52 of the EBERRON *Campaign Setting*. A dragon totem ritual requires 1 uninterrupted hour of meditation by all those participating in the ritual, as well as the sacrifice of a quantity of Siberys dragonshards at the conclusion of the ceremony. If anything interrupts the concentration of any participant, the entire ritual is disrupted and no benefits are bestowed (the dragonshards to be sacrificed are not affected by a failed ritual).

When the ritual is completed, each participant gains the indicated benefits for the ritual. (A character performing the ritual can choose to gain no benefit from the ritual; in this case he need not invest any dragonshards in the sacrifice.) These benefits last for 24 hours. If the ritual grants a limited number of uses, these must be used within 24 hours or they are lost.

Multiple dragon totem rituals can be combined into a single ceremony. Doing this has no effect on the time required for the ritual, but all dragonshard costs are cumulative.

A few of the known dragon totem rituals are described below, using the following format:

Prerequisites: To gain the benefit of a dragon totem ritual, you must meet any prerequisites given here.

Benefit: The benefit gained by completing the dragon totem ritual.

Dragon Totem: Characters with the Dragon Totem feat can choose to gain a slightly improved benefit from the ritual. In the case of multiple rituals combined into a single ceremony, this decision can be made separately for each benefit gained.

Cost: This entry is the gp cost in Siberys dragonshards required for each person to benefit from the ritual. For

TOTEM BEACH TEMPLE

Altar
Observation
Reliquary
Dragonshard Vault
Entry Guardians

ONE SQUARE ≈ 5 FEET

every multiple of the amount required to provide the benefit to all the participants, the ritual's effect lasts for an additional 24 hours. The amount must be increased in complete multiples of the minimum amount of dragonshards; one character can't pay extra to gain the benefit for 48 hours unless all participants do so.

Ritual of . . .	Prerequisites	Benefit
Breath	Con 11 or Concentration 1 rank, 5 HD	Gain breath weapon
Fangs	Str 11, 6 HD	Gain secondary bite attack
Presence	Cha 11 or Intimidate 1 rank, 5 HD	Render enemy shaken for 1 minute
Prophecy	Int 11 or Knowledge (arcana) 1 rank, Speak Language (Draconic), 2 HD	Gain Dragon Prophesier feat
Resistance	5 HD	Gain resistance 20 to energy type
The Totem Guardian	Cha 11, 14 HD	Call dragon to fight for you
Vision	Wis 11 or Spot 1 rank, 8 HD	Gain darkvision
Wings	Dex 11, 10 HD	Fly at land speed

RITUAL OF BREATH

A dragon's breath weapon is its most legendary ability. Fire, lightning, cold, and acid are wielded with ease by true dragons, requiring only an exhalation. The ritual of breath focuses on the energy of a dragon's breath, granting the participating warriors a modicum of this power.

Prerequisites: Con 11 or Concentration 1 rank, 5 HD.

Benefit: You feel the energy of a dragon burning within your lungs. You can release a breath weapon up to three times during the ritual's 24-hour duration. The shape of the breath weapon and the type of damage dealt matches the dragon totem of the individual performing the ritual.

Dragon	Energy	Shape
Black	Acid	60-ft. line
Blue	Electricity	60-ft. line
Brass	Fire	60-ft. line
Bronze	Electricity	60-ft. line
Copper	Acid	60-ft. line
Gold	Fire	30-ft. cone
Green	Acid	30-ft. cone
Red	Fire	30-ft. cone
Silver	Cold	30-ft. cone
White	Cold	30-ft. cone

Your breath weapon deals 4d6 points of damage of the indicated energy type to all creatures in its area. Creatures caught in your breath weapon take half damage if they succeed on a Reflex save. The DC of the saving throw is 10 + 1/2 your Hit Dice + your Con modifier.

Dragon Totem: You can choose to match the breath weapon to the dragon of your dragon totem. In this case your breath weapon deals 6d6 points of damage.

Cost: Siberys dragonshards worth 800 gp.

RITUAL OF FANGS

The dragon teeth found discarded along Totem Beach are prized by the Seren tribes, whose members fashion them into deadly weapons. The Seren can only imagine the deadliness of a mouthful of those teeth. Through the ritual of fangs, the Seren warriors can mimic the attacks of their revered patrons, gaining dangerous bites of their own. Dragon totem warriors consider defeating a foe with the fangs granted by this ritual to be a sacred act.

Prerequisites: Str 11, 6 HD.

Benefit: You grow long, sharp teeth. You can make a bite attack as a secondary natural attack (using your normal attack bonus −5). The bite deals 1d6 points of damage + 1/2 your Str bonus.

If you already have a bite attack, you can choose to replace your existing bite attack with this attack; otherwise you gain no benefit from the ritual.

Dragon Totem: Your bite attack deals 1d8 points of damage.

Cost: Siberys dragonshards worth 1,000 gp.

RITUAL OF PRESENCE

Powerful dragons can unsettle their foes with their mere presence. Warriors who undergo this ritual gain some semblance of that ability, able to strike fear into the hearts of their enemies.

Prerequisites: Cha 11 or Intimidate 1 rank, 5 HD.

Benefit: As a standard action, you can render a single enemy shaken for 1 minute. Your enemy must be able to see you and must be within 30 feet. A successful Will save (DC 10 + 1/2 your HD + Cha modifier) negates this effect; if you have at least 5 ranks in Intimidate, the save DC increases by 2. Any enemy who successfully saves against this effect is immune to your use of this ability for 24 hours. Multiple uses of this ability don't stack.

Dragon Totem: When you use this ability, you can choose to have it affect all enemies within 30 feet who can see you.

Cost: Siberys dragonshards worth 500 gp.

RITUAL OF PROPHECY

Dragons are obsessed with the draconic Prophecy. Creatures that undergo this ritual gain some insight of the Prophecy, and can claim some ability to read signs and portents themselves.

Prerequisites: Int 11 or Knowledge (arcana) 1 rank, Speak Language (Draconic), 2 HD.

Benefit: You gain the Dragon Prophesier feat (see page 46) as a bonus feat, or if you already have that feat, any one of the feats that require Dragon Prophesier as a prerequisite. This feat can't be used as a prerequisite to qualify for another feat, prestige class, or other special ability. See Feats in this chapter for details.

Dragon Totem: Your Wisdom is treated as 2 points higher for the purpose of determining how many times you can enter a state of prophetic favor each day.

Cost: Siberys dragonshards worth 1,500 gp.

RITUAL OF RESISTANCE

The power of the dragons can be harnessed to protect the dragon totem warriors against the energy of a dragon's breath weapon, as well as other sources that generate the same type of energy.

Prerequisite: 5 HD.

Benefit: You gain resistance 20 to the type of energy associated with the dragon totem of the character leading the ritual. This effect manifests as a shimmering outline of barely visible flowing sigils, much like the script of a dragonmark, that flows around you in the shape of a draconic form and intensifies when it prevents you from taking energy damage you would otherwise by subjected to.

Dragon Color	Energy
Black, copper, green	Acid
Blue, bronze	Electricity
Brass, gold, red	Fire
Silver, white	Cold

Dragon Totem: You can choose instead to gain immunity to the type of energy associated with your own dragon totem.

Cost: Siberys dragonshards worth 400 gp.

RITUAL OF THE TOTEM GUARDIAN

Few among the Seren dragon totem warriors have ever witnessed a totem guardian, because only the most powerful among them are even capable of conducting this ritual. A totem guardian is a quasi-real manifestation of a dragon totem.

Prerequisites: Cha 11, 14 HD.

Benefit: Once per day, you can call forth a dragon totem guardian that closely resembles a dragon of a kind that matches the totem of the ritual leader. Though it resembles a living creature, the totem guardian is actually a creation of magical energy. Close examination reveals that the hide of the dragon actually resembles a tightly scripted dragonmark.

Regardless, the dragon functions identically to a dragon of the indicated kind and age. It attacks your enemies to the best of its ability. (If you can speak Draconic, you can give it more complex commands.) The totem guardian lasts for a number of rounds equal to your HD, after which it discorporates into a flurry of dragonmark slivers that flare brightly before slowly winking out.

Dragon	Age
Black	Juvenile
Blue	Juvenile
Brass	Juvenile
Bronze	Young
Copper	Young
Gold	Very young
Green	Juvenile
Red	Young
Silver	Young
White	Young adult

Dragon Totem: The totem guardian can match your dragon totem instead of the totem of the ritual's leader; in this case the totem guardian gains a +2 morale bonus on attack rolls, damage rolls, and saving throws.

Cost: Siberys dragonshards worth 6,000 gp.

RITUAL OF VISION

Dragons are known for their keen ability to detect foes, even those they cannot see. Seren tribal members who undergo this ritual are granted great visual acuity. This ritual is commonly performed before a night assault on enemies.

Prerequisites: Wis 11 or Spot 1 rank, 8 HD.

Benefit: You gain darkvision out to 60 feet. You also gain a +2 competence bonus on Spot checks.

Dragon Totem: In addition to the above benefit, you also gain blindsense with a range of 10 feet.

Cost: Siberys dragonshards worth 1,200 gp.

RITUAL OF WINGS

Dragons are at their most majestic when soaring through the air. They are masters of the sky, raining fire and ice down upon their foes. With the ritual of wings, dragon totem warriors can take to the air in a semblance of their draconic patrons.

One totem ritual grants wings

Prerequisites: Dex 11, 10 HD.

Benefit: A flowing sigil, much like a dragonmark, emerges from your shoulders. This sigil briefly wraps about you before unfurling into a pair of wings attached to your back. These wings give you a limited ability to fly. You can fly at your standard land speed, with poor maneuverability (see page 20 in the *Dungeon Master's Guide* for more on flying and aerial combat).

Dragon Totem: Your fly speed is equal to your land speed + 10 feet, and you have good maneuverability.

Cost: Siberys dragonshards worth 1,500 gp.

FEATS

The feats in this section are nearly all tied to a specific region or field of magic in Eberron. They focus on the diversity of the various magical (or psionic) energies that run rampant across Eberron, and provide characters with a multitude of options for focusing on one or more of these schools of magical theory. For example, Shae-ahm Rhen Skyshadow (a gnome elemental scion of Zilargo) might be interested in choosing the Augment Elemental feat, which makes summoned elementals more powerful, or the Elemental Smite feat, which allows her to channel the energy of an elemental graft into her attacks.

The feats described in this chapter follow the rules and format for feats as described in the *Player's Handbook*. Item creation feats are described in the *Player's Handbook*. Psionic feats and psionic item creation feats are described in the *Expanded Psionics Handbook*.

No new feat types are presented here, though some subsets of feats share certain rules or themes in common. Several feats are concerned with how attuned a character is to the draconic Prophecy, while others augment your ability to benefit from dragon totem rituals (described earlier in this chapter).

AUGMENT ELEMENTAL

Your knowledge of planar magic allows you to imbue your summoned elementals with extraordinary combat prowess and durability.

Prerequisite: Knowledge (the planes) 2 ranks.

Benefit: Each elemental you conjure with a *summon* spell gains a +2 enhancement bonus on attack rolls and damage rolls, and temporary hit points equal to twice its Hit Dice.

CULL WAND ESSENCE

You can focus the raw magical energy of a wand or staff into a beam of energy.

Prerequisite: Use Magic Device 4 ranks.

Benefit: When using a spell trigger device, such as a wand or staff, you can expend a charge from the device and produce a ray of magical energy that you can fire at a single target within 60 feet. With a successful ranged touch attack, the ray deals amage based on the level of the spell normally produced by the magic item, according to the table below.

Spell Level	Damage
1st	1d6
2nd	3d6
3rd	6d6
4th	10d6

For example, a charge from a *wand of cure moderate wounds* could be used to deal 3d6 points of damage to a target.

This attack benefits from Weapon Focus (ranged spells) and similar feats and effects. The ray is treated as a spell of the same level as the spell normally produced by the magic item. Spell resistance applies to the damage, using the caster level of the spell trigger item.

DEATHLESS FLESHGRAFTER [ITEM CREATION]

You can grow and graft the tissues and body parts of deathless creatures onto others, granting the recipients of your grafts new, potent abilities.

Prerequisites: Aereni elf, Knowledge (religion) 2 ranks, caster level 5th.

Benefit: You can create and attach any deathless graft whose prerequisites you meet (see individual grafts in Chapter 5 for prerequisites). Creating and attaching a deathless graft follows the normal rules for creating a graft (see page 127).

DORJE MASTERY [ITEM CREATION]

Psionic dorjes are more potent in your hands.

Prerequisites: Craft Dorje, manifester level 9th.

Benefit: When you use a dorje, the power manifested is treated as if augmented by 4 additional power points. If the power cannot be augmented, then the DC of saving throws against the dorje's effect is increased by 2.

DRAGON PROPHESIER

The sky above, the pits and caverns below, and the land between contain signs and portents for those with the skill to see them. The dragons of Argonnessen seek meaning in the patterns they observe all around them, looking for omens of the draconic Prophecy.

Like the dragons, you seek to untangle and perceive the record of everything that has been, and more important, what will be. The world is the record, and you are the perennial student. This openness to knowledge infuses you with additional foresight—you have prophetic favor.

Prerequisites: Knowledge (arcana) 2 ranks, Speak Language (Draconic).

Benefit: With a full-round action, you can place yourself in a state of openness and insight into the world around you. This state is referred to as prophetic favor, and it lasts for a number of rounds equal to 3 + 1/2 the number of Knowledge (arcana) ranks you have.

While in prophetic favor, you gain a +1 insight bonus on saves. Dragon Prophesier also enables you to take additional feats that grant you extra benefits while in a state of prophetic favor.

You can enter a state of prophetic favor a number of times per day equal to 1/2 your HD (round up) + your Wis bonus (if any).

DRAGON TOTEM FOCUS

Your focus allows you to enjoy the benefit of a dragon totem ritual longer than normal.

Prerequisites: Base attack bonus +4, Concentration 2 ranks, Dragon Totem.

Benefit: Whenever you benefit from a dragon totem ritual (see page 43), the effects last for an additional 24 hours.

DRAGON TOTEM LOREKEEPER

You have been instructed in how to perform the rituals of dragon totem magic.

Prerequisites: Knowledge (history) 15 ranks, Dragon Totem, ability to spontaneously cast 1st-level arcane spells.

Benefit: You can perform dragon totem rituals (see page 43).

DRAGON TOTEM SCION

You are naturally attuned to the magic of the dragon totem ritual.

Prerequisites: Dragon Totem.

Benefit: You can treat your Hit Dice and all ability scores as two higher for the purpose of meeting prerequisites for dragon totem rituals.

ELDEEN PLANTGRAFTER
[ITEM CREATION]

You can create and apply plant grafts onto others, granting the recipients of your grafts new, potent abilities.

Prerequisites: Knowledge (nature) 4 ranks, caster level 5th.

Benefit: You can create and attach any plant graft whose prerequisites you meet (see individual grafts in Chapter 5 for requirements). Creating and attaching a plant graft follows the normal rules for creating a graft (see page 127).

ELEMENTAL GRAFTER
[ITEM CREATION]

You can create and apply elemental grafts onto others, granting the recipients of your grafts new, potent abilities.

Prerequisites: Knowledge (the planes) 2 ranks, caster level 5th.

Benefit: You can create and attach any elemental graft whose prerequisites you meet (see individual grafts in Chapter 5 for prerequisites). Creating and attaching an elemental graft follows the normal rules for creating a graft (see page 127).

ELEMENTAL HELMSMAN

You are more capable of piloting an elemental vessel.

Benefit: You gain a +4 bonus on opposed Charisma checks when you attempt to control an elemental vessel. If you use *lightning reins* or a *wheel of wind and water* (depending on the nature of the vessel you are attempting to pilot), your bonus increases to +10. If you fail the opposed Charisma check, the vessel continues its current motion, though you can try again the following round.

Even characters not of House Orien or House Lyrandar sometimes take this feat, in an effort to pilot airships and earth sleds without the auspices of the dragonmarked houses.

ELEMENTAL SMITE

You can channel the energy associated with one of your elemental grafts into your melee attacks.

Prerequisites: Cha 11, Knowledge (the planes) 3 ranks, at least one elemental graft.

Benefit: You can attempt to smite a creature with one normal melee attack. You deal 1 extra point of energy damage per character level. The graft donor of one of your elemental grafts determines the type of energy damage: electricity for an air graft, acid for an earth graft, fire for a fire graft, and cold for a water graft. If you have more than one elemental graft, you choose one of the graft's associated energy types when you make the elemental smite attack.

If you accidentally smite a creature that has immunity to the type of energy damage you deal, the smite has no effect, but the ability is still used up for that day. Likewise, a missed smite attack means the smite attempt is used for the day.

You can use this smite attack once per day, plus one additional time per five levels gained (two times per day at 5th, three times per day at 10th, and so on).

ETCH SCHEMA [ITEM CREATION]

You can create a minor schema.

Prerequisite: Caster level 10th.

Benefit: You can create a schema of a spell or infusion. Etching a minor schema takes one day for each 1,000 gp in its base price. The base price of a minor schema is its spell or infusion level × its caster level × 400 gp. To etch a minor schema, you must spend 1/25 of this base price in XP and use up raw materials costing one-half of this base price.

For rules on minor schemas, see page 122.

With the proper training, spellcasters can learn to etch minor schemas

NEW FEATS

General Feats	Prerequisites	Benefit
Augment Elemental	Knowledge (the planes) 2 ranks	Summoned elementals gain +2 bonus on attack and damage and +2 hp per Hit Die
Cull Wand Essence	Use Magic Device 4 ranks	Expend wand or staff charge to deal damage with ray attack
Dragon Prophesier	Knowledge (arcana) 2 ranks, Speak Language (Draconic)	Enter prophetic favor to gain +1 insight bonus on saves
Dragon Totem Focus	Base attack bonus +4, Concentration 2 ranks, Dragon Totem	Dragon totem ritual benefit lasts extra 24 hours
Dragon Totem Lorekeeper	Knowledge (history) 15 ranks, Dragon Totem, ability to spontaneously cast 1st-level arcane spells	You can perform dragon totem rituals
Dragon Totem Scion	Dragon Totem	Meet dragon totem ritual prerequisites as if +2 HD and +2 ability scores
Elemental Helmsman	—	+4 on Cha checks to control elemental vessels
Elemental Smite	Cha 11, Knowledge (the planes) 3 ranks, at least one elemental graft	Add energy damage to melee attack
Heroic Companion	Companion creature	Companion can use your action points
Improved Homunculus	Craft Construct or craft homunculus class feature, Craft (any) 6 ranks	Your homunculus's natural armor improves, and you can give it new special abilities
Prophecy's Artifex	Knowledge (arcana) 2 ranks, Speak Language (Draconic), Craft Wand or Craft Staff, Dragon Prophesier	Enter prophetic favor to use wand or staff as swift action
Prophecy's Explorer	Base attack bonus +2, Knowledge (arcana) 2 ranks, Speak Language (Draconic), Dragon Prophesier	Enter prophetic favor to increase your speed and AC
Prophecy's Hero	Knowledge (arcana) 2 ranks, Speak Language (Draconic), Dragon Prophesier	Gain 1 temporary action point when in prophetic favor
Prophecy's Shaper	Knowledge (arcana) 4 ranks, Speak Language (Draconic), Dragon Prophesier, ability to cast 2nd-level spells	Enter prophetic favor to empower one spell per round
Prophecy's Shepherd	Knowledge (arcana) 4 ranks, Speak Language (Draconic), Dragon Prophesier, ability to spontaneously cast *cure* or *inflict* spells	Enter prophetic favor to quicken *cure* or *inflict* spells
Prophecy's Slayer	Base attack bonus +2, Knowledge (arcana) 2 ranks, Speak Language (Draconic), Dragon Prophesier	Enter prophetic favor to deal +1d6 damage against flanked or flat-footed enemies
Psiforged Body*	Warforged, 1st level only	Become psiforged, gain 1 power point, and store power points in your body as if it were a cognizance crystal
Quicken Dragonmark	Least Dragonmark	Use dragonmark abilities as a swift action
Rapid Infusion	Artificer level 3rd	Hasten an infusion without spending an action point
Symbiont Mastery	Wis 11	+4 bonus on Will saves to control symbiont; +2 hp per symbiont
Wand Surge	Caster level 3rd	Expend action point instead of wand or staff charge

HEROIC COMPANION

Your luck extends to your companion creature.

Prerequisite: Companion creature, such as an animal companion, familiar, special mount, or homunculus.

Benefit: Your animal companion, special mount, homunculus, or other companion creature can draw from your pool of action points when resolving a roll. (Cohorts and followers cannot benefit from this feat.)

You and your companion creature can each draw a maximum of 1 action point per round from your pool of action points.

You also gain 1 extra action point each time you attain a level.

HEROIC FOCUS [PSIONIC]

Despite the dangers all around, you can quickly regain your psionic focus.

Benefit: As a move action, you can spend an action point to automatically regain your psionic focus.

You also gain 1 extra action point each time you attain a level.

Special: If you have the Psionic Meditation feat (see the *Expanded Psionics Handbook*), you can spend an action point to automatically regain your focus as a swift action.

Item Creation Feats	Prerequisites	Benefit
Deathless Fleshgrafter	Aerenal elf, Knowledge (religion) 2 ranks, caster level 5th	You can create deathless grafts
Dorje Mastery*	Manifester level 9th	You gain 4 power points to augment dorje's effects
Eldeen Plantgrafter	Knowledge (nature) 4 ranks, caster level 5th	You can create plant grafts
Elemental Grafter	Knowledge (the planes) 2 ranks, caster level 5th	You can create elemental grafts
Etch Schema	Caster level 10th	You can create minor schemas

Psionic Feats	Prerequisites	Benefit
Heroic Focus*	—	Spend action point to quickly regain psionic focus
Prophecy's Mind*	Knowledge (arcana) 2 ranks, Speak Language (Draconic), Dragon Prophesier	Expend focus while in prophetic favor to avoid death
Psionic Luck*	—	Expend focus to get more from action points
Psychic Rush*	—	Spend an action point to reduce the cost of a power

*These feats require the use of the *Expanded Psionics Handbook*.

IMPROVED HOMUNCULUS

You are adept at improving and modifying your homunculus. Whenever you advance your homunculus's Hit Dice, you can also imbue it with special supernatural abilities.

Prerequisites: Craft Construct or craft homunculus class feature, Craft (any) 6 ranks.

Benefit: Your homunculus gains natural armor and special abilities based on its HD (see chart). If you use the Craft Construct feat to construct a homunculus, it gets these abilities when you create it. If you use the craft homunculus class feature of the artificer class, your homunculus gains natural armor and special abilities based on its current HD, and additional natural armor or special abilities if you later increase its HD.

All special abilities are described below; those requiring additional information follow the chart. Unless otherwise specified, an ability can only be taken once.

Each time the homunculus gains a HD, you can choose to remove any one special ability already granted from this feat and select another ability to replace the lost one. For example, an artificer with a 4-HD homunculus that has the climber special ability could choose to give it sneak attack instead if the homunculus's Hit Dice were increased to 5.

This feat applies to the character's homunculus regardless of its type. For new types of homunculi, see Chapter 6.

Hit Dice	Natural Armor	Total Special Abilities
1–2	+0	0
3–5	+2	1
6–8	+4	2
9–11	+6	3
12–14	+8	4
15–17	+10	5
18+	+12	6

HOMUNCULUS ABILITIES

Ability	Effect
Climber[1]	Gains climb 20 ft. or existing climb speed improves by 20 ft.
Dextrous	Gains +2 Dexterity
Durable[1]	Gains 10 hp
Evasion	As monk class feature
Flyer[1]	Gains fly 20 ft. (good) or existing fly speed improves by 20 ft. and maneuverability improves by one category
Skilled[2]	Gains +3 competence bonus on chosen skill check
Sneak attack[1]	Gains sneak attack +1d6 (as rogue class feature)
Store infusion	Homunculus can store one infusion of up to 3rd level
Strong	Gains +2 Strength
Swimmer[1]	Gains swim 20 ft. or existing swim speed improves by 20 ft.
Telepathy range	Range of telepathy between homunculus and creator increases to 1 mile/level of the creator
Weapon ability[2]	Natural weapons gain special ability

1 May be chosen more than once. Multiple selections stack.
2 May be chosen more than once. Multiple selections do not stack; instead, each selection of the ability applies to a new skill or weapon ability.

Store Infusion: At the beginning of each day, the artificer can store one infusion of up to 3rd level in the homunculus. This infusion must be one that the artificer could normally imbue the homunculus with. This infusion does not take effect when it is first stored. Instead, the homunculus can use a standard action to imbue itself with the infusion. No homunculus can store more than one infusion at a time.

Weapon Ability: When this ability is granted, choose a weapon special ability with a base price modifier of "+1 bonus," such as ghost touch, keen, or shock. The homunculus's natural weapons are treated as if they had this special ability.

PROPHECY'S ARTIFEX

Your perception of the draconic Prophecy gives you insights into that allow you to transcend the normal limits of magic item use.

Prerequisites: Knowledge (arcana) 2 ranks, Speak Language (Draconic), Craft Wand or Craft Staff, Dragon Prophesier.

Benefit: While in prophetic favor (see Dragon Prophesier), you can activate a wand or staff that you created as a swift action (as long as the item's normal activation time is no greater than a standard action).

PROPHECY'S EXPLORER

Your perception of the draconic Prophecy imbues you with a preternatural sense of your surroundings, enabling you to move easily and quickly through dangerous areas.

Prerequisites: Base attack bonus +2, Knowledge (arcana) 2 ranks, Speak Language (Draconic), Dragon Prophesier.

Benefit: While in prophetic favor (see Dragon Prophesier), your base land speed increases by 10 feet. In addition, if you end your turn at least 10 feet away from where you started your turn, you gain a +1 insight bonus to AC until the start of your next turn.

While in prophetic favor, you also gain a +2 insight bonus on Balance, Climb, and Move Silently checks.

PROPHECY'S HERO

Your perception of the draconic Prophecy charges you with the will to prevail, providing you with the opportunity to see a way to victory even when the odds are stacked against you.

An artificer can upgrade the abilities of his homunculus

Prerequisites: Knowledge (arcana) 2 ranks, Speak Language (Draconic), Dragon Prophesier.

Benefit: When you enter prophetic favor (see Dragon Prophesier), you gain 1 temporary action point. When you use this action point, your prophetic favor ends even if its duration has not yet elapsed. If you don't use this action point during your prophetic favor, it disappears when your prophetic favor ends.

PROPHECY'S MIND [PSIONIC]

You meld your perception of the draconic Prophecy with a mental focus that provides you with momentary warning when death is at hand.

Prerequisites: Knowledge (arcana) 2 ranks, Speak Language (Draconic), Dragon Prophesier.

Benefit: While psionically focused and in prophetic favor (see Dragon Prophesier), you can lessen the damage dealt by a potentially lethal attack. Any time an attack would reduce your hit points to −10 or fewer, you can expend your psionic focus to instead be reduced to 0 hp. Doing this also ends your prophetic favor.

This feat cannot protect you from an effect that slays you without reducing your hit points to −10.

PROPHECY'S SHAPER

Your perception of the draconic Prophecy is such that you can disrupt reality and make your spells more powerful than reality would normally allow.

Prerequisites: Knowledge (arcana) 4 ranks, Speak Language (Draconic), Dragon Prophesier, ability to cast 2nd-level spells.

Benefit: While in prophetic favor (see Dragon Prophesier), you can empower one spell per round without any adjustment to the level or casting time of the spell. You can't empower any spell of the highest spell level you can cast (for example, a 3rd-level wizard can't empower 2nd-level spells).

PROPHECY'S SHEPHERD

Your perception of the draconic Prophecy is such that you can alter the natural flow of the world by connecting your knowledge of life-force with the world around you.

Prerequisites: Knowledge (arcana) 4 ranks, Speak Language (Draconic), Dragon Prophesier, ability to spontaneously cast *cure wounds* or *inflict wounds* spells.

Benefit: While in prophetic favor (see Dragon Prophesier), you can quicken one *cure wounds* or *inflict wounds* spell per round (see below) without any adjustment to the level of the spell. You can use this ability even on spontaneously cast spells.

If you are capable of spontaneously casting *cure wounds* spells, you can use this feat to quicken any *cure wounds* spell.

If you are capable of spontaneously casting *inflict wounds* spells, you can use this feat to quicken any *inflict wounds* spell.

PROPHECY'S SLAYER

Your perception of the draconic Prophecy includes a keen appreciation of life. You recognize how fragile and tenuous life truly is when balanced against your lethal foreknowledge.

Prerequisites: Base attack bonus +2, Knowledge (arcana) 2 ranks, Speak Language (Draconic), Dragon Prophesier.

Benefit: While in prophetic favor (see Dragon Prophesier), you gain a +1d6 insight bonus on melee damage rolls made against flat-footed living opponents, or living opponents you are flanking. Creatures with immunity to critical hits or sneak attacks have immunity to this extra damage.

PSIFORGED BODY

As a warforged, your body can be crafted using trace amounts of psionically resonant deep crystal, providing you with increased psionic power and the ability to store psionic energy in your body. If you take this feat, you will often be referred to as a psiforged. For more information on the psiforged and their outlook, see page 39.

Prerequisites: Warforged, 1st level only.

Benefit: You gain 1 extra power point at 1st level, regardless of whether you choose a psionic class.

As you gain experience, you can attune the crystals infused in your body to the psionic energies of your mind. You can treat your body as a *cognizance crystal*, storing up to 1 power point plus 1 power point per two character levels (up to a maximum of 11 power points at 20th level), and withdrawing those stored power points at some later time. For more details on cognizance crystals, see page 167 of the *Expanded Psionics Handbook.*

Special: Unlike most feats, this feat must be taken at 1st level during character creation.

PSIONIC LUCK [PSIONIC]

Your psionic focus improves your luck.

Benefit: When you expend your psionic focus as part of spending an action point, you roll d10s instead of d6s and add the result to the d20 roll.

If you have the Action Boost feat and the Psionic Luck feat, you roll d12s when you spend an action point and expend your psionic focus.

PSYCHIC RUSH [PSIONIC]

You can occasionally manifest a psionic power with less effort.

Benefit: When you manifest a power, you can spend an action point to reduce the power point cost of that power by 1d6 power points, to a minimum cost of 1 power point.

The cost of the power before the reduction cannot exceed your manifester level.

QUICKEN DRAGONMARK

You can use your dragonmark abilities more quickly.

Prerequisite: Least Dragonmark.

Benefit: You can use your least dragonmark spell-like ability as a swift action, as if casting a quickened spell.

All spell-like abilities of your least dragonmark are quickened, should you have more than one spell-like ability from your mark (for instance, if have two levels in the dragonmark heir prestige class).

Special: You must carry a Siberys shard attuned to your dragonmark, and worth at least 50 gp, for this ability to function.

You can select this feat multiple times. To take this feat a second time, you must have the Lesser Dragonmark feat, and to take it a third time, you must have the Greater Dragonmark feat. The second time you select it, you can quicken the spell-like abilities of your lesser dragonmark. The third time you select it, you can quicken the spell-like abilities of your greater dragonmark. Siberys marks and aberrant dragonmarks are unaffected by this feat.

RAPID INFUSION

You can imbue an item with an infusion more quickly than normal.

Prerequisite: Artificer level 3rd.

Benefit: Once per day, you can hasten one infusion, imbuing it in 1 round, without spending an action point to do so.

Normal: You can spend an action point to imbue an infusion in 1 round, even if the casting time is normally longer than 1 round.

Special: You can choose this feat as an artificer bonus feat.

SYMBIONT MASTERY

You have stronger control over an attached symbiont than regular creatures, and you gain vitality for each symbiont attached to you.

Prerequisite: Wis 11.

Benefit: You gain a +4 bonus on Will saves made during any personality conflict that might erupt between you and your symbiont.

You gain 2 bonus hit points per symbiont attached to you. If you detach a symbiont, you lose these hit points immediately.

WAND SURGE

You can squeeze more magic out of charged items.

Prerequisite: Caster level 3rd.

Benefit: You can spend an action point instead of a charge when you activate a charged spell trigger item, such as a wand or staff. To use this ability, the item must have at least one charge remaining.

Special: If two or more charges would normally be subtracted from the charged spell trigger item, then the number of charges required is reduced by one when you spend your action point.

Yesrin stood in the midst of the dragons of Argonnessen and cast his spell to get their attention. "Hear me, o great ones!" Yesrin shouted. "I bring news of your unfolding Prophecy and would speak with you as an equal. . . ."

The dragons gazed upon the lesser creature with disdain, but at least one of them was intrigued. "You presume much, small one," a huge black dragon snarled, "but if you truly speak of the Prophecy, you may live to see another day. . . ."

CHAPTER THREE
PRESTIGE CLASSES

The weave of the world is maintained by magic. At least, so all prominent practitioners of that grandest of arts believe in their hearts. How could it be any different? From the most primitive glimmerings of magic light to the most staggering feats of celestial manipulation, magic is the force supreme that the mute firmament of the natural world must obey.

Chasms can be called into existence (or repaired), great fires that burn with the fury of the daystar can be ignited (or quenched), creatures of devilish or divine strength can be summoned (or dispatched), items of surpassing mastery can be forged (or destroyed) and the minds of even the greatest kings can be commandeered (or guarded), all through the use of the proper spell, ritual, or magic relic.

Are there also not as many varieties of magic as there are species of insect in the dank jungles of Xen'drik? Knowing just what sort of magic to employ can be a task in itself, though of course such a choice is largely dependent on factors of history, background, circumstance, culture, and aptitude. Merely wanting to practice a particular type of magic is not enough. With desire must also come opportunity.

Even the straightforward magic of the arcanist hides complexity of choice behind its incanted spells. Should a would-be caster choose the way of the wizard, whose spell-book is deep? Or perhaps he doesn't have a choice, and is born to the way of the sorcerer, who can bring to bear the brute force of repetition? What about the artificer, a caster neither arcane nor divine, who can invest inanimate objects with the soul of magic?

This chapter presents eight new prestige classes, each of which focuses on a particular area of magic or psionics. Specialists of magic, mind, skill, life, death, or alien philosophy, these classes can be found on the furthest continents of Eberron, as well as on the most trodden streets of the capital cities of the Five Nations. Some expand an arcane spellcaster's tactics, while others grant combatants new magical abilities. Each class includes expansive tips on making it part of an EBERRON campaign, such as roleplaying advice, organizational notes, and a sample NPC.

ALCHEMIST SAVANT

"Life is a mixture of happiness and sadness, of good and evil. The trick is finding the perfect measure of each."

—Janmari d'Cannith, alchemist savant

Since the Last War, House Cannith has been divided into three major branches. The southern branch, led by Merrix d'Cannith from Sharn, emphasizes specific types of magic craft, including alchemy. In Merrix's view, alchemy combines an awareness of natural laws, a talent for careful attention, and a familiarity with magic into the perfect science. Indeed, the most advanced alchemical practitioners of House Cannith are truly formidable opponents. These alchemist savants excel in the capacity to break down the normal barriers that lie between alchemy and magic, between potion and alchemical fluid, between science and art.

ARTIFICERS AND PRESTIGE CLASSES

Artificers benefit in a specific way from prestige classes that have "+1 level of existing spellcasting class" as a level advancement benefit. An artificer taking levels in such a prestige class does not gain any of his class abilities, but he does gain an increased caster level when using his infusions. Levels of prestige classes that provide +1 level of spellcasting effectively stack with the artificer's level to determine his effective caster level. An artificer gains access to higher-level infusions at these prestige class levels as though he had gained a level in the artificer class.

An artificer can qualify for prestige classes with spell-casting level requirements (as long as they do not specifically require arcane or divine casting), even though his infusions aren't spells. Prestige classes with caster level requirements are also well suited to the artificer. An artificer's caster level for his infusions fulfills this requirement.

Classes that advance only arcane or divine spellcasting classes, specifically, would not benefit an artificer, because infusions are neither arcane nor divine in nature. Likewise, a prestige class with a prerequisite to cast a specific spell would be unavailable to an artificer.

The first deadgrim, a half-orc named Taarak Half-Ear (LN male rogue 3/cleric of Dol Arrah 3/barbarian 1/deadgrim 5), still roams Karrnath, and he has begun actively recruiting those interested in taking the fight to the undead for the Red Watchers. As a new organization, the Watchers do not have a strong presence in any one locale, and they are still somewhat disorganized. However, this lack of organization sometimes works to the order's advantage in a land so thoroughly influenced by the group the Red Watchers deem their archnemesis: the Blood of Vol.

As a member of the Red Watchers, you are mostly expected to keep your eyes and ears open for evidence of undead activity. As a deadgrim, when you find such activity, you destroy it. This process might not be as simple as walking into a dank crypt and smiting the undead inhabitants (although that is certainly part of your job description). The way to go about a given task is the prerogative of each individual deadgrim, but those who have had the most success typically rely on stealth and negotiation as much as force of arms.

Most deadgrim serve a sort of apprenticeship under an older member of the Red Watchers, who may or may not be another deadgrim. This individual schools you in the basic art of tracking, identifying, and destroying undead. Once this basic training is done, each member is turned loose, although Watchers are encouraged to check in with the order as often as possible.

You will want to keep adding ranks to Knowledge (religion) as you gain levels in the deadgrim class, because you will need to recognize ever more obscure and deadly types of undead—some perhaps never encountered before by another member of your organization. You will also want to keep magic items on hand capable of dealing with the undead you face and the effects they might have on your companions. Scrolls, potions, and wands that negate the terrible abilities of undead are key, since your allies are likely not nearly as prepared for encounters with undead as you are. If you take them on a Red Watchers mission, you are especially responsible for their safety. While you might warn them of the terrors they will face, ultimately only you know the depths, depravity, and horror to which undead creatures can aspire.

Resources

When you visit a Red Watcher outpost, you can usually expect to find basic resources available that will enable you to rid yourself of any lingering effects of a battle against undead. Potions or scrolls of *restoration, remove curse, align weapon, protection from evil,* and *break enchantment* can nearly always be found for sale at 20% or more off the normal price, depending on your reputation within the organization. You can almost always find fierce allies at these locations, ready to take the fight to any identified undead in the area.

DEADGRIM IN THE WORLD

"Zombies, wights, vampires, or whatever else the Blood of Vol cooks up—I'll be happy to give them their 'eternal rest.'"

—Akaana Lightwind, deadgrim

Deadgrim make an excellent source of adventure hooks whenever undead are involved. Any time the players find themselves battling the unholy forces of the undead, or if they come into conflict with the Blood of Vol, the Order of the Emerald Claw, or other minions of Vol, they might encounter a member of the Red Watchers. The deeper

into such a conflict they get, the more likely they are to meet a deadgrim.

Player characters on a particularly difficult quest against undead might seek out an organization dedicated to defeating such creatures, coming into contact with the Red Watchers as a result. As a young order, the Red Watchers do not require a great deal of modification to bring them into a campaign, and their background, motives, and organization can be molded according to the players' needs.

The Red Watchers (and their deadgrim members in particular) are extremely dedicated to their cause, and could also come into conflict with the PCs if their goals run counter to the order's—an extremely likely situation given how manipulative the Blood of Vol and its agents can be.

Organization

Deadgrim typically work alone, but this is mostly due to the fact that so few of them yet exist. Spread as thin as they are, deadgrim tend to form alliances with other creatures that also share their abhorrence for the undead. While many are localized to Karrnath, some have spread their search outside that country's borders, seeking out their hated foes wherever they can be found. Higher-ranking members of the Red Watchers sometimes give assignments to local deadgrim (often involving leads on new undead activity), but for the most part, they are treated as roving freelance agents. The Red Watchers know that even working on their own, the deadgrim are furthering the goals of the greater group, and thus the greater good.

Taarak Half-Ear was the first deadgrim. One of the first members of the Red Watchers organization, the half-orc lost his family and home near the end of the Last War, when a band of Karrnathi zombies mistakenly attacked his village on the other side of Scions Sound from Thrane. The contingent of zombies was ordered into Taarak's small village in the first hours after dawn by a confused and battle-weary commander, who had lost his way on the sound that night and ended up on his own country's side. By the time an alarm was raised, it was too late, and the handful of survivors, Taarak among them, headed for the hills.

Taarak's only real superior in the Red Watchers is Esel Abreik (NG male human rogue 3/fighter 3). Esel, called the First Watcher, acts as the current head of the organization at large, setting long-term goals for the Red Watchers and trying to implement a tighter organization for the group.

Members of the Red Watchers do not have ranks, per se. They elect the First Watcher (Esel is currently in his fourth month of service) and report to Red Watcher outposts wherever they travel. Members are expected to try to check in as often as possible, although exceptions are frequent. Missions are typically assigned only rarely, and for the most part, Esel and other members of the Red Watchers expect their members to seek out undead where they can, report the activity, then find a way to disrupt or destroy it.

All members are expected to track any new undead specimens, tactics, or powers they encounter, recording every detail when they do check in. These notes are compiled by the Watchers' scribe—a dwarf named Sharp (LN male dwarf expert 2/fighter 2) whose missing arm and leg bear testament to a battle with a mummy long ago. Sharp is sent the reports of every member of the Red Watchers, and he compiles them into an archive of undead lore that rivals any in Khorvaire, including the continent's greatest libraries and research institutions.

RED WATCHERS OUTPOST

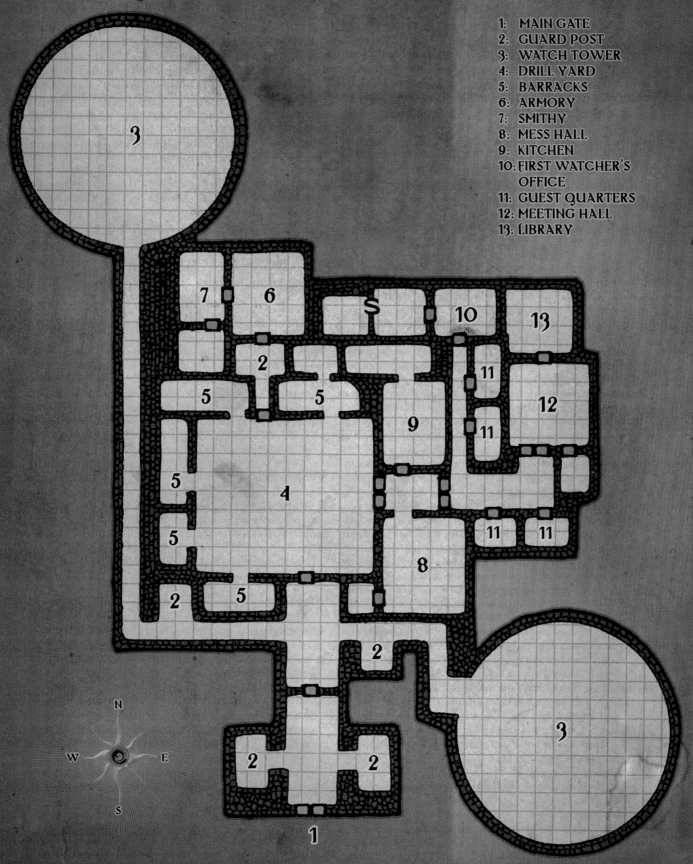

1: MAIN GATE
2: GUARD POST
3: WATCH TOWER
4: DRILL YARD
5: BARRACKS
6: ARMORY
7: SMITHY
8: MESS HALL
9: KITCHEN
10: FIRST WATCHER'S OFFICE
11: GUEST QUARTERS
12: MEETING HALL
13: LIBRARY

ONE SQUARE ≈ 5 FEET

might be mistaken for one by someone unfamiliar with dragonmarks.

Each ability description gives a minimum class level that you must attain in order to select it. In addition, some abilities require you to be in a state of prophetic favor (see the Dragon Prophesier feat, page 46).

These abilities are extraordinary unless otherwise specified.

Aasterinian: This is the dragon deity of invention and trade. If you attune to this constellation, creating magic items becomes easier for you. You can select one of the following feats (found in the EBERRON *Campaign Setting*) as a bonus feat: Exceptional Artisan, Extraordinary Artisan, or Legendary Artisan. You must still meet all prerequisites for a bonus feat. Minimum class level 1st.

Astilabor: This is the dragon deity of wealth. If you attune to this constellation, your dragon mentor sends you a magic item from its hoard to aid you in finding more connections and clues to the Prophecy. The item selected by the DM and should be worth no more than 5,000 gp. Minimum class level 5th.

Bahamut: This is the dragon deity of protection and good fortune. If you attune to this constellation, whenever you are in prophetic favor, you can reroll one check or saving throw that you have just made before the DM declares whether the roll results in success or failure. You must take the result of the reroll, even if it is worse than the original roll. Using this ability immediately ends your prophetic favor. Minimum class level 9th.

Chronepsis: This is the dragon deity of fate and prophecy. If you attune to this constellation, you gain the spell-like ability to use *commune*, as the spell, once per week at a caster level equal to your arcane caster level or infusion caster level. You commune with no single deity when you use this ability, but rather with the power of the draconic Prophecy itself. In addition, you gain a +2 insight bonus on Sense Motive checks, as you gain frequent premonitions about what people or creatures you communicate with mean to say before a word is spoken. Minimum class level 5th.

Falazure: This is the dragon deity of death and decay. If you attune to this constellation, you gain +2 bonus on saving throws against death effects, disease, and poison. While in prophetic favor, you can force a creature that has confirmed a critical hit against you to reroll the confirmation roll. If this second confirmation roll fails, the attack

is not a critical hit (though it deals damage normally). Using this ability ends your prophetic favor. Minimum class level 1st.

Garyx: This is the dragon deity of chaos and destruction. If you attune to this constellation, you can deal devastation with a moment's thought. While in prophetic favor, you can cast a single evocation spell as a swift action, as long as the spell's casting time is no more than 1 round. Using this ability ends your prophetic favor. Minimum class level 5th.

Hlal: This is the dragon deity of humor. If you attune to this constellation, the save DC against your illusion spells increases by 1. You also gain a +2 insight bonus on Bluff checks. Minimum class level 1st.

Io: This is the dragon deity of magic and knowledge. If you attune to this constellation, all Knowledge skills become class skills for you. In addition, any Knowledge check you make is treated as a trained check, even if you have no ranks in the skill. While in prophetic favor, you gain an insight bonus on Knowledge checks equal to one-half your class level (minimum +1). Minimum class level 1st.

Lendys: This is the dragon deity of justice and law. If you attune to this constellation, you gain the ability to magically strike back against an enemy that has injured you. While in prophetic favor, if you are dealt damage by another creature (whether by weapon, spell, or other effect), you can cast a single spell or use a spell-like ability in response as an immediate action. The spell or spell-like ability must target only that creature, and must have a casting time of one standard action. For example, if an enemy archer hits you with an arrow, you could cast *magic missile* as an immediate action, though all missiles from the spell would have to target the archer. However, you couldn't cast *fireball*, even if no other enemies were in the area, since *fireball* is not a targeted spell. Using this ability ends your prophetic favor. Minimum class level 5th.

Tamara: This is the dragon deity of life. If you attune to this constellation, you gain fast healing 1 (see page 309 of the *Monster Manual*) whenever you are in prophetic favor. Minimum class level 5th.

Tiamat: This is the dragon deity of greed and power. If you attune to this constellation, you can attempt to steal a spell as it is being cast by another spellcaster. You must be in prophetic favor and must ready an action to use this ability, though you need not designate a spellcaster target

THE DRAGON PROPHET   HIT DIE: d4

Level	Base Attack Bonus	Fort Save	Ref Save	Will Save	Special	Spellcasting
1st	+0	+0	+0	+2	Constellation power	—
2nd	+1	+0	+0	+3	—	+1 level of existing arcane spellcasting or infusion-imbuing class
3rd	+1	+1	+1	+3	Constellation power	+1 level of existing arcane spellcasting or infusion-imbuing class
4th	+2	+1	+1	+4	Bonus feat	+1 level of existing arcane spellcasting or infusion-imbuing class
5th	+2	+1	+1	+4	Constellation power	+1 level of existing arcane spellcasting or infusion-imbuing class
6th	+3	+2	+2	+5		+1 level of existing arcane spellcasting or infusion-imbuing class
7th	+3	+2	+2	+5	Constellation power	+1 level of existing arcane spellcasting or infusion-imbuing class
8th	+4	+2	+2	+6	Bonus feat	+1 level of existing arcane spellcasting or infusion-imbuing class
9th	+4	+3	+3	+6	Constellation power	+1 level of existing arcane spellcasting or infusion-imbuing class
10th	+5	+3	+3	+7	Ageless	+1 level of existing arcane spellcasting or infusion-imbuing class

Class Skills (4 + Int modifier per level): Appraise, Concentration, Craft, Diplomacy, Gather Information, Knowledge (arcana), Knowledge (history), Profession, Search, Spellcraft, Use Magic Device.

until the ability is activated. The spellcaster must be within 60 feet of you, and you must have line of effect to the caster. You steal the spell with a successful caster level check (DC 10 + the target's caster level). If you are successful, the spell is cast to no effect by the targeted caster, with any material components consumed and any costs to the caster paid as normal. Using this ability immediately ends your prophetic favor.

You immediately know which spell you have stolen, and at any time in the next hour, you can activate the stolen spell as a spell-like ability. You use the original caster's caster level, but for all other purposes, you treat the spell as if you had cast it. If you steal a second spell before casting the first, the first spell is lost.

Stealing a spell in this manner is a supernatural ability. Minimum class level 9th.

Bonus Feat: Your exploration of the Draconic Prophecy reveals many secrets to you. At 4th and 8th level, you gain a bonus feat, which must be selected from the following list: Prophecy's Artifex, Prophecy's Explorer, Prophecy's Hero, Prophecy's Mind, Prophecy's Shaper, Prophecy's Shepherd, Prophecy's Slayer. (All these feats are presented in Chapter 2.) You must still meet all prerequisites for a bonus feat.

Ageless (Ex): Upon reaching 10th level, you no longer take penalties to your ability scores for aging, you cannot be magically aged, and your natural life span becomes four times normal for your race. Any aging penalties that you have already taken remain in place. Ability bonuses still accrue, and you still die of old age when your extended time is up.

PLAYING A DRAGON PROPHET

Each dragon prophet is unique, and you are no exception. You are driven primarily to find new pieces of the massive, millennia-spanning puzzle that is the draconic Prophecy, but your means for doing so likely differ from any of the Prophecy's other followers. Dragons of every type recruit dragon prophets, though not every dragon has a dragon prophet working for it. Your personality and methods are strongly dictated by your dragon mentor, and many dragon prophets share at least one alignment component and certain aspects of their dragon mentor's personality (greedy if red, stately and distant if silver, scheming and manipulative if black, and so on).

The one trait you share with all other dragon prophets, however, is your ability to make long-term plans. The knowledge of the health and extended life span you gain when you reach the pinnacle of your class makes you sure that any plans you lay will have ample time to come to fruition.

You are not a member of any specific organization. Each dragon prophet furthers the agendas of her dragon mentor and herself (in that order), and you are no exception. In fact, it is extremely likely that at some point in your career, you will come into conflict with another dragon prophet who seeks some bit of knowledge you have gained, or who is competing for access to a single resource important to your understanding of the Prophecy.

How you handle such an encounter is up to you. Many prophets cooperate (though almost always briefly) if they run into one another, while others loathe their dragon prophet peers and fight on sight. Some dragons recruit prophets as part of a larger organization, however, and if

A dragon prophet seeks portents concerning the draconic Prophecy

you are such a prophet, you might be ordered to work with other dragon prophets from time to time on a particularly important portion of the Prophecy.

Combat

Like other arcane spellcasters, you rely on your spells to see you through difficult battles. Your style in combat is different from that of any other prophet, given your individual magical specialties and the allies you adventure with. Choosing constellation abilities that complement your companions' fighting styles will help keep them (and yourself) alive longer.

You should plan for battles whenever possible by scouting the territory (magically or otherwise), and preparing accordingly. Spells that improve your allies' fighting capabilities can be cast before a conflict, allowing you to lurk near the fringes of a battle, locate the most significant threat (likely a rival spellcaster), and focus your energies there. Ready counterspells frequently and keep plenty of *dispel magic* and *greater dispel magic* spells on hand. In addition, ready actions to cast damaging spells whenever possible in an effort to disrupt enemy casters' spells.

Once you have mastered five of the draconic constellations, you have an abundance of options at your fingertips to help you overcome adversaries. Play to the strengths you have identified and heightened with your constellation abilities, and remember that you have the time to be patient in your planning. You are usually better off laying siege than storming the main gates.

Advancement

Like other dragon prophets, you were recruited to your important work by a dragon of Argonnessen. This recruitment was likely handled by the dragon in humanoid form, although recruitment stories vary from prophet to prophet. However, because such offers are not extended until a dragon knows that a subject is likely to accept (often because he or she had previously demonstrated an interest in the Prophecy or dragons in general), your own acceptance might have been more a formality than anything else.

The dragon that recruited you became your mentor, and still routinely sends you bits of advice and tips on places to research. You might be required to keep in touch on a regular basis, or you might not hear from your mentor for months at a time. However, you know that your mentor keeps track of your progress, and if that were not incentive enough, the tantalizing hints and fragments of the Prophecy itself lure you on.

In general, you would have been provided with only rudimentary instruction by your mentor upon accepting the role of dragon prophet—to seek out signs of the draconic Prophecy, make attempts to decipher their meaning, and report your findings to your mentor as quickly as possible. A dragon mentor also provides its prophet with its full name, so that it can be contacted by *sending* and similar spells. Doing this puts the dragon at risk, but you know that betraying that trust by revealing your mentor's name would result in swift and merciless destruction. Dragon mentors have message centers hidden in nearly every populated portion of Khorvaire, and prophets wandering far from such areas for extended periods are expected to find other ways to stay in touch.

You should continue to add ranks to your Knowledge (arcana) skill at each level, because doing so gives you the best chance of deciphering dragonmarks and other signs of the

Prophecy, as well as extending the duration of your prophetic favor. Taking additional prophecy feats beyond your bonus feats is useful, because they better enable you to survive the challenges your searches will inevitably lead you to face.

Resources

Because dragon prophets lack a formal organization, you are effectively isolated. You must rely on your own skills and initiative most of the time, since your dragon mentor will not be able to aid you often from its home on distant Argonnessen. You should consider buying or building a magic item capable of accessing a *sending* spell or similar magic, so that you can stay in touch with your mentor. Otherwise, bond with other adventurers and look to those friendships for aid. Whether you reveal your affiliation to them is up to you, but beware indifference—or betrayal—from those who do not understand the importance of your mission.

DRAGON PROPHETS IN THE WORLD

"No one knows everything. No one understands everything. But there's no harm in trying."

—Yesrin Lieng, dragon prophet

The dragon prophet prestige class enables you to have the most fascinating creatures in D&D—the dragons—play a pivotal role in a campaign. Dragon prophet characters can set out on countless adventures in search of clues to the Prophecy, and can be used to introduce all manner of villains interested in discerning the mysteries of the Prophecy for their own ends.

Organization

Dragon prophets do not affiliate with one another for the most part. Driven not only by their own unique motivations but by their dragon mentors' agendas, dragon prophets are extremely complex characters. Because they have no set organization, no single prophet claims leadership over others. However, the relationship between prophets and their mentors changes the prophets, making them a little more like their mentors each day.

Each mentor treats its prophet in a different manner, however. Evil dragons tend to think of their prophets as property—a useful and active extension of their hoard. Most prophets willing to deal with evil dragons accept a de facto role as their mentors' slaves, and some become slave owners themselves in mimicry of this relationship. Good dragons, on the other hand, tend to see prophets as useful (albeit inferior) partners. These dragons expect just as much from their prophets as any evil dragons, but are more forgiving of failures.

Dragon prophets are, without exception, adventurers. They seek out signs of the Prophecy wherever they go, sending word to their mentors whenever they find an important piece of information. A dragon prophet might spend months or even years at a single place engaged in research, but she is always ready to pack up in pursuit of the next clue. As a result, nearly all prophets are solitary individuals, though rumors of a few who have established romantic relationships with their dragon mentors persist.

NPC Reactions

Most NPCs have little reason to view a dragon prophet as anything other than an arcane spellcaster. If NPCs manage to spot a prophet's constellation marks, they might assume the character to be a member of one of the dragonmarked houses and react accordingly. However, NPCs who become aware of a dragon prophet's nature might have very different views. Those interested in arcane lore might seek to quiz the prophet on her duties, while those afraid of Argonnessen's intent toward Khorvaire might seek to have a dragon prophet restrained or even killed.

Generally, the worst enemies of dragon prophets tend to be other dragon prophets. Competing for access to new appearances of dragonmarks or other signs of the Prophecy, dragon prophets often come into conflict. Representatives of other groups interested in magical activity might also clash with a dragon prophet from time to time, though unless prophets are under some sort of time constraint, most are generally willing to let a different group go about its business before performing their own investigations.

DRAGON PROPHET LORE

Characters with Knowledge (arcana) can research the dragon prophets to learn more about them. When a character makes a skill check, read or paraphrase the following, including the information from lower DCs.

DC 10: "Some spellcasters are especially interested in the appearance of dragonmarks where none were before."

DC 15: "Dragon prophets work for the dragons, looking for dragonmarks wherever they appear and investigating dragon lore."

DC 20: "A dragon prophet seeks out signs of import to dragons, then reports those signs back to the dragons on Argonnessen."

DC 30: "A dragon prophet seeks signs of the draconic Prophecy. These signs take many forms and appear in many unusual places, so these prophets wander all over the place. They maintain close contact with their dragon masters, using both magical and mundane methods."

DRAGON PROPHETS IN THE GAME

Dragon prophets can show up wherever magical activity occurs. Dragonmarks have begun appearing in odd places in the last several hundred years, so wherever such a mark manifests, a dragon prophet probably won't be far off. Likewise, any general information on dragonkind is likely to be investigated by a dragon prophet, and even magical activity that has nothing to do with dragonmarks or dragons might draw a prophet to an area. They see signs and hints of the Prophecy everywhere, and only they and their mentors know these signs when they see them.

A dragon prophet PC should be encouraged to explore, which is easily done by dropping the occasional odd sign or newly appeared dragonmark into the game. You shouldn't be afraid to use a dragon mentor as a mentor or teacher figure for the entire party, giving players the opportunity to send their PCs on missions at the request of a dragon. Weaving a primary or secondary story element into a campaign about the Prophecy isn't that difficult, either. The point is not to try to create the entire Prophecy (for not even the dragons know entirely what the Prophecy portends), but to focus on a small

DRAGON PROPHET'S RETREAT

OBLIQUE VIEW

PLAN VIEW

ONE SQUARE = 50 FEET

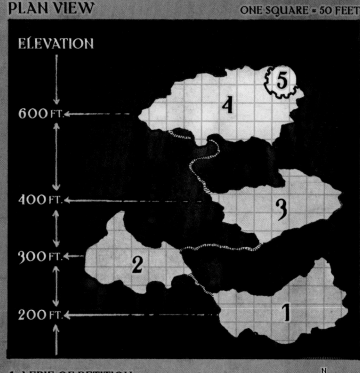

1: AERIE OF PETITION
2: AERIE OF PURIFICATION
3: AERIE OF GRAND CONVERSATION
4: AERIE OF PROPHECY
5: TOWER OF DESTINY

aspect of it, presenting hooks relating to that aspect for a prophet to follow.

Adaptation

While the dragon prophet class is focused on a unique feature of Eberron, it can function just as well in any setting. Using dragons as mentors and adversaries can be quite rewarding, and with the Eberron-specific references removed, this prestige class can fit virtually any campaign. Doing so means either losing the ties to the draconic Prophecy (perhaps replacing it with some other unique legend), or incorporating the Prophecy into your game. Doing so is easier than it might seem, since it is unlikely that the PCs will have heard of every obscure prophecy or omen in the campaign world.

SAMPLE ENCOUNTER

Characters are likely to encounter a dragon prophet anywhere they find new magical activity. A newly discovered dungeon that hides lost artifacts of ancient civilizations might be home to one or more adventuring prophets. A dragonmark appearing in a prominent place on an existing structure might inspire dragon prophets to show up in large numbers, leading to inevitable conflicts between them.

Yesrin Lieng (EL 9)

Yesrin Lieng is a human dragon prophet who has been serving his bronze mentor for nearly five years. He has advanced rapidly in the class as he wanders Khorvaire on his quest to unravel a portion of the Prophecy.

YESRIN LIENG	CR 9

Male human sorcerer 6/dragon prophet 3
LN Medium humanoid
Init +6; **Senses** Listen +0, Spot +0 (+2 to both if familiar within 5 ft.)
Languages Common, Draconic

AC 18, touch 13, flat-footed 16 (includes *mage armor*); +1 AC when in prophetic favor
hp 42 (9 HD)
Fort +5, **Ref** +5, **Will** +8; +1 when in prophetic favor

Speed 30 ft. (6 squares); 40 ft. when in prophetic favor
Melee dagger +4 (1d4–1/19–20) or
Ranged mwk light crossbow +7 (1d8/19–20)
Base Atk +4; **Grp** +3
Atk Options prophetic favor 5/day (9 rounds)
Combat Gear scroll of *fly*, scroll of *lightning bolt* (10th), scroll of *teleport*, 2 *potions of cure moderate wounds*
Sorcerer Spells Known (CL 8th):
  4th (4/day)—*scrying* (DC 18)
  3rd (6/day)—*fireball* (DC 17), *major image* (DC 18)
  2nd (7/day)—*invisibility*, *scorching ray* (+6 ranged touch), *web* (DC 16)
  1st (7/day)—*detect secret doors*, *mage armor*, *magic missile*, *ray of enfeeblement* (+6 ranged touch), *shield*
  0 (6/day)—*arcane mark*, *detect magic*, *light*, *mage hand*, *open/close*, *read magic*, *resistance*, *touch of fatigue* (+4 melee touch)
Abilities Str 8, Dex 14, Con 14, Int 12, Wis 10, Cha 18
SQ constellation of Hlal, constellation of Io, familiar, share spells
Feats Alertness[B] (if familiar within 5 ft.), Great Fortitude, Dragon Prophesier*, Improved Initiative, Prophecy's Explorer*, Prophecy's Shaper*
*New feats described in Chapter 2.

Skills Balance +2 (+4 in prophetic favor), Bluff +18, Climb –1 (+1 in prophetic favor), Concentration +14, Diplomacy +6, Disguise +4 (+6 to act in character), Gather Information +7, Intimidate +6, Knowledge (arcana) +13 (+14 in prophetic favor), Knowledge (history) +5 (+6 in prophetic favor), Knowledge (religion) +4 (+5 in prophetic favor), Listen +0 (+2 if familiar within 5 ft.), Move Silently +2 (+4 in prophetic favor), Spellcraft +10, Spot +0 (+2 if familiar within 5 ft.)

Possessions combat gear plus dagger, masterwork light crossbow with 20 bolts, *cloak of Charisma +2, amulet of natural armor +1, ring of protection +1, scrying* mirror (not usually carried), 150 gp

Prophetic Favor (Ex) Yesrin can enter a state of prophetic favor as a full-round action. He can empower one spell each round of up to 3rd level without any adjustment to the level or casting time of the spell while in a state of prophetic favor.

ATEK, SNAKE FAMILIAR	CR ~

Tiny viper
N Tiny magical beast
Init +7; **Senses** scent; Listen +6, Spot +6
Languages empathic link, speak with master

AC 20, touch 15, flat-footed 17
hp 21 (9 HD)
Resist improved evasion
Fort +3, **Ref** +6, **Will** +9

Speed 15 ft. (3 squares), climb 15 ft., swim 15 ft.
Melee bite +9 (1 plus poison)
Space 2-1/2 ft.; **Reach** 0 ft.
Base Atk +4; **Grp** –7
Special Actions deliver touch spells

Abilities Str 4, Dex 17, Con 11, Int 8, Wis 12, Cha 2
Feats Improved Initiative, Weapon Finesse[B]
Skills Balance +11, Climb +11, Hide +15, Listen +6, Spot +6, Swim +5

ELEMENTAL SCION OF ZILARGO

"I understand the true nature of energy—how it flows and changes, ebbs like the tide. I know where raw magic is found. It is within me."

—Shae-ahm Rhen Skyshadow,
elemental scion of Zilargo

The elemental scion of Zilargo attempts to understand the true nature of the elements through bizarre methods. She has at least one elemental graft (see page 129) that is extremely special to her, because it is alive. As she grows in power, so does her graft, until she and it are like twin souls inhabiting the same body.

BECOMING AN ELEMENTAL SCION OF ZILARGO

Most elemental scions are melee combatants of one stripe or another. Fighters, barbarians, and even rogues might all find reasons to pursue this class, though they might enter with very different combinations of grafts. A majority of scions hail from Zilargo, and many of those are ex-soldiers who served in the defense of their homeland at one time or another. Others are simply wanderers drawn to the essential building blocks of energy and life.

Though the class doesn't appeal to many spellcasters, those willing to sacrifice advanced spell knowledge for the class's other benefits can achieve a unique level of power (particularly those with one or more levels of elemental savant, a prestige class presented in *Complete Arcane*). Some bards also find exploring the mysteries of the elements a worthwhile journey, although they must give up some progression in bardic music and spellcasting to take levels in this class.

ENTRY REQUIREMENTS

Base Attack Bonus: +5.
Skills: Knowledge (nature) 2 ranks, Knowledge (the planes) 2 ranks, Speak Language (Auran, Aquan, Ignan, or Terran). The elemental language known must match the type of elemental that provides the scion's graft; see Special.
Special: Must have at least one elemental graft.

CLASS FEATURES

Elemental scions believe that raw elemental power forms the foundation of life. As such, they seek to grow closer to the elements in their most basic form. Elemental scions of Zilargo nurture elemental growth within their very flesh. This growth, which begins as an elemental graft, soon becomes sentient and develops a rudimentary awareness of its surroundings. The graft essentially becomes a living, independently thinking being, fused to the body of the scion. Eventually, this graft can itself create an elemental creature inhabited by its own intelligence. As elemental scions gain levels in this prestige class, the graft grows across more of their body, making them look even more like the elementals they revere (though they never entirely lose their humanoid appearance).

Elemental Graft Affinity (Ex): Though you might have a variety of elemental grafts (both before and after entering this class), you create a bond with a particular kind of elemental (air, earth, fire, or water). The elemental chosen must match the type of one of your existing elemental grafts, and you must speak the language of the chosen elemental.

This bond allows you to more easily take on other grafts of the same kind. Any time that you receive an elemental graft of the same kind as your chosen element, determine the time required, gp cost, and XP cost as if the normal cost were reduced by 25% (as if the creator had the Exceptional Artisan, Extraordinary Artisan, and Legendary Artisan feats from the EBERRON *Campaign Setting*). These reductions do not stack with the benefits of those feats.

Elemental Spellcasting (Ex): Whenever you cast a spell with an elemental or energy descriptor that matches your chosen element, you add your elemental scion class level to your caster level. For the purpose of this ability, spells with the air or electricity descriptor match the air element, spells with the acid or earth descriptor match earth, spells with the fire descriptor match fire, and spells with the cold or water descriptor match water.

Graft Awareness (Ex): At 2nd level, one of your elemental grafts becomes sentient. The sentient graft is chosen by you, and must be of the type chosen for your elemental graft affinity. It gains an Intelligence, Wisdom, and Charisma score equal to 3 + your class level.

Your graft can communicate telepathically with you. Its sensory abilities are too limited for it to clearly perceive the outside world (it can't make Listen or Spot checks, for example), but its presence aids your senses slightly, granting you a +2 bonus on your Listen and Spot checks.

Grafted Health (Ex): As your elemental grafts increasingly integrate themselves into your body, you become slightly more robust. Beginning at 3rd level, you gain +1 hit point per graft that matches your chosen element.

Grow Elemental (Su): Eventually the synergistic relationship between you and your elemental graft attains a startling new level. Beginning at 4th level, you can grow a Large elemental (of the type chosen for your elemental graft affinity) as a standard action, using your own graft's substance as a seed. The elemental appears adjacent to you and can act immediately. It has the mental ability scores of your intelligent elemental graft (which might affect its Will save and skill check modifiers), but is otherwise identical to a normal elemental (see page 95 of the *Monster Manual*).

Though your graft provides a "seed" for the new elemental, the graft remains in place. The elemental you grow is created from surrounding matter and inhabited by the sentience of your intelligent graft. The various abilities of your elemental graft are not affected, but the graft is rendered nonintelligent for the duration of the effect.

You can communicate telepathically with the elemental, which follows your commands completely. If reduced to 0 hp, the elemental disappears and its sentience returns to the graft from which it came. Otherwise, the elemental remains for a number of rounds equal to your Constitution modifier plus the number of elemental grafts you have of that kind (minimum 1 round).

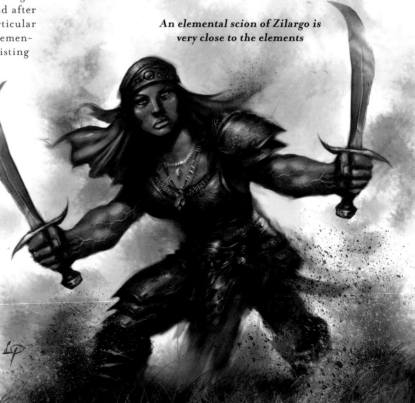

An elemental scion of Zilargo is very close to the elements

HIT DIE: d8

Level	Base Attack Bonus	Fort Save	Ref Save	Will Save	Special
1st	+0	+2	+0	+0	Elemental graft affinity, elemental spellcasting
2nd	+1	+3	+0	+0	Graft awareness
3rd	+2	+3	+1	+1	Grafted health
4th	+3	+4	+1	+1	Grow elemental (Large)
5th	+3	+4	+1	+1	Uncanny dodge
6th	+4	+5	+2	+2	Grow elemental (Huge)
7th	+5	+5	+2	+2	Elemental merge
8th	+6	+6	+2	+2	Grow elemental (greater)
9th	+6	+6	+3	+3	Improved uncanny dodge
10th	+7	+7	+3	+3	Grow elemental (elder)

Class Skills (2 + Int modifier per level): Climb, Craft, Intimidate, Jump, Knowledge (nature), Knowledge (the planes), Profession, Survival, Swim.

You can use this ability once per day at no risk to yourself, but additional uses take a toll on your health. Creating a second elemental within 24 hours of the first renders you fatigued and deals 1d4 points of Constitution drain. Creating a third elemental within the same 24-hour period renders you exhausted (even if you are not already fatigued) and deals 2d4 points of Constitution drain. Each additional use in the same 24-hour period deals an amount of Constitution drain equal to the previous drain +1d4 (3d4 for the fourth use, 4d4 for the fifth, and so on). Characters with immunity to Constitution drain or without a Constitution score cannot create more than one elemental in a 24-hour period.

At higher levels, the elemental you create is increasingly more powerful, at your option. The elemental you grow is Huge beginning at 6th level, a greater elemental at 8th level, and an elder elemental at 10th level.

Uncanny Dodge (Ex): The awareness of your sentient elemental graft improves your reactions. At 5th level, you cannot be caught flat-footed and react to danger before your senses would normally allow you to do so. If you already have uncanny dodge from another class, you gain improved uncanny dodge instead (see below). See the barbarian class feature, page 26 of the *Player's Handbook*.

Elemental Merge (Su): Starting at 7th level, you can physically merge with the body of any elemental that you summon, call, or grow (using your grow elemental class feature), as long as the elemental matches your chosen affinity. The elemental must be at least two size categories larger than you. Entering the elemental requires a move action, and you must be adjacent to the elemental to merge with it.

Once you have merged with the elemental, you can no longer take any actions other than communication. Instead, you control the elemental as easily as if it were you (though the elemental retains all its own ability scores and other statistics). The elemental doesn't benefit from (and cannot use) any of your special abilities, magic items, or continuous effects while you are merged; however, any temporary effects (such as spells) active on you when you merge are continued on the elemental, assuming that it would be a legal target for the effect.

For example, the elemental wouldn't benefit from your *+1 full plate armor*, *ring of protection*, *gauntlets of ogre power*, or uncanny dodge ability, nor could it activate your *ring of invisibility*. It would, however, share the benefit of the *bless* spell cast on you by your cleric ally, as well as the *bull's strength* and *stoneskin* spells cast on you by a sorcerer. If you had already activated your *ring of invisibility* before merging, it would gain that effect as well.

While inside an elemental, you have immunity to all effects both beneficial and harmful; effectively, you no longer exist as a separate physical body. If the elemental that you inhabit is killed or dismissed, you appear in a randomly determined square within its space.

You can remain inside the elemental for a number of rounds equal to your class level, though there is no limit to the number of times per day that you can use this ability.

This ability cannot be used to merge with a bound elemental that you have previously called.

Improved Uncanny Dodge (Ex): The awareness of your sentient elemental graft continues to improve your reactions. From 9th level on, you can no longer be flanked. See the barbarian class feature, page 26 of the *Player's Handbook*.

Ex-Elemental Scions of Zilargo

An elemental scion of Zilargo who loses all the elemental grafts of her chosen element loses all class features of this prestige class, and cannot gain any further levels in the class until she gains a new elemental graft of that type.

PLAYING AN ELEMENTAL SCION OF ZILARGO

You are consumed with learning more about elementals, elemental energy, and especially those elementals that match your affinity. You are so immersed in the mysteries you constantly ponder that some might think you slow-witted or befuddled. However, you are constantly aware of your surroundings, both physically and spiritually. As you gain levels as an elemental scion, your graft gains power, eventually beginning to aid in your goals of discovery.

While you are mostly left alone to explore the connections between elementals and the world, you are expected to report your discoveries to your leaders in the Inmost (see the Advancement and Organization sections). If you are a native of Zilargo, you will be expected to come to that nation's defense should it ever be threatened. Native elder scions are often regarded as elite soldiers of Zilargo by some members of its government, because the nation has no standing army on the scale of its peers. Even if you are not a gnome, your education in the mysteries of the elements (as well as your first elemental graft) probably came from a grafter in Zilargo. If you encounter a threat to Zilargo, you are expected to do what you can to protect the homeland (of your graft, if not yourself), whether that means taking direct action or alerting someone else in your organization.

Combat

Elemental scions of Zilargo most often have a martial focus, but you might still feel some hunger for the esoteric powers of the universe. You might have possession of items that allow you to call elemental allies forth to battle at your side, and you count on being able to withstand damage with your grafts and class abilities when trouble finds you. You likely favor medium or heavy armor and shields, preferring to chip away at an enemy with a single weapon than take the risk of two-handed or two-weapon attacks.

Most scions do not venture into combat alone, and even a scion who seems alone probably has other scion or elemental allies nearby. As a member of the Inmost, you can usually call for help when you need it, but you might prefer to make friends of other sorts. Branching out and finding allies with complementary or varied abilities benefits everyone involved. You are probably the bulwark of your adventuring party, guarding the forward approach while more nimble allies try to flank foes, and ranged attacks are launched from behind your defenses.

Once you have reached the pinnacle of your career, you are even more capable of defending yourself and your allies. The second awareness provided by your elemental graft enables you to more effectively watch out for surprise attacks. Your graft is almost like another ally for your party, giving the group another host of abilities to capitalize on.

Advancement

Elemental scions of Zilargo are all affiliated in some way with a group called the Inmost, a subsect within the Power of Purity organization (see page 34). This group, even more than the Power of Purity at large (which finds itself increasingly devoted to the running of an elemental binding business), is dedicated to understanding the mysteries of elemental magic, as well as negotiating on good terms with the elementals they bind into items, vessels, and themselves. Those interested in these pursuits typically seek out a Power of Purity workshop (see the map on page 34) and apply for membership to the Inmost. A would-be member must demonstrate some rudimentary knowledge of elementals, but sometimes sheer eagerness is enough for an applicant to qualify.

The secrets of the group are never revealed to low-ranking members. In fact, you likely discover your own secrets, refining new ideas or inspirations until they can be unveiled as a new application of elemental binding (whether in the form of graft, item, or something entirely new).

You might have been recruited from the ranks of elemental binders in another part of Khorvaire, or you might be native to Zilargo. In recent years, the nongnome population of the Inmost (and of the elemental scions) has begun to inch upward.

You and other members of the Inmost are always afforded a place to work in whatever workshop you find yourself. The space might be small and have few tools, but you are expected to find ways to fund your own research. This funding sometimes comes in the form of grants from the government of Zilargo, but private investors are almost as common. You can also rent a room from a local workshop for 1 sp per night, which includes one hot meal per day. Allies and companions can rent the same sort of room for 2 sp per night, but those unaffiliated with the Inmost are typically not welcome (as spies are common in the elemental binding industry).

You are expected to find your own path on your quest to understand the elements, and so elemental scion training is haphazard at best. Novices must seek out more experienced members if they want instruction; official classes are never held, although some members might offer the occasional workshop or clinic on a particular theory. Many novices find work with more experienced members, but they are afforded plenty of time to pursue their own studies.

A few Inmost novices elect to better understand elementals and their abilities by traveling the world and seeing those forces at work. While not discouraged, such members are still expected to report in with new discoveries from time to time. Elemental scions form the largest percentage of this group, because they often have a lack of direct magical knowledge that hinders them in the workshop laboratories and summoning chambers.

Resources

Any sort of elemental graft and most kinds of elemental vessels are available at an Inmost workshop provided you have the cash (and often the time, since most vessels are constructed on demand). Most members of the Inmost have at least one elemental graft, while you and most other elemental scions have several of various types. Bound-elemental weapons, armor, and other items are also common among members, and can be bought for 10% off the market price by members of the Inmost at organization workshops. Selection varies, however, so if you desire a specific item, you must usually put in a request well in advance.

ELEMENTAL SCIONS OF ZILARGO IN THE WORLD

"Elementals live and die, just as we do. But our elemental allies—grafted to our very flesh and bone—live as we live, and die as we die."

—Shae-ahm Rhen Skyshadow,
elemental scion of Zilargo

Elemental scions of Zilargo are becoming slowly more common outside that nation. Though characters are liable to encounter one at any time within the borders of Zilargo, they can also be found in any places ripe with potent elemental energy, from an elemental vessel to the wildest reaches of Eberron. Industrial espionage is a common occurrence in the elemental binding industry, so a character with levels in this class might be approached repeatedly by members of the Inmost or other factions from Zilargo with requests to recover stolen inventions (or perhaps even to steal one herself).

Organization

Elemental scions are rare, so they do not often work together. However, they are readily identifiable to one another, and most are on friendly terms. Some competition between all members of the Inmost exists, but as most are interested in knowledge before recognition, it tends to stay good-natured.

The Inmost is led by Harkra Loivaerl Lonadar (N female gnome wizard 14). She is the group's founder, as well as the founder of the Inmost's parent organization, the Power of Purity, and she still conducts research in a large, sprawling workshop complex in Korranberg near the Library. Harkra ceded general control of the Power of Purity only a few months ago to focus on the Inmost and her research. The group has no strict hierarchy or formal structure. Members tend to recognize their more innovative peers and defer to them when decisions must be rendered. The organization is quite wealthy from the sale of elemental-bound items, allowing its members the freedom to pursue whatever studies interest them most. Harkra has seen no reason as yet to change this informality, although some of her immediate advisors have told her that since the group is growing rapidly, they can see a day when a more traditional structure will need to be adopted.

The elemental scions ultimately report to another gnome, a male ranger named Agraefa Fekk Earthheart. One of the first to discover that an elemental graft could assume a sentient state, Agraefa is almost revered by other scions, who believe that he has discovered the truths of elemental unity and embodies them within himself. Multiple grafts of many sorts adorn Agraefa's body, and his flesh has been nearly consumed by the extensive work. Beneath Agraefa, who answers only loosely to Harkra Loivaerl Lonadar, other scions come and go as they please in the loose network that seems to suit them. Like all those who work within the Inmost, both leaders seek to understand the truths of elemental power as they bind themselves more closely to what they see as the basic building blocks of all reality.

Like all members of the Inmost, elemental scions earn recognition for their deeds and discoveries. New theories and applications of elemental magic receive a great deal of attention, and most members aren't considered more than novices until they present such a discovery to their peers. The group is thus split along basically two lines: novices and masters. Within the ranks of the masters, there are many subtle grades that only members seem to understand, based on the weight of a master's body of work, its overall importance to the organization and Zilargo at large, and many other factors.

NPC Reactions

Virtually all folk across Khorvaire know of elemental vessels and Khyber shard items, and that the bulk of these come out of the gnome nation of Zilargo. However, while almost no one outside Zilargo knows (or cares) about the Inmost or the elemental scions, within Zilargo is a different story. Most gnomes and other Zil know of the elemental scions, especially within the industry built around the creation of elemental items. Most spellcasters and nobles likewise know of the group and their more bizarre members.

Though scions are often seen as peculiar, the transformation and power they represent is clear enough to anyone who gets a close look, and the effects the Inmost have had on the elemental binding industry are well known. More commoners know of elemental grafts than of the scions in particular, but the gnomes are blessed with an impressive tolerance for strangers. Scions in Zilargo will find themselves welcomed in most towns and villages, if for no other reason than the chance to study and question them.

Like all groups on the rapid rise to impressive power, the members of the Inmost have their share of enemies. The world of elemental binding is cutthroat, and industrial espionage and sabotage are common. The Inmost leadership keeps a close eye on these activities but they are not omniscient, and many groups have tried to steal (so

far unsuccessfully) the secrets of becoming an elemental scion. What all these thieves have yet to realize is that doing so requires more than control of the graft. Negotiation with it is vital—an elemental scion must accept the graft as a potential life force worth nurturing, rather than something to be forced into submission.

ELEMENTAL SCIONS OF ZILARGO LORE

Characters with Knowledge (arcana) can research the elemental scions of Zilargo to learn more about them. (Within Zilargo itself, the Gather Information skill can be used to uncover the same information.) When a character makes a skill check, read or paraphrase the following, including the information from lower DCs.

DC 10: "A new group of elemental binders started up not too long ago. They apparently have been receiving lots of new contracts lately."

DC 15: "This group believes that elementals should be negotiated with peacefully rather than just bound into an item. They even think that elementals are part of all of us, and should be treated respectfully."

DC 20: "The Power of Purity has some new way to bind elementals. One segment of the group is called the Inmost, and they bind elementals into living creatures!"

DC 30: "A ranger named Agraefa Earthheart has bound an elemental into his own body, and is so covered in elemental grafts that you can hardly tell he was a gnome at some point."

ELEMENTAL SCIONS OF ZILARGO IN THE GAME

Elemental scions can be introduced whenever the PCs have reason to use one of the numerous elemental vessels of Khorvaire. Scions routinely travel in airships or on the lightning rail, considering it almost a rite of passage to see and understand these remarkable vessels that many folk have come to take for granted. Even if not recognized as such, a scion is easily distinguished by the elemental grafts that cover her body, providing an interesting topic of conversation for a passing spellcaster or any other curious character. Alternatively, a scion might approach one of the PCs if they have openly displayed an affectation for a type of spell or item that uses elemental magic.

An elemental scion PC should occasionally be given options to learn something new about one or more of the elements with which she is so fascinated. Trips to other planes might accomplish this, and ties to the elements and elementals are already common across Khorvaire in the form of Khyber shards and the power they bind. The scion will want to seek out new techniques of elemental magic or new ways to apply old knowledge. Occasional trips to Zilargo will also help such a character stay in touch with her peers.

Adaptation

The easiest way to customize this prestige class is by making it dependent on another type of graft (see Chapter 5). Perhaps a sect of elves in Aerenal seeks to become more like the deathless by growing a living deathless graft, or a group of druids in the Eldeen Reaches might have found some benefit to nurturing a plant graft into sentience.

The class could also be given a stronger spellcasting flavor by toning down some of the special abilities (perhaps removing the elemental graft affinity, uncanny dodge, and elemental merge abilities), giving the class only a good Will save (instead of good Fortitude and Will saves), and dropping the Hit Dice to d6 or d4. The class can then have increased spellcasting progression at every level except those where the graft gains special powers. These elemental scion caster variants might be yet another faction within the Inmost, or perhaps a rival group within Zilargo.

SAMPLE ENCOUNTER

Elemental scions of Zilargo might be encountered anywhere that elemental vessels, items, and grafts are made. The odds of the PCs running into a scion increase dramatically within the borders of Zilargo, especially if the characters are near a binding facility. The PCs might also find elemental scions anywhere they might perceive that elementals are being exploited, as well as in areas where strong elemental forces are at work, such as near a volcano. Scions are also drawn to areas devastated by powerful elements, seeking to spread awareness of their allies and aid victims unprepared for such onslaughts of nature.

Shae-ahm Rhen Skyshadow (EL 10)

Shae-ahm Skyshadow is a gnome elemental scion. She has been a member of the Inmost for nearly two years, and wanders Khorvaire seeking to unravel the secrets of elemental magic. She spends a great deal of time on airships, conversing with bound elementals and seeking to discover the secrets of their souls. When her fire graft achieved sentience, she named it Kaervan (Gnome for *dedicated fire*).

SHAE-AHM RHEN SKYSHADOW	CR 10

Female gnome rogue 7/elemental scion 3
N Small humanoid
Init +2; **Senses** low-light vision; Listen +15, Spot +3
Languages Common, Gnome, Ignan

AC 18, touch 13, flat-footed 18; +2 against traps, +4 against giants
hp 57 (10 HD)
Resist evasion
Fort +7, **Ref** +8 (+10 against traps), **Will** +4; +2 against illusions

Speed 20 ft. (4 squares)
Melee mwk short sword +12/+7 (1d4+2/19–20) or
Melee mwk short sword +10/+5 (1d4+2/19–20) and mwk short sword +10 (1d4+1/19–20) or
Melee touch +10 (1d6 fire)
Base Atk +8; **Grp** +6
Atk Options hands of flame +1d6 fire damage, sneak attack +4d6
Spell-Like Abilities (CL 1st):
    1/day—*speak with animals* (burrowing animals only)

Abilities Str 14, Dex 15, Con 14, Int 10, Wis 13, Cha 8
SQ elemental graft affinity (fire), graft awareness, grafted health, trapfinding, uncanny dodge
Feats Iron Will, Two-Weapon Defense, Two-Weapon Fighting, Weapon Focus (short sword)
Skills Climb +11, Disable Device +12, Hide +15, Jump +5, Knowledge (nature) +2, Knowledge (the planes) +2, Listen +15, Move Silently +11, Open Lock +9, Search +5, Spot +3

Possessions masterwork chain shirt, two masterwork short swords, hands of flame (elemental graft), masterwork thieves' tools
Graft Awareness (Ex): Shae-ahm's hands of flame elemental graft is sentient. It has Int 6, Wis 6, and Cha 6, and can communicate telepathically with Shae-ahm. It grants her a +2 bonus on Listen and Spot checks (included).
Hands of Flame: Shae-ahm can activate her hands of flame elemental graft as a swift action. For 1 round, her melee touch attacks and melee attacks with metallic weapons deal an extra 1d6 points of fire damage.

IMPURE PRINCE

"Let every tool be brought to bear on the abominations that push their way into our world. Even the tools of our enemies, in our hands made pure, will be used to eradicate the daelkyr and their servitors."

—Aldred Enduru, impure prince

The threat represented by aberrations and their masters is one that has assailed the world from time out of mind. But some individuals have always singled out aberrations as special enemies. As the wise instruct, those most effective in fighting against an enemy must come to know the ways, tools, and philosophies of that enemy in an intimate fashion. Of those who make it their special mission to rid the world of illithids, beholders, dolgaunts, dolgrim, and dolghasts (a new monster found on page 143), only impure princes can claim the distinction of using daelkyr-inspired corruptions and symbionts as their most effective tool in aberration cleansing.

Impure princes travel across and under Eberron, certain in their task and unswayed by the methods to which they resort. Their decision to accept the imprimatur of a symbiont and the pain that accompanies that symbiotic relationship merely fuels their resolve in their campaign of suppression.

BECOMING AN IMPURE PRINCE

Impure princes are most often rangers or druids, although many have at least one level of rogue or bard to better meet the skill requirements. Though they sometimes work alone, impure princes are always happy to form teams to bolster their chances at taking down an aberration. Because aberrations often turn up as masterminds behind many evil plots in the world, an impure prince is usually patient enough to follow many seemingly unrelated adventures through to their conclusion in the hope that underlying factors, once discovered, point to daelkyr influence.

ENTRY REQUIREMENTS

Skills: Gather Information 4 ranks, Knowledge (dungeoneering) 8 ranks, Search 4 ranks, Speak Language (Daelkyr).
Feat: Symbiont Mastery*.
Special: Favored enemy (aberrations) or Gatekeeper Initiate feat (from the EBERRON *Campaign Setting*).
*New feat described on page 51.

CLASS FEATURES

The impure prince's class features focus on hunting down and destroying aberrations, but they simultaneously change your mind and body to be more like those of your hated foes.

THE IMPURE PRINCE
HIT DIE: d8

Level	Base Attack Bonus	Fort Save	Ref Save	Will Save	Special	Spellcasting
1st	+1	+0	+0	+2	Expanded spell list, lure symbiont	—
2nd	+2	+0	+0	+3	Favored enemy aberrations +2	+1 level of existing spellcasting class
3rd	+3	+1	+1	+3	Aberrant anatomy (25%)	+1 level of existing spellcasting class
4th	+4	+1	+1	+4	Aberrant fortitude	+1 level of existing spellcasting class
5th	+5	+1	+1	+4	Otherworldly surge	+1 level of existing spellcasting class
6th	+6	+2	+2	+5	Aberrant anatomy (50%), favored enemy aberrations +4	—

Class Skills (4 + Int modifier per level): Bluff, Climb, Concentration, Disguise, Gather Information, Hide, Jump, Knowledge (dungeoneering), Knowledge (local), Knowledge (the planes), Listen, Move Silently, Search, Sense Motive, Spot, Survival.

Spellcasting: At each level except 1st and 6th, you gain new spells per day and an increase in caster level (and spells known, if applicable) as if you had also gained a level in a spellcasting class to which you belonged before adding the prestige class level. You do not, however, gain any other benefit a character of that class would have gained. If you had more than one spellcasting class before becoming an impure prince, you must decide to which class to add each level for the purpose of determining spells per day, caster level, and spells known.

Expanded Spell List: The impure prince learns a variety of magical techniques for rooting out and destroying aberrations. Add the following spells to any one of your class spell lists:

1st—*disguise self, protection from evil, remove fear.*
2nd—*calm emotions, lesser restoration, zone of natural purity*.*
3rd—*daylight, remove disease.*
4th—*nature's wrath*, restoration.*

*Spell found in the EBERRON *Campaign Setting.*

Lure Symbiont (Ex): Due to your extensive study of aberrations and their ilk, you can lure a symbiont to yourself chosen from the following list: breed leech, crawling gauntlet, stormstalk, throwing scarab, or winter cyst (all detailed in Chapter 6). Luring a symbiont for your personal use requires 8 hours of preparation and an expenditure of resources with a cost of 100 gp. The symbiont arrives 24 hours later.

If this symbiont is lost or killed, you can gain a new one using the same method. However, as long as you lack your symbiont, you cannot gain further levels in the impure prince class, and you lose access to the aberrant fortitude and otherworldly surge class abilities. If you are at least 5th level, you can choose to lure a shadow sibling, spellwurm, or tentacle whip instead of the options given above (the shadow sibling and spellwurm appear in Chapter 6; the tentacle whip is found in the EBERRON *Campaign Setting*). The lured symbiont willingly joins with you; any other character who attempts to join with the symbiont must succeed on a personality conflict every day until the symbiont wins, at which point it detaches from the host.

You can also possess symbionts obtained through other means (such as by being a member of the daelkyr half-blood race, presented on page 37).

Favored Enemy (Aberrations) (Ex): Beginning at 2nd level, you gain aberrations as a favored enemy. At 6th level, the bonuses against aberrations increases by 2. The bonus from this ability stacks with those from other favored enemy class features. See the ranger class feature, page 47 of the *Player's Handbook.*

Aberrant Anatomy (Ex): Your internal anatomy reshapes in subtle and disturbing ways as you become more like the creatures you hate. Beginning at 3rd level, any time you are struck by a critical hit or sneak attack, there is a 25% chance that the extra damage from the critical hit or sneak attack is negated.

At 6th level, this chance increases to 50%.

Aberrant Fortitude (Su): As you taint your body with aberrant traits, your mental power begins to exert influence over your physical form. Beginning at 4th level, you can choose to apply your Wisdom modifier instead of your Constitution modifier on Fortitude saves. You lose access to this class feature if your symbiont is lost or killed. Once you lure a new symbiont, the ability returns.

Otherworldly Surge (Su): At 5th level, you become able to channel the power of Xoriat, the Realm of Madness. As a standard action, you can radiate a burst of mind-twisting energy drawn from the plane of Xoriat. This effect deals 1d6 points of damage per class level to all living, intelligent creatures within a 20-foot-radius burst (not including you or any of your symbionts) and confuses any creatures damaged by the burst for 1 round. A successful Will save (DC 10 + class level + Wis modifier) halves the damage dealt and negates the confusion. Aberrations are particularly vulnerable to this surge and take a −4 penalty on saves to resist it. This is an enchantment (compulsion), mind-affecting effect.

You can use this ability a number of times per day equal to 3 + your Wis modifier (minimum once). You lose access to this class feature if your symbiont is lost or killed. Once you lure a new symbiont, the ability returns.

PLAYING AN IMPURE PRINCE

If the will is strong enough, great burdens can be borne if a greater good is accomplished. Such is the choice you made when you learned the lore necessary to lure a daelkyr-bred symbiont to yourself. With it, you have unparalleled insight into the workings of the crazed minds of aberrations. It is a constant balancing act—you must pull back from full immersion in their philosophies and spastic manner of thinking, lest you cross that fine line and become one of them. As a result, you might seem frenzied and energized at times, and at other times dour and contemplative to your companions, if any.

These mood shifts are only your outward visage reflecting the status of your constant internal struggle. This struggle is one that you can never forget, because it is embodied in the symbiont you host. Hated, yet needed, you have a relationship with your symbiont that the term ambivalence hardly manages to begin describing. Without it, your ability to fight that which you hate most is circumscribed. But with it, you carry that which you hate most. It is a matter of rationalization, you convince yourself. Sometimes lesser evils are necessary in the eradication of the greater. If impurity is something you must take into your soul, then you are allowing the chance for far greater purity to be claimed by the rest of those who live on Eberron.

To accomplish your lifelong quest, you must seek your enemy in the wild lands and below the earth. Because there is strength in numbers, you are not averse to teaming with others, and because aberrations are often behind the evils in the world, you can force yourself to remain patient enough to follow seemingly unrelated adventures through to their conclusion, hoping all the while that underlying factors, once discovered, point to daelkyr influence.

Sometimes you will encounter those who, seeing your demeanor and methods, and especially your symbiont, will assume that you are one of the dark creatures you hunt. Though you might attempt to disabuse them of their fallacious views at first, in the end it sometimes proves easier to merely expunge them, lest they interfere with your true mission. These meddlers get what they deserve in delaying your ongoing quest.

Combat

Already a skilled warrior, you can reinforce your martial ability with your spells and class abilities. Depending on the symbiont that you lure and host, your options on offense and defense are myriad. For instance, you might find a shadow sibling the perfect protector, or instead opt for a spellwurm, especially one that harbors a particularly potent spell.

You first can use your abilities to hunt and track aberrations, then finish the job with either martial skill at arms or an application of your spells and otherworldly surge. Many of the spells to which you have access serve to either protect, disguise, or lift deleterious conditions that aberrations are capable of inflicting.

While you will certainly have cause to curse the lack of specificity that causes your otherworldly surge to slop over and effect nonaberrations, sometimes you will find that this ability is an effective surprise against enemies that, while not spawned by daelkyr, are just as interested in tearing out your vitals.

Advancement

As you continue to gain levels in the impure prince class, your ability to wield your primary weapon should not be set aside. To this end, continue to take feats that enhance your fighting ability, perhaps even starting (or continuing) down the Two-Weapon Fighting feat tree.

Because of the foes you face, it isn't a bad idea to bolster your ability to shrug off mental effects. Consider taking Iron Will despite your otherwise good Will save.

Resources

It is not unknown for two impure princes to trade symbionts for short periods, if one knows that a special ability of a comrade's symbiont might come in handy during an upcoming mission. Sometimes trades are permanent.

IMPURE PRINCES IN THE WORLD

"I wouldn't trust them. They're too much like the creatures they should be hunting."

—Ickthelos, Sharn Magistrate

Impure princes can rise from nearly any locale, but they are thickest in and around areas bordering on the Shadow Marches or other areas of aberration incursion.

While on the hunt, the life of an impure prince involves travel, camping, weathering the elements, and braving unrelated dangers along the way. Most impure princes find it reasonable to hide their symbionts when at all possible. They're more likely to be accepted in small communities they pass through while hunting aberrations.

An impure prince uses the fruit of corruption to fight the same

formerly did, and it does not inconvenience you in the least.

You are considered proficient with your battlefist, and you can make a natural slam attack with your battlefist that deals 1d6 points of damage plus your Strength modifier. If your base attack bonus is +6 or higher, you can attack more than once in a round with your battlefist, just as you would with a wielded weapon. You can also use spells or infusions on your battlefist as if it were a both a natural and a manufactured weapon.

At 2nd level, your battlefist becomes a magic weapon and gains a +1 enhancement bonus on attack rolls and damage rolls. This bonus improves by 1 at 5th level and again at 9th level. A battlefist with a +1 or greater enhancement bonus can be further enhanced or improved with Craft Magic Arms and Armor just as if it were a magic weapon.

Craft Master (Ex): You are extremely skilled at construction and repair. You add your renegade mastermaker level to all Craft checks you make.

Self-Repair (Su): Starting at 2nd level, you can channel your spells or infusions into repairing damage that you have taken. As a full-round action, you can expend a spell or infusion; you heal 1d6 hit points per level of the spell or infusion sacrificed. You can only use this ability on yourself.

Supporting Construction (Ex): By the time you reach 3rd level, you have incorporated so many artificial parts into your body that you can be the target of *repair damage* spells and infusions. You heal half the result of the *repair* spell or infusion when it is cast upon you.

At 6th level, your supporting construction is even more pervasive, and you gain the full benefit of *repair damage* spells, but you also become vulnerable to spells and infusions that deal damage to constructs, such as *inflict damage* and *disable construct*.

Damage Reduction (Ex): As you incorporate pieces of adamantine and other reinforcing materials into your body, you become somewhat resistant to physical damage. At 4th level, you gain damage reduction 1/adamantine. This benefit increases to damage reduction 2/adamantine at 8th level.

Embed Component (Ex): Starting at 7th level, you gain the ability to embed or attach warforged components to yourself, including docent and artifact components, as long as a component does not affect your battlefist.

Each warforged component you embed or attach grants you 1 bonus hit point.

Construct Exemplar: At 10th level, you have reached your version of perfection and become a living construct. Your type changes to living construct and you gain all the traits of that type (see the EBERRON *Campaign Setting*). You are treated as a warforged for the purpose of meeting any requirements or prerequisites.

You also gain a bonus warforged feat. You can even select a warforged feat that normally requires you to be 1st level, such as Mithral Body.

PLAYING A RENEGADE MASTERMAKER

Warforged are the next step in the evolution of humanity. They are the most magnificent creation to emerge from the forges, the perfection of Cannith craft, and you are actively attempting to become one. What better goal is there than the pursuit of perfection?

As a renegade mastermaker, you dabble in forbidden knowledge, using the secrets of the creation forges to slowly transform yourself into a warforged. Others, especially most members of House Cannith, frown upon your actions, but they simply don't understand the enlightenment of the path you deign to follow. Some call you mad, crazed by too much machine and not enough soul, but you are mostly certain that you are perfectly sane.

Combat

Your abilities make you harder to damage and more resilient than your more fleshy companions. As you advance, you maintain most of your spellcasting ability, so the role you fill doesn't change significantly from that of your earlier adventures. Your battlefist is a reasonable weapon if you find yourself in melee, and even with a low attack bonus you might be able to aid your comrades in melee using the aid another action or taking up a flanking position.

As you attain levels as a renegade mastermaker, you become even harder to hurt. You can take advantage of this by using touch spells in combat, without fearing the occasional blow that lands. If you are an artificer, using

RENEGADE MASTERMAKER   HIT DIE: d6

Level	Base Attack Bonus	Fort Save	Ref Save	Will Save	Special	Spellcasting
1st	+0	+2	+0	+2	Battlefist, craft master	—
2nd	+1	+3	+0	+3	Battlefist (+1), self-repair	+1 level of existing spellcasting class
3rd	+2	+3	+1	+3	Supporting construction	+1 level of existing spellcasting class
4th	+3	+4	+1	+4	Damage reduction 1/adamantine	+1 level of existing spellcasting class
5th	+3	+4	+1	+4	Battlefist (+2)	+1 level of existing spellcasting class
6th	+4	+5	+2	+5		+1 level of existing spellcasting class
7th	+5	+5	+2	+5	Embed component	—
8th	+6	+6	+2	+6	Damage reduction 2/adamantine	+1 level of existing spellcasting class
9th	+6	+6	+3	+6	Battlefist (+3)	+1 level of existing spellcasting class
10th	+7	+7	+3	+7	Construct exemplar	+1 level of existing spellcasting class

Class Skills (4 + Int modifier per level): Appraise, Concentration, Craft, Disable Device, Knowledge (arcana), Knowledge (architecture and engineering), Knowledge (the planes), Open Lock, Profession, Search, Spellcraft, Use Magic Device.

personal weapon augmentation and similar infusions can make your battlefist a devastating weapon.

If you really want to focus on your battlefist attack, take advantage of Attune Magic Weapon and feats that increase your attack rolls and damage rolls. Further enhance your weapon with a *weapon augmentation* infusion (or, if an arcane spellcaster, *greater magic weapon*), and your attack and damage can be on par with that of a fighter, though you might not have as many attacks.

Once you become a living construct, take advantage of your newfound immunities by placing yourself in harm's way, making yourself a target for those poison or paralysis attacks that would incapacitate one of your less-resilient companions.

Advancement

Renegade mastermakers come primarily from groups of disillusioned artificers and magewrights of House Cannith, who were promised the secrets of creation forges, but then forbidden to use that knowledge. Other crafters and spellcasters also began experimenting with warforged parts culled from the scattered battlefields of the Last War. You might be one of these individuals, but you could just as easily be an artisan with a desire to incorporate the strengths of the warforged into your own body.

Renegade mastermakers as a group are not particularly social, so you might find yourself traveling to foreboding towers in distant lands to meet another mastermaker. There you might glean some additional secrets of the warforged creation process, perhaps by analyzing the completed portions of your fellow mastermaker. However, advancing in your class is not contingent on learning such secrets directly from your peers; many renegade mastermakers perfect their craft through experimentation, using standard warforged or other constructs as learning subjects.

As you attain more levels in the renegade mastermaker prestige class, you will want to keep increasing your Craft skill, since your daily healing depends upon it. If you are an artificer, choose a homunculus that fits your style, such as a furtive filcher if you require stealth, or an arbalester (see page 152) if you need ranged support. You can also transform your battlefist into a formidable weapon if you further improve it using your Craft Magic Arms and Armor feat and later take the Attune Magic Weapon feat (from the EBERRON *Campaign Setting*). With or without enhancing your battlefist, if you are an artificer, your *weapon augmentation* infusions can also be very effective.

Resources

With no organization willing to support them directly, most renegade mastermakers are forced to find their own workshops in which to perform their experiments. In many cases, such workspace is provided by benefactors as a reward for completing quests or missions. Even in those cases, a benefactor eventually becomes concerned about the dubious legality of a mastermaker's work, and might be forced to close his doors.

Some of the more advanced renegade mastermakers have found solace in the Mournland, and while it is unclear if the Lord of Blades supports them directly, these mastermakers seem to be less disturbed by the construct denizens of that region.

RENEGADE MASTERMAKERS IN THE WORLD

"We made them to be like us, so it is only fitting that we also make ourselves to be like them."

—Morran d'Cannith, before his expulsion from the Cannith Forgehold

Renegade mastermakers see themselves as a self-made link between the humanoid races and the warforged. Those races seldom share that perception, instead believing most renegade mastermakers to be dangerous mad scientists, obsessed with corrupting the natural order of life. That said, many members of House Cannith secretly admire the ingenuity of the mastermakers, and the house tries to keep tabs on any new technologies the mastermakers stumble into.

Renegade mastermakers have found a way to replace their bodies with warforged parts

Organization

Most renegade mastermakers find the constant persecution to be a detriment to research, and so move to remote or secluded locations where they can attempt to work in peace. They still occasionally deal with inquisitive neighbors and the threat of assassination by any number of private or government organizations, or even by other mastermakers seeking to add to their own libraries.

Some renegade mastermakers fund adventuring groups to handle routine tasks such as retrieving extra warforged parts or gaining access to lost or secret texts and schemas. In these cases, a mastermaker might provide his envoys with various items, some experimental and of questionable reliability. These mastermakers sometimes form a mentor relationship with an adventurer, extolling the virtues of construct life while the adventurer completes the task at hand.

A dirty secret of House Cannith is that Morran d'Cannith, a prominent artisan within the ranks of the house, has started down the path of the renegade mastermaker. At first, his obsession with the warforged was praised as a demonstration of a healthy appetite and enthusiasm for his work in the great creation forge in the depths of Sharn. But his experiments grew beyond the boundaries of propriety, and the house began to question his sanity. After an incident involving the disassembly of some recently created warforged, Morran was banned from the House Cannith Forgehold in the depths of Sharn. However, Morran was a close friend of Merrix d'Cannith, who could not bring himself to issue an execution order, so he instead provided Morran with an underground laboratory deep within Undersharn, where he continues his experiments and adapts his body to his construct ideal.

Because many of the secrets used by the renegade mastermakers pertain to knowledge that House Cannith jealously guards, they have a certain interest in keeping track of these renegades to ensure that the knowledge remains secret. At the same time, members of the house recognize that the renegades provide a new avenue for research that isn't available to the house through standard venues. Thus, the house is conflicted. The insular nature of the mastermakers protects them, in a way. In general, House Cannith turns a blind eye to the activities of renegade mastermakers as long as they remain isolated. But at the same time, the house is poised to deal swiftly with the mastermakers should they become a threat.

NPC Reactions

During the first few levels, a renegade mastermaker appears no different from a typical adventurer, albeit one with an oversized metallic hand. Most people stare at the replaced appendage with morbid curiosity and feel uncomfortable speaking to a renegade mastermaker, darting periodic glances at the metal hand. Such situations can be avoided by covering the hand or hiding it within a cloak or robe. Many other folk are simply indifferent to a mastermaker's appearance.

At the middle levels of the class, a renegade mastermaker begins to experience persecution and disdain, as his body incorporates more mechanical portions than most people are comfortable with. Many common folk perceive mastermakers as abominations, so attempted interactions are likely to garner an unfriendly response, if not outright hostility.

At the pinnacle of his advancement, a renegade mastermaker closely resembles a warforged, and so is afforded the same courtesy (or lack thereof) offered those living constructs. Those folk who have a fear or loathing of warforged might have similar feelings toward high-level mastermakers, and are usually unfriendly, at best.

In Thrane and Karrnath, mastermakers are treated with suspicion, because they are an uncomfortable reminder that warforged might, in fact, not be slaves. The members of House Cannith also afford the mastermakers a degree of respect, even while they attempt to silence those renegades who threaten to spread the secrets of warforged creation.

Many mastermakers find solace working under the auspices of the Lord of Blades in the Mournland, because that warforged scion and his followers are less likely to be hostile toward mastermakers simply because of their apparent mechanical nature.

RENEGADE MASTERMAKER LORE

Characters with Knowledge (arcana) or Knowledge (architecture and engineering) can research the renegade mastermakers to learn more about them. When a character makes a skill check, read or paraphrase the following, including the information from lower DCs.

DC 10: "Those mastermakers are mad! Who, in their right mind, would chop off his hand and strap a gauntlet on the bloody stump?"

DC 15: The renegade mastermakers have found a way to replace their bodies with warforged parts. They are also some of the best smiths around—too bad they aren't entirely stable.

DC 20: "Renegade mastermakers want to be warforged, the Host knows why. House Cannith doesn't seem to mind, but they should. Creating warforged is illegal, after all."

DC 30: Characters who achieve this level of success can learn details about specific mastermakers in your campaign, potentially including how to contact them. They also learn some of the more gruesome details regarding the entry requirements.

In Sharn, a DC 25 Gather Information check can uncover Morran d'Cannith's name as a prominent renegade mastermaker. At any Cannith enclave in or near Sharn, a Diplomacy check with a helpful result can facilitate a meeting with Morran. A member of House Cannith gains a +2 circumstance bonus on the check, and the bonus increases to +4 if the member also bears the Mark of Making.

RENEGADE MASTERMAKERS IN THE GAME

Renegade mastermakers have only recently begun to appear outside the creation forges. During the Last War, a few mastermakers of House Cannith were significantly involved in the operation of the creation forges that churned out warforged and other material. Once the war ended, the mastermakers found their way out into the world, though eventually they sought refuge in isolated workshops where they could continue their experiments unmolested. Their relative anonymity allows them to be easily added to an ongoing campaign.

A player who chooses this prestige class likely sees the benefits of changing her character's type to living construct and enjoys the roleplaying aspects of incorporating more mechanical parts into her PC's body. You should play up these physical features, allowing a player to more fully develop how her PC feels about the world. While many renegade mastermakers have workshops or laboratories, such facilities are not actually required for a PC to advance in the class.

Adaptation

Renegade mastermakers can fit the role of a mad wizard in any campaign world. While the prestige class is tailored for an artificer, there is no reason why a wizard or cleric could not gain the same benefits. In a world without warforged, the renegade mastermaker could idolize golems or some other construct form. In such cases, replace the Embed Component ability with the ability to wear up to two magic items about the neck (amulet, brooch, medallion, necklace, periapt, or scarab).

SAMPLE ENCOUNTER

The PCs might encounter a renegade mastermaker while journeying near the Mournland, or they might have been sent to find him to deliver a message or bring him back to a nearby settlement.

Thalas (EL 8)

Thalas, a hot-headed renegade mastermaker, has gotten himself in hot water, and finds himself staring up at a warforged titan ordered to kill him. If the PCs rescue or help him, he invites them back to his workshop: a hollow buried under the rubble of an abandoned town, with all manner of instruments and tools strewn about. Once there, he might be willing to spend some time enhancing a weapon or two for his saviors.

Thalas	**CR 8**

Male human artificer 7/renegade mastermaker 1
LN Medium humanoid
Init +0; **Senses** Listen −1, Spot −1
Languages Common, Draconic, Dwarven

AC 19, touch 10, flat-footed 19
hp 46 (8 HD)
Fort +7, **Ref** +3, **Will** +7

Speed 20 ft. (4 squares)
Melee battlefist +6 (1d8+1) or
Ranged mwk light crossbow +6 (1d8/19–20)
Base Atk +5; **Grp** +6
Atk Options Empower Spell
Combat Gear *wand of magic missile* (CL 5th, 37 charges)

Artificer Infusions (CL 7th, DC 13 + level of infusion):
  4/day—2nd, 1st*
  3/day—3rd*
  *See Chapter 4 and page 103 of the EBERRON *Campaign Setting* for available artificer infusions
Spell-Like Abilities (CL 1st):
  1/day—*repair serious damage**
  1/day—*make whole**
*See page 114 of the EBERRON *Campaign Setting*

Abilities Str 12, Dex 10, Con 14, Int 16, Wis 8, Cha 14
SQ artificer knowledge +10, artisan bonus, craft homunculus, craft master, disable trap, item creation, metamagic spell trigger, retain essence
Feats Brew Potion[B], Craft Magic Arms and Armor[B], Craft Wand[B], Craft Wondrous Item[B], Empower Spell, Exceptional Artisan[B], Least Dragonmark (Mark of Making), Lesser Dragonmark (Mark of Making), Rapid Infusion*, Scribe Scroll[B]

*New feat; see Chapter 2.
Skills Appraise +3 (+5 armor), Concentration +13, Craft (armorsmithing) +15, Disable Device +14, Knowledge (arcana) +14, Knowledge (the planes) +8, Search +14, Spellcraft +16 (+18 scrolls), Survival −1 (+1 other planes), Use Magic Device +13 (+15 scrolls)
Possessions combat gear plus *+1 breastplate*, *+1 light steel shield*, battlefist, masterwork light crossbow with 20 bolts, *cloak of resistance +1*, *amulet of natural armor +1*
Warforged Titan: hp 106; EBERRON *Campaign Setting* page 302.

VIGILANT SENTINEL OF AERENAL

"We watch the world, letting none know who we are or what we do. Are we lonely? Yes. But our families, our people, are safe."

—Jabreki Osluuhn,
vigilant sentinel of Aerenal

Vigilant sentinels of Aerenal serve an important function for their island nation. Part spy, part assassin, and completely loyal to the Sibling Kings and Aerenal's undying rulers, the sentinels roam across Eberron. Their duty is to keep their eyes and ears open for any rumor or whisper of a threat to their nation, as well as to perform the tasks and missions requested by their leaders. The vigilant sentinels of Aerenal are essentially roving sleeper agents, focused on their nation's well-being over any other consideration.

BECOMING A VIGILANT SENTINEL OF AERENAL

Rogues, bards, and monks most frequently become vigilant sentinels of Aerenal, since each of these classes can meet the requirements by 5th level. Fighters and rangers are also sometimes drawn to the vigilant sentinel path, although the skill requirements typically require them to multiclass.

ENTRY REQUIREMENTS

Race: Aerenal elf or half-elf.
Skills: Diplomacy 8 ranks, Hide 4 ranks, Move Silently 4 ranks, Sense Motive 8 ranks.
Special: Must have been accepted into the Order of the Vigilant Sentinels and accept an oath to obey its masters in all you do (see Code of Conduct, below).

THE VIGILANT SENTINEL OF AERENAL
HIT DIE: d8

Level	Base Attack Bonus	Fort Save	Ref Save	Will Save	Special
1st	+0	+0	+2	+2	Code of conduct, master of disguise, nondetection
2nd	+1	+0	+3	+3	Sneak attack +1d6
3rd	+2	+1	+3	+3	Thought theft
4th	+3	+1	+4	+4	Sneak attack +2d6
5th	+3	+1	+4	+4	*Dimension leap*

Class Skills (6 + Int modifier per level): Bluff, Climb, Concentration, Craft, Diplomacy, Disguise, Escape Artist, Forgery, Gather Information, Hide, Intimidate, Jump, Knowledge (local), Listen, Move Silently, Open Lock, Perform, Profession, Search, Sense Motive, Sleight of Hand, Speak Language, Spot, Tumble, Use Magic Device.

CLASS FEATURES

Vigilant sentinels of Aerenal are trained to uncover threats to their nation before they have an opportunity to manifest. Their abilities allow them to sneak into environments where they might not normally be welcome, gleaning information from those who probably don't want it shared.

Code of Conduct: Vigilant sentinels of Aerenal must always obey the directives and orders of their commanders. If you ever willingly violate a directive in a way that endangers Aerenal, the order, or any of its members, you are expunged from the order and declared a threat to the survival of Aerenal. Other vigilant sentinels are ordered to slay you on sight, and it is almost certain that at least one sentinel will quickly be given the task of hunting you down.

Vigilant sentinels must also be willing to lay down their lives for their nation, though you are not expected to act foolishly or sacrifice yourself needlessly. However, failure to act honorably and protect your people to the best of your ability will likely result in your being recalled to Aerenal for debriefing, an investigation into your conduct, and possible expulsion from the order.

Master of Disguise (Ex): Part of your job as a vigilant sentinel is to make your way into places you shouldn't be, and without being detected as a vigilant sentinel. You gain a bonus on Disguise checks equal to your class level.

Nondetection (Su): The vigilant sentinels of Aerenal must be able to protect their minds from enemy spies and spellcasters. You are constantly protected by a *nondetection* effect (as the spell), at a caster level equal to your character level. You can raise or lower this effect as a standard action.

Sneak Attack (Ex): Beginning at 2nd level, you deal extra damage when you are flanking an opponent or at any time when the target would be denied its Dexterity bonus. This extra damage applies to ranged attacks only if the target is within 30 feet. See the rogue class feature on page 50 of the *Player's Handbook.* Your sneak attack damage increases at 4th level.

Thought Theft (Su): Beginning at 3rd level, your ability to use Sense Motive has progressed to the point where you can obtain secret information from creatures with which you interact. You can use your Sense Motive skill to glean elements of culture and even bits of knowledge from your target, enabling you to more thoroughly blend into your surroundings.

As a standard action, you can make a Sense Motive check to detect the vague surface thoughts of a creature with which you can communicate (DC 10 + target creature's HD + target creature's Cha modifier). If you succeed on the check, you gain scattered bits of information that the creature might expect you to know (a password, a hand gesture of identification, a name), the subject of a particular gathering, or even particular modes of speech or dress. This translates into a +4 insight bonus on Bluff, Diplomacy, Disguise, and Gather Information checks made against the target creature and in social situations with that creature.

If the check fails by 5 or more, the target instantly realizes that you were probing its thoughts. Among other consequences, this typically changes the creature's attitude toward you to unfriendly or even hostile, depending on the situation.

Creatures protected from mind reading or similar effects (such as by *nondetection*) have immunity to this ability. This is a mind-affecting, language-dependent ability.

Dimension Leap (Sp): At 5th level, you learn to transport yourself instantly to another nearby location. You can use *dimension leap* (see page 95) as a spell-like ability, with a caster level equal to your class level. You can use this ability once per minute.

Ex-Vigilant Sentinels of Aerenal

A vigilant sentinel who betrays the order or Aerenal does not lose any of the abilities he gained as a result of taking levels in the prestige class, but he cannot continue to advance in the class. In addition, he is now hunted (as described under Code of Conduct, above). The Order of Vigilant Sentinels will stop at nothing to see such renegades captured or slain, since their knowledge of the inner workings of the order is considered a threat to the elven nation. Such characters will mysteriously find no safe harbor in any elven community that knows anything of the vigilant sentinels, even in Valenar or other nations. Needless to say, the order selects its members carefully, and rarely does one choose this path.

PLAYING A VIGILANT SENTINEL OF AERENAL

As a vigilant sentinel of Aerenal, you are the first line of defense for your often misunderstood (and sometimes feared) people. The rest of Eberron stands against you (or at least that is what you are trained to assume), and uncovering threats to Aerenal is always your primary motivation. Years might pass between your missions, allowing you to pursue your own personal or professional agenda, but when the call for duty comes, you must respond immediately.

You are expected to keep your skills sharp, and you probably do so by moving in powerful circles, engaging in the endless parry and thrust of court intrigue. As a vigilant sentinel, you often find yourself in a position where you must assume a role to further your nation's cause. The machinations of court life keep you on your toes and allow you to establish contacts that will help you when you receive a mission. You should also seek to establish relationships with individuals whose skills complement your own. Forging these bonds will provide you with allies willing to stand by you in a tight spot.

You do not live within your nation, although you might be summoned there to receive a particularly important assignment or debriefing. Instead, you call some other country home. Your skills are best suited to blending into the world around you with little or no foreknowledge of the situation in which you find yourself. You must manage to convince those around you (hostile or otherwise) that you are who you appear to be, even as you uncover information that will aid your mission.

At first, you are likely to be given simple charges, perhaps even as mundane as a courier assignment. But as you rise within the silent ranks of the sentinels, you will be entrusted with more sensitive missions that require an increasingly delicate touch. At the highest levels, you might someday be the only one who stands against the certain destruction of your homeland.

Combat

Like rogues, vigilant sentinels rely on misdirection and finesse in battle rather than brute force. Feats that improve your ability to negotiate a tricky battlefield (such as Mobility or Spring Attack) are a plus, as is the Two-Weapon Fighting feat, since it increases the sneak attack damage you can deal in a round.

You lack the hit points (and probably the AC) of heavier armored fighters, so try to remain on the outskirts of a battle, picking your moments to strike with care and patience. When you do enter the fray, use Tumble to set up flanking positions with allies, maximizing the effectiveness of your sneak attack damage.

At higher levels, you can use *dimension leap* to set up flank attacks or surprise your foes, possibly getting the opportunity to attack an enemy while it is still flat-footed.

Advancement

When you entered the order of the vigilant sentinels, you were likely recruited, though some members learn of the group through family connections and ask to join. The ranks of the vigilant sentinels of Aerenal are filled with rehabilitated criminals, former petty thieves or burglars, and more than a few wandering bards. Taught that their personal concerns pale besides those of their nation, these individuals must swear an oath to obey the masters of the order, the Sibling Kings, and the Undying Court in all things. As a result, the initial training of an initiate of the order is more mental and emotional than physical. Recruited members already possess a solid foundation in the skills they need to succeed at the order's bidding, and so their teachers focus more on instilling strong feelings of loyalty and devotion in their charges.

Even despite the oath and training, new members are not trusted with much information. Turned loose and told to notify the order when you settle in another land, you might then wait months or even years for your first assignment. During this time, the order observes you, taking note of your behavior and whether you use this opportunity to

good purpose. You are expected to establish a network of contacts in many fields of interest, as well as keep an ear to the social and political ground for signs of plots against Aerenal.

When you finally receive your first assignments, they are likely short, even tedious affairs. You might be asked to make a simple courier run or simply sit in a public place for a day and observe passing citizens. These missions all have a purpose in the greater schemes of the order and of Aerenal, however, and those who shirk the simple duties soon find that all ties with the order have been cut. Such characters cannot continue to advance in this class, but will not typically be hunted unless their actions involve betrayal of the group or another member (see Ex-Vigilant Sentinels of Aerenal, above).

As a vigilant sentinel, you are expected to always keep your eyes and ears open, and to pass on any information of value to your nation. This obligation might lead to conflict with your closest friends or companions at times, which is why most members of the order keep the details of their duty secret, even from those they trust the most. Many sentinels claim to be natives of Valenar, and your abilities easily allow you to pass yourself off as a Valenar elf (even among the Valenar themselves).

Take opportunities to expand your horizons. Vigilant sentinels are encouraged to travel, although they must remain in contact with other members of the order. Expand your network of contacts and knowledge of other cultures and

The agents of the island nation of Aerenal are called vigilant seninels

nations, meeting with other members of your order and exchanging information when you can.

Resources

All members of the vigilant sentinels are taught specific techniques to identify other members through subtle body language and inflections of speech. Identifying a member of the order requires you to be familiar with these techniques and succeed on a DC 25 Sense Motive check. Members are also expected to have some method of staying in contact with their masters back on Aerenal. This often takes the form of some magic device, but many members use more mundane means of communication. Such messages are always encoded, however, and frequently employ alchemical devices to conceal their true nature.

VIGILANT SENTINELS OF AERENAL IN THE WORLD

"I've heard of these elves—sentinels they call themselves. The idea of those death-lovers creeping around in civilized company gives me chills. Wait, where did you say you were from?"

—Gazdran Illeiope, merchant of Sharn

Characters who are involved in any level of espionage in an EBERRON campaign are likely to cross paths with a vigilant sentinel of Aerenal at some point. Vigilant sentinels can look (and act) like anyone, so virtually any elf or half-elf NPC in the campaign might be revealed as a vigilant sentinel at some point. If the PCs are working for someone interested in prying the secrets of Aerenal loose from the island nation, they are even more likely to encounter a vigilant sentinel, though not necessarily in a positive way. An elf PC with levels in this prestige class makes an excellent source of ongoing campaign hooks, as his masters send him on missions across Eberron.

Organization

The Order of Vigilant Sentinels is run by an elf named Sha'aret Gaazikshi (LN female elf rogue 3/fighter 3/vigilant sentinel of Aerenal 5), who works out of the order's headquarters in Pylas Talaear. Their proximity to the merchants and envoys of other nations suits the order's leadership well, providing them with countless opportunities to send agents and messages off the island aboard merchant or diplomatic vessels.

Sha'aret's loyalty to the Undying Court is absolute. Her father, Rethret Gaazikshi, led the order for nearly two centuries before she took over at the end of the Last War (and it is unlikely that she would have done so if he hadn't gone missing in an exploratory expedition to Xen'drik just as the war concluded).

She works closely with the governor of the city, Syraen Melideth, to ensure that her agents' movement through the city is unimpeded (though Syraen frankly wouldn't know who to impede unless Sha'aret shared their names with her). Syraen is instrumental in seeing to it that agents have transport to Khorvaire and the other corners of the world.

An average day for a vigilant sentinel varies. They are mostly allowed (even encouraged) to pursue their own agendas, as long as those do not conflict with the protection of Aerenal. Many act as courtesans in courts across Khorvaire, while others are merchants (some small, some prominent) in various cities. However, when not actively undertaking a mission for the order, most vigilant sentinels adventure. Many sentinels have learned that a powerful strike team of adventurer allies can be an invaluable asset to the missions they are called on to perform. The bonds established from sharing the extreme risks of adventuring last through even the most difficult times, and many of these alliances have proven as important to the protection of Aerenal as any based in a royal court.

While the order doesn't have ranks per se, those with more levels in the prestige class are typically deferred to by lower-level members. However, a low-level sentinel who has performed a particularly daring or important mission is recognized for her deeds, and perhaps even called upon to lead the Ivek Nath, or Sentinels Elite. These are teams of vigilant sentinels brought together when the order perceives a threat greater than any one agent can handle. Only twice in the last one hundred and fifty years has such a group been called together, the last time when the former leader of the order, Rethret Gaazikshi, led the vanished mission to Xen'drik.

As with any large, widespread organization, some of the older sentinels frown on the way Sha'aret (the "young elf") runs the Vigilant Sentinels. Most have given her the benefit of the doubt out of respect for her father (and, some whisper, in the vain hope that he will return from Xen'drik someday), but a murmur has recently surfaced of a small faction of vigilant sentinels based in Valenar who seek to break from the larger group. These dissidents are led by Trevak Larieen (N male elf rogue 5/vigilant sentinel of Aerenal 3), who has been a member of the organization for over two hundred years. He doesn't go on missions much anymore, but that hasn't stopped him from wooing several older Valenar agents to his cause. He hopes to remove Sha'aret from power gently in the coming years, but as with everything relating to elves, "the coming years" might prove to be a long time.

NPC Reactions

Outside Aerenal, few know of the existence of the vigilant sentinels—and the order prefers it that way. In fact, learning anything about the order is extremely difficult outside Aerenal, but most Aereni who do know of the sentinels' existence see them as heroes. They know of the tremendous sacrifice involved in living for so long outside one's homeland, and that these folk have kept their people secure time and again. Within the borders of Aerenal, a member of the class who encounters a normal citizen of the nation will be met with indifference, but an NPC who knows of the group meets members with an initial attitude of helpful.

The enemies of Aerenal are the enemies of the vigilant sentinels, and the Blood of Vol (along with their Aerenal pawns, the Stillborn) are often subject to sentinel attention. In fact, if not for the actions of the sentinels in years past, the Blood of Vol's foothold in Aerenal might be much stronger than it is.

VIGILANT SENTINELS OF AERENAL LORE

Characters with the Gather Information or Knowledge (history) skill can research the vigilant sentinels of Aerenal to learn more about them. The DCs below are for checks made within Aerenal; add 10 to the DCs anywhere outside the elven nation. When a character makes a skill check, read or paraphrase the following, including the information from lower DCs.

DC 10: "The elves of Aerenal aren't as content as everyone thinks to live alone on their island nation. They have spies everywhere."

DC 15: "The agents of the island of Aerenal are called vigilant sentinels. It's their job to make sure the nation is safe from external threats."

DC 20: "The vigilant sentinels of Aerenal are all over Khorvaire, and even on other continents. They can blend in among other races and cultures, and some say they even have the power to read minds."

DC 30: "The sentinels are led by a female elf named Sha'aret, and their base can be found in the city of Pylas Talaear. Her father disappeared at the end of the Last War, and he was the leader before her. She has sent other expeditions to Xen'drik in the hope of learning his whereabouts, but none have had any success."

VIGILANT SENTINELS OF AERENAL IN THE GAME

As NPCs, vigilant sentinels can be worked into a campaign at virtually any time. Any elf or half-elf NPC might be a sentinel in disguise, even a character with whom the PCs have had a longstanding relationship. The prestige class is more interesting for PCs, however, and an elf character from Aerenal with the necessary skill set (and the requisite loyalty to the homeland) might be approached at any time by a member of the order for recruitment.

Player character sentinels should be allowed to adventure as they please most of the time, but being given missions on occasion can help them feel more immersed in the class. These characters are excellent sources of adventure hooks, since Aerenal is not a well-understood nation, and its enemies are many.

Such missions can be undertaken as short solo adventures during party down time (while spellcasters scribe scrolls or craft magic items, for example), or even as group adventures. When running an adventure that also happens to be a sentinel mission, you might let only the player of the vigilant sentinel know the true nature of the adventure. You can leave it to the sentinel's player to reveal the information to his companions at the right time.

Adaptation

This class can easily be adapted for races other than elves. A goblinoid version of the class might serve the nation of Darguun, while a halfling version might defend the Talenta Plains. Any alternative versions of the class can retain the class features of the vigilant sentinel.

SAMPLE ENCOUNTER

Characters visiting any major court or city on Eberron are likely to encounter a vigilant sentinel, although they are equally unlikely to notice.

Jabreki Osluuhn (EL 7)

Jabreki Osluuhn is a mid-level member of the Order of Vigilant Sentinels. He currently works out of Fairhaven, in Aundair, although he has also worked in Sharn and Taer Vlaestas at times. In Aundair, he is known as Ubeth Gratios, a human wine merchant. He is currently between missions, but could be introduced to the PCs as an employer. Alternatively, they might run afoul of him if he receives orders from home to pursue a mission contrary to the PCs' current goals.

JABREKI OSLUUHN	CR 7

Male elf rogue 5/vigilant sentinel of Aerenal 2
CG Medium humanoid
Init +4; **Senses** low-light vision; Listen +5, Spot +11
Languages Common, Elven

AC 20, touch 14, flat-footed 16; +1 against traps
hp 29 (7 HD)
Immune sleep
Resist evasion
Fort +1, **Ref** +11 (+12 against traps), **Will** +3 (+5 against enchantments)

Speed 30 ft. (6 squares)
Melee *+1 rapier* +9 (1d6+2/19−20) or
Ranged dart +8 (1d4+1)
Base Atk +4; **Grp** +5
Atk Options sneak attack +4d6
Combat Gear *potion of invisibility*

Abilities Str 12, Dex 18, Con 11, Int 10, Wis 8, Cha 17
SQ able to notice secret or concealed doors, nondetection
Feats Investigate*, Investigator, Weapon Finesse
Skills Bluff +13, Diplomacy +13, Disguise +9 (+11 to act in character), Gather Information +13, Hide +14, Intimidate +5, Listen +5, Move Silently +12, Search +8, Sense Motive +7, Spot +11
Possessions combat gear plus *+1 chain shirt*, masterwork buckler, *+1 rapier*, 6 darts, *cloak of Charisma +2*, 20 gp
*See the EBERRON *Campaign Setting*.

Nondetection (Su) Jabreki is constantly protected by a *nondetection* effect (as the spell) at caster level 7th. He can activate or lower this ability as a standard action.

Throndred nearly perished during the quori's initial onslaught, but he was prepared. In has staff was a splinter of Khyber dragonshard—with it, he sprung his *Khyber trap*.

CHAPTER FOUR
SPELLS AND POWERS

Magic is a cornerstone of everyday life in Khorvaire, as well as the currency in which many of the more combative and adventurous elements of society trade. While this chapter presents a number of new spells and infusions for spellcasters and artificers alike, it also considers what life might be like in the magic-suffused society that is Eberron.

LIFE IN A MAGIC-SUFFUSED SOCIETY

Without the inroads of the "technology" of magic that saturates Eberron, the shape of society in Khorvaire and elsewhere would be far simpler. But though Eberron has much in common with other traditional medieval fantasy worlds, make no mistake—Eberron is not a typical medieval society. Whether king or commoner, the people of Eberron almost universally rely on magic to protect their health and conduct their day-to-day lives (sometimes without even being aware of it). Even so, Eberron is by no means a modern society, and though magic grants many of the same benefits as industrialization, it generally does so in very different ways.

POST-MEDIEVAL WORLD

In many ways, Eberron's pseudo-medieval culture already shares many elements of a later renaissance society. This is an important point, because it underscores the fact that the benefits granted by the wide-scale manipulation of magic are not provided by arcane factories of mass production. Instead, Eberron's magical wonders remain the purview of individual practitioners, artisans, and expert crafters.

While skycoaches fly among the soaring towers of Sharn, it is important to remember that each skycoach is the product of individual effort by skilled designers, builders, and spellcasters. Though blacksmiths might chant spells to improve they way they work, their individual forges continue to spit out items just one at a time. While airship travel allows fast, safe, and expensive transport across large distances, each airship is a one-of-a-kind product produced by Zilargo workshops that are themselves unique foundries of often-competitive talent. While the streets of many cities are illuminated with *everbright lanterns*, their magic is individually cast and maintained by ranks of professional spell chandlers. No central reservoir of magical energy powers these and other wonders through some sort of industrial-age magical "grid."

PROFESSIONAL SPELLCASTERS

Professional spellcasters differ from adventuring spellcasters in that they earn a daily living by casting spells for payment. Without the daily spell maintenance of magewrights and others, Eberron would seem a very different place. While the possession of dragonmarks nearly guarantees a professional spellcaster economic viability in one of the houses that dominate the trade and industry of Khorvaire, unmarked spellcasters can still earn a living by working for various guilds (though dragonmarked houses often have controlling interests in these enterprises).

Because of professional spellcasters, most people in Khorvaire enjoy a standard of living above that which they could otherwise normally attain. Most people have cash enough to purchase transport on a short-range skycoach, and all citizens benefit from the *everbright lanterns* set along the major thoroughfares of large Khorvarien cities. Of course, services for which only the wealthy and motivated can afford to pay also exist.

NEW SPELLS AND INFUSIONS

The spells and infusions described below augment the repertoire of the wizards, clerics, magewrights, artificers, and other spellcasters of Eberron. Some are associated closely with particular dragonmarks or dragonmarked houses, and have additional effects when cast by characters with the proper marks or affiliated with those houses.

NEW ARTIFICER INFUSIONS

1st Level

Ablative Armor: Reduce damage from next attack by 5 + caster level (max 15).

Indisputable Possession: Call an item back to your hand if it leaves your possession.

Metamagic Scroll: Imbue spell completion item with metamagic feat.

Pending Potion: Target potion or oil takes effect at a later time.

2nd Level

Elemental Prod: Move an elemental creature a short distance.

Lucky Blade: Weapon grants a single reroll of an attack.
Reinforce Construct: Construct gains 1d6 + 1/level temporary hit points.
Suppress Dragonmark[F]: Suppress the spell-like abilities of target's dragonmark.

3rd Level

Adamantine Weapon: Transform weapon into adamantine.
Blast Rod: Infused rod stores 1d8/level destructive energy.
Lucky Cape: Cape grants a single reroll of a saving throw.
Spell Snare: Dragonshard absorbs a spell or spell-like ability of up to 3rd level.

4th Level

Censure Elementals: Deal 2d4 + 1/level damage each round to elementals.
Concurrent Infusions: Cast three 1st-level infusions simultaneously.

5th Level

Slaying Arrow: Creates a projectile deadly to a specific creature type.

6th Level

Spell Snare, Greater: Dragonshard absorbs a spell or spell-like ability of up to 6th level.

NEW BARD SPELLS

1st Level

Ancient Knowledge: Gain a +5 insight bonus on a single Knowledge check.
Distracting Shadows: −5 penalty on Search and Spot checks in a 20-ft.-radius spread.
Hidden Ward: Hide magical effects on an object.

2nd Level

Clothier's Closet: Conjure several sets of clothing.
Dimension Leap: Teleport 10 ft./level.

4th Level

Watchful Ancestors: Spiritual manifestations prevent you from being flanked and grant insight bonus on one Reflex save.

5th Level

Glimpse of Eternity: Target takes 1d6 nonlethal damage/level and is *confused*.

6th Level

Glimpse of the Prophecy: Gain +1 insight bonus to AC and on saves; gain insight bonus equal to 1/2 caster level on one save, or enter prophetic favor as immediate action.

NEW CLERIC SPELLS

1st Level

Detect Dragonmark: Detect and identify dragonmarks within 60 ft.

2nd Level

Expose the Dead: Gain insight bonuses to locate undead or when investigating a corpse.
Magic Weapon, Legion's: Allies' weapons gain +1 enhancement bonus.
Sense Weakness: Automatically confirm one critical hit.
Shared Healing: Subject creature can cure up to twice your caster level of its own hit points.

4th Level

Watchful Ancestors: Spiritual manifestations prevent you from being flanked and grant insight bonus on one Reflex save.

5th Level

Orb of Dancing Death: Orb you control bestows 1 negative level each round.
Scry Trap: Scry attempts against target deal 1d6/level damage and blind scrying creature.
Undying Aura: Subject gains immunity to death effects, energy drain, and negative energy; can harm one undead or heal one deathless.

6th Level

Glimpse of the Prophecy: Gain +1 insight bonus to AC and on saves; gain insight bonus equal to 1/2 caster level on one save, or enter prophetic favor as immediate action.
Magic Weapon, Greater Legion's: Allies' weapons gain +2 or greater enhancement bonus.
Semblance of Life: Undead take 3d6 damage per round; intelligent undead also dazed 1 round.

7th Level

Leech Undeath: Harm undead to gain temporary hit points.

NEW DRUID SPELLS

2nd Level

Leap Into Animal: Merge with animal and control its actions.

3rd Level

Wind's Favor: Create strong wind for 1 hr./level.

NEW PALADIN SPELLS

2nd Level

Expose the Dead: Gain insight bonuses to locate undead or when investigating a corpse.
Magic Weapon, Legion's: Allies' weapons gain +1 enhancement bonus.

NEW RANGER SPELL

2nd Level

Leap into Animal: Merge with animal and control its actions.

New Sorcerer/Wizard Spells

1st Level

Ancient Knowledge: Gain a +5 insight bonus on a single Knowledge check.

Detect Dragonmark: Detect and identify dragonmarks within 60 ft.

Distracting Shadows: −5 penalty on Search and Spot checks in a 20-ft.-radius spread.

Hidden Ward: Hide magical effects on an object.

2nd Level

Clothier's Closet: Conjure several sets of clothing.

Dimension Leap: Teleport 10 ft./level.

Expose the Dead: Gain insight bonuses to locate undead or when investigating a corpse.

Magic Weapon, Legion's: Allies' weapons gain +1 enhancement bonus.

Mindburn: Target loses a spell or infusion each round.

Sense Weakness: Automatically confirm one critical hit.

Speaking Stones: Pass a 25-word message between two magically linked stones.

Suffer the Flesh^M: Take Constitution damage to make your spellcasting more potent.

Suppress Dragonmark^F: Suppress the spell-like abilities of target's dragonmark.

3rd Level

Khyber Trap: Trap extraplanar creature within a Khyber dragonshard.

4th Level

Spell Snare: Dragonshard absorbs a spell of up to 3rd level.

Watchful Ancestors: Spiritual manifestations prevent you from being flanked and grant insight bonus on one Reflex save.

5th Level

Glimpse of Eternity: Target takes 1d6 nonlethal damage/level and is *confused*.

Magic Weapon, Greater Legion's: Allies' weapons gain +2 or greater enhancement bonus.

Orb of Dancing Death: Orb you control bestows 1 negative level each round.

Scry Trap: Scry attempts against target deal 1d6/level damage and blind scrying creature.

Storm Touch: Touch deals 9d6 electricity damage and stuns victim for 1 round; usable a number of times equal to level.

6th Level

Control Elemental: Gain control of an elemental creature.

Glimpse of the Prophecy: Gain +1 insight bonus to AC and on saves; gain insight bonus equal to 1/2 caster level on one save, or enter prophetic favor as immediate action.

Overwhelming Revelations: Creatures take a −2d6 penalty to Wisdom, are *confused* for 1 round.

7th Level

Scalding Touch: Touch deals 13d6 fire damage and dazes victim; usable a number of times equal to level.

Spell Snare, Greater: Dragonshard absorbs a spell or spell-like ability of up to 6th level.

8th Level

Leech Undeath: Harm undead to gain temporary hit points.

Spells and Infusions

The spells herein are presented in alphabetical order (with the exception of those whose names begin with "greater" or "legion's").

ABLATIVE ARMOR

Abjuration
Level: Artificer 1
Components: S, M
Casting Time: 1 minute
Range: Touch
Target: Suit of armor touched
Duration: 10 minutes/level
Saving Throw: None (object)
Spell Resistance: No (object)

Armor imbued with this infusion absorbs 5 points of damage from the next attack that deals damage to the creature that wears it (treat this as one-time damage reduction 5/—). Forms of damage that aren't affected by damage reduction likewise overcome *ablative armor*. Once the infused item has prevented damage from a single attack (even if not all the damage reduction is needed), the magic fades.

The damage reduction increases by 1 for every caster level above 1st, to a maximum of 15/— at 10th level.

Special: A character with any Mark of Sentinel dragonmark, or with the Favored in House feat (Deneith), casts this infusion at +1 caster level.

Material Component: A shard of scrap metal from a forge.

ADAMANTINE WEAPON

Transmutation
Level: Artificer 3
Components: S, M
Casting Time: 1 minute
Range: Touch
Target: Weapon touched
Duration: 1 minute/level
Saving Throw: Will negates (harmless, object)
Spell Resistance: No (object)

This infusion temporarily alters the substance of one weapon, transforming it into adamantine. This effect replaces the properties of any other special material the weapon might be constructed from. Only weapons made of metal can benefit from this infusion.

Material Component: A pinch of powdered adamantine.

ANCIENT KNOWLEDGE

Divination
Level: Bard 1, sorcerer/wizard 1
Components: V, S, F
Casting Time: 1 minute
Range: Personal
Target: You
Duration: 1 hour/level or until discharged

You tap the ancient knowledge of fate and fortune, giving you a greater ability to focus on a particularly difficult academic problem. Before making a Knowledge check, you can decide to discharge this spell as an immediate action to give yourself a +5 insight bonus on the check. If you do not have any ranks in the Knowledge skill, it is still treated as an untrained check.

Special: A character with any Mark of Finding dragonmark, or with the Favored in House feat (Tharashk), treats any Knowledge check made in conjunction with this spell as a trained check, even if he doesn't have any ranks in the skill.

Focus: A piece of ivory worth at least 100 gp.

BLAST ROD

Evocation
Level: Artificer 3
Components: S, F
Casting Time: 1 minute
Range: Touch
Target: Rod touched
Duration: 10 minutes/level
Saving Throw: None (object)
Spell Resistance: Yes

You store energy within a rod, then unleash it in rays of destructive power. The *blast rod* can deal a total of 1d8 points of damage per caster level (maximum 10d8), either focused into a single blast or divided up among multiple blasts.

To use the rod, you designate how many dice of damage you wish to release, then make a ranged touch attack as a standard action against any target within 60 feet. Regardless of whether the attack hits or not, the damage dice you specified are subtracted from the total stored in the rod.

Focus: The rod to be infused.

CENSURE ELEMENTALS

Abjuration
Level: Artificer 4
Components: S, M
Casting Time: 1 standard action
Range: Touch
Target: Object touched
Duration: 1 minute/level
Saving Throw: None (object) or Will half; see text
Spell Resistance: No (object) or Yes; see text

When artificers began construction of some of the first great elemental vessels, they wanted a way to keep elementals from wreaking havoc prior to being bound. This infusion was developed as a means of conditioning the elementals through negative reinforcement.

Typically cast into a pole or other prod, this infusion creates a field that can harm elemental creatures. When held aloft (a standard action), the infused item deals 2d4 points of damage plus 1 point per caster level (maximum +15) to any elemental creatures within a 20-foot-radius area. This damage repeats each round at the start of the artificer's turn as long as the item is held aloft (a standard action). A successful Will save halves this damage, and spell resistance applies against this effect.

The caster can designate up to one elemental creature per level to have immunity to the effects of the infusion.

Special: A character with any Mark of Making dragonmark, or with the Favored in House feat (Cannith), casts this spell at +1 caster level.

Material Component: A pinch of kiln-hardened mud.

CLOTHIER'S CLOSET

Conjuration (Creation)
Level: Bard 2, sorcerer/wizard 2
Components: V, S, M
Casting Time: 10 minutes
Range: Close (25 ft. + 5 ft./2 levels)
Effect: One or more sets of clothes
Duration: 1 hour/level (D); see text
Saving Throw: None
Spell Resistance: No

When you and your companions need to attend a gala reception at the last minute, you need not despair over your clothing. When you cast *clothier's closet*, you conjure a 3-inch-diameter wooden rod up to 10 feet long between any two upright supports you choose. For example, you could summon the rod to appear between two walls of a corridor or alcove. On the rod hang a number of outfits as determined by you, each of a size and type you specify while the spell is cast.

The conjured rod can hold a variety of separate outfits whose total price does not exceed 100 gp. The outfit types that you can specify include the following: artisan's outfit (1 gp), cleric's vestments (5 gp), cold weather outfit (8 gp), courtier's outfit (30 gp), entertainer's outfit (3 gp), explorer's outfit (10 gp), monk's outfit (5 gp), noble's outfit (75 gp), scholar's outfit (5 gp), or traveler's outfit (1 gp).

The conjured clothing is normal in all respects and does not radiate magic. Even after the duration elapses and the rod and hangers disappear, the clothes remain.

Special: A character with any Mark of Hospitality dragonmark, or with the Favored in House feat (Ghallanda), can cast this spell without the material component, but the conjured clothes last only as long as the spell's duration.

Material Component: A gem worth at least 100 gp.

CONCURRENT INFUSIONS

Transmutation
Level: Artificer 4
Components: S, M
Casting Time: 1 minute
Range: Touch
Target: Object touched
Duration: Instantaneous
Saving Throw: None (object)
Spell Resistance: No (object)

You channel your artificer talents through an increased number of minor infusions. When you cast this infusion, you can imbue the target object with the effects of three different 1st-level infusions chosen at the time of casting. The infusions function exactly as if you had cast them on the object, and do not count against your daily allotment.

Material Component: An oak twig with at least three forks along its length.

CONTROL ELEMENTAL

Enchantment (Compulsion) [Mind-Affecting]
Level: Sorcerer/wizard 6
Components: V, S
Casting Time: 1 standard action
Range: Close (25 ft. + 5 ft./2 levels)
Target: One elemental with HD no greater than twice your caster level
Duration: 1 minute/level
Saving Throw: Will negates
Spell Resistance: Yes

This spell enables you to command an elemental for a short period of time. While a spellcaster does not normally have line of effect to a bound elemental, which remains bound by a Khyber shard, a caster can establish line of effect by maintaining physical contact with the dragonshard while casting this spell. In such a case, the caster of *control elemental* would also need to have contact with the Khyber shard binding the elemental, or in the case of an elemental vessel, access to the helm, whenever he wished to give the elemental an order.

The elemental is commanded by voice and understands you, no matter what language you speak. Even if vocal communication is impossible (in the area of a *silence* spell, for instance), the targeted elemental does not attack you. When the spell's duration expires, the target elemental reverts to its normal behavior and remembers that you controlled it.

DETECT DRAGONMARK

Divination
Level: Cleric 1, sorcerer/wizard 1
Components: V, S, M/DF
Casting Time: 1 standard action
Range: 60 ft.
Area: Cone-shaped emanation
Duration: Concentration, up to 10 minutes/level (D)
Saving Throw: None
Spell Resistance: No

You can sense the presence of dragonmarks. The amount of information you receive about a particular dragonmark depends on how long you study a particular area or subject.

1st Round: Presence or absence of dragonmarks.

2nd Round: Number of dragonmarks (on creatures or objects) in the area, and the type (aberrant, least, lesser, greater, or Siberys) of the most potent dragonmark.

3rd Round: The location and type of each dragonmark. If the objects or creatures bearing the dragonmarks are in line of sight, you can attempt Spellcraft checks to determine the name of the spell-like ability granted by the mark (see page 47 of the Eberron Campaign Setting for the

appropriate DC). If you beat the DC by 5 or more, you also learn whether the mark's spell-like ability has any remaining uses for the day.

Arcane Material Component: A scale from a true dragon.

DIMENSION LEAP

Conjuration (Teleportation)
Level: Bard 2, sorcerer/wizard 2
Components: V
Casting Time: 1 standard action
Range: 10 ft./level
Target: You and touched objects
Duration: Instantaneous
Saving Throw: None
Spell Resistance: No

You instantly transfer yourself from your current location to another spot within range. The distance traveled must be an increment of 10 feet (10 feet, 20 feet, 30 feet, and so on). You always arrive at exactly the spot desired, whether by simply visualizing the area or by stating direction and distance. You can bring along any objects you are touching as the spell is cast, so long as their weight doesn't exceed your maximum load. You cannot bring along other creatures.

If this spell would put you in a place that is already occupied by a solid body, the spell fails.

Special: A character with any Mark of Passage dragonmark, or with the Favored in House feat (Orien), uses his character level rather than his caster level to determine the distance teleported.

DISTRACTING SHADOWS

Evocation [Darkness]
Level: Bard 1, sorcerer/wizard 1
Components: V, M
Casting Time: 1 standard action
Range: Touch
Target: Object touched
Duration: 24 hours (D)
Saving Throw: None
Spell Resistance: No

This spell causes an object to radiate distracting shadows in a 10-foot-radius spread. Casual scrutiny of an affected area doesn't reveal anything out of the ordinary; however, cracks, crannies, corners, hidden traps, and secret entrances or exits within the area become harder to spot.

Creatures within the area or looking into it are subliminally confused by the *distracting shadows*, and take a −5 penalty on all Spot and Search checks. However, the shadows do not provide sufficient concealment for a creature to make a Hide check.

Distracting shadows counters or dispels any *light* or *darkness* spell of equal or lower level.

Distracting shadows can be made permanent with a *permanency* spell (minimum caster level 10th; cost 1,000 XP).

Special: A character with any Mark of Shadow dragonmark, or with the Favored in House feat (Phiarlan or Thuranni), can cast this spell to fill a 20-foot-radius spread.

Material Component: A bit of bat fur and either a drop of pitch or a piece of coal.

ELEMENTAL PROD

Abjuration
Level: Artificer 2
Components: S
Casting Time: 1 minute
Range: Touch
Target: Staff or pole touched
Duration: 1 minute/level
Saving Throw: None (object)
Spell Resistance: No (object)

The need to control elementals more easily during the binding process led to the creation of an infusion that imbues a staff or pole with the ability to move elementals.

As a standard action, the wielder of an *elemental prod* can gesture with the staff, indicating the starting and ending position for a target elemental creature. The total distance covered must be no greater than 10 feet + 5 feet/2 caster levels. The target creature immediately understands the command to move, and it can elect to be pushed along without resisting. Elementals that choose to resist take 1d6 points of damage and are moved only 5 feet in the desired direction.

EXPOSE THE DEAD

Divination
Level: Cleric 2, paladin 2, sorcerer/wizard 2
Components: V, S, M/DF
Casting Time: 1 standard action
Range: Personal
Target: You
Duration: 1 minute/level (D)

You gain a sixth sense that allows you to better locate undead creatures, as well as to investigate corpses. Your eyes turn white while under the effect of the spell, making it seem as though you were blind (although you can see as well as normal).

While this spell is in effect, you gain an insight bonus equal to your caster level (maximum +10) on Survival checks made to track undead, and you can follow undead tracks with a DC above 10 as if you had the Track feat. You gain the same insight bonus on Listen and Spot checks made against undead creatures.

In addition, you gain an insight bonus equal to your caster level (maximum +10) on Search checks made when examining a dead body, and you are treated as if you had the Investigate feat (see page 55 of the EBERRON *Campaign Setting*) when doing so.

Finally, while this spell is active, increase the save DC of any *speak with dead* spell you cast by 2.

Arcane Material Component: A dwarf's fingerbone.

GLIMPSE OF ETERNITY

Enchantment (Compulsion) [Mind-Affecting]
Level: Bard 5, sorcerer/wizard 5
Components: V, S, M
Casting Time: 1 standard action
Range: Close (25 ft. + 5 ft./2 levels)
Target: One creature
Duration: 1 round/3 levels
Saving Throw: Will partial; see text
Spell Resistance: Yes

You call upon the ancestral memory and experience of the long-lived elves, visiting all the burden of that knowledge on a single creature. The target of the spell takes 1d6 points of nonlethal damage per caster level (maximum 15d6) and is *confused* for the duration of the spell unless it makes a Will save. A successful save results in half damage and negates the confusion.

Elves and similarly long-lived creatures are affected normally by this spell. No creature can experience millennia of knowledge in such a short time without feeling its weight.

Material Component: A pinch of dust from an hourglass.

GLIMPSE OF THE PROPHECY

Divination
Level: Bard 6, cleric 6, sorcerer/wizard 6
Components: V, S
Casting Time: 1 standard action
Range: Personal
Target: You
Duration: 1 hour/level or until discharged

You gain powerful insight into the workings of the draconic Prophecy, granting you inner strength and a potent sixth sense in relation to your surroundings. You gain a +1 insight bonus to Armor Class and a +1 insight bonus on saving throws for the duration of the spell.

Once during the spell's duration, you can gain an insight bonus equal to one-half your caster level (maximum +10) on any saving throw. Activating this effect is an immediate action, but it must be done before you make the roll to be modified. Once this ability is used, the spell ends.

If you have the Dragon Prophesier feat (see page 46), you can enter a state of prophetic favor as an immediate action instead of a full-round action while this spell is in effect. This still counts as one of your daily uses of prophetic favor. Once this ability is used, the spell ends.

You cannot have more than one *glimpse of the Prophecy* spell active on you at the same time.

HIDDEN WARD

Illusion (Glamer)
Level: Bard 1, sorcerer/wizard 1
Components: V, S, M
Casting Time: 10 minutes
Range: Touch
Target: Object touched
Duration: 24 hours; see text
Saving Throw: None
Spell Resistance: No

This spell helps disguise the presence of any spells (including *glyph of warding*) that have been cast upon the target object. If *detect magic* or a similar effect is used to detect the presence of magical auras on the object, the caster must succeed on a caster level check (DC 10 + your caster level) to find any magical auras that are the result of active spells. (The DM should make this roll in secret to prevent suspicion by the players.) A single successful check will reveal both the *hidden ward* and the spells it hides.

In addition, casting this spell on a magic trap (such as a *fire trap* spell cast on an object) increases the Search DC to find the trap by one-half your caster level (maximum +5). This spell cannot be used to conceal nonmagical traps, nor does it hide the magical properties of an item that aren't dependent on active spells (such as the magic aura of a *+1 longsword*).

Special: When cast by a character with any Mark of Warding dragonmark, or with the Favored in House feat (Kundarak), the duration increases to one day per level.

Material Component: Lead shavings and powdered diamond worth 100 gp.

INDISPUTABLE POSSESSION

Conjuration (Teleportation)
Level: Artificer 1
Components: V, S
Casting Time: 1 minute
Range: Touch
Target: Object touched
Duration: 10 minutes/level
Saving Throw: None (object)
Spell Resistance: No (object)

This infusion creates a bond between you and an object. If that item ever leaves your possession, you can call it back to your hand as a move action. The bond is severed if the item is out of your possession for more than 1 minute per artificer level. A creature holding onto an item you are trying to retrieve can make a Will save to retain its grasp on the item, but that creature must be holding or wearing it, not merely carrying the object among its possessions.

KHYBER TRAP

Abjuration
Level: Sorcerer/wizard 3
Components: S, F
Casting Time: 1 standard action
Range: Close (25 ft. + 5 ft./2 levels)
Target: One outsider or extraplanar creature
Duration: 1 round/level (D)
Saving Throw: Will negates
Spell Resistance: Yes

This spell draws upon the binding power of a Khyber dragonshard to trap an extraplanar creature for a short duration. If the creature fails its Will save, it is drawn into the Khyber shard. It can take no actions inside the shard, though it can communicate if it is capable of telepathy. If the dragonshard containing the creature is broken, the creature is released.

Focus: A Khyber dragonshard worth at least 100 gp per HD of the target creature. The focus can hold only one trapped creature at a time.

LEAP INTO ANIMAL

Transmutation
Level: Druid 2, ranger 2
Components: V, S
Casting Time: 1 standard action
Range: 10 ft.
Target: You and one willing animal; see text

Duration: 1 minute/level (D)
Saving Throw: Will negates
Spell Resistance: Yes

Leap into animal enables you to meld your body and up to 100 pounds of nonliving gear into a single willing animal (such as an animal companion). The animal must be your size category or larger. To any observer, you appear to leap and phase into the animal; you are gone, while the animal remains. For all intents and purposes, you no longer exist while merged with the animal, and you cannot be detected or affected by anything as long as you remain within it.

While melded with the animal, you mentally direct its actions. You can make it attack, run, or take any other action it could normally physically accomplish. However, because you are directing the animal with your own intelligence, it can undertake actions normally beyond its own instincts (such as manipulating objects with its claws or mouth). Suicidal or self-destructive commands (including an order to attack a creature two or more size categories larger) are ignored. You receive direct sensory input from the creature using its normal senses and skill modifiers.

You cannot take any mental actions while within the animal other than directing it or dismissing the effect (such that you cannot manifest a psionic power or cast a spell, even if it has no components).

Injury to the animal has no effect on you. If the animal is killed, if the spell is dispelled or dismissed, or if the spell's duration expires, you appear (as if leaping forth from the animal) in an open space of your choice within 10

Khyber trap draws upon the power of a Khyber dragonshard to trap an outsider or extraplanar creature

When someone protected by a scry trap becomes the target of attempted scrying . . .

OVERWHELMING REVELATIONS

Evocation

Level: Sorcerer/wizard 6
Components: V, S, M
Casting Time: 1 standard action
Range: Close (25 ft. + 5 ft./2 levels)
Area: 20-ft.-radius burst
Duration: Instantaneous
Saving Throw: Will partial
Spell Resistance: Yes

You tap the incredible complexity of the draconic Prophecy, granting creatures in the area a burst of insight powerful enough to threaten their sanity. Creatures in the area take a –2d6 penalty to Wisdom and are *confused* for 1 round. A successful Will save reduces the penalty by half and negates the confusion.

Special: Characters with the Dragon Prophesier feat (see page 46) have immunity to the effect of this spell. Furthermore, if within the area of the spell, such a character can choose to enter prophetic favor as an immediate action. This counts as one of the character's daily uses of prophetic favor.

Characters with a dragonmark take a –2 penalty on their saving throw against this spell.

Material Component: A scale from an adult or older dragon.

PENDING POTION

Transmutation

Level: Artificer 1
Components: S, M
Casting Time: 1 minute
Range: Touch

Target: Vial of potion or oil touched
Duration: 10 minutes/level
Saving Throw: None (object)
Spell Resistance: No (object)

You magically delay the effects of a potion or oil. Once imbued with this infusion, a potion can be consumed or an oil applied, but the effects of the potion or oil do not take place immediately. Instead, the creature that consumed the potion or had the oil applied to it can activate its effects as a swift action at any time before the end of the infusion's duration. If the consumed potion or oil is not activated before the duration expires, it takes effect at that point.

An oil that is applied to an object is normally activated by the wielder of the object, rather than the character who applied the oil. However, if an oil imbued with this infusion is applied to an intelligent construct (such as a warforged or homunculus), only the construct can activate the effects of the oil. If an oil imbued with this infusion is applied to a nonintelligent construct (such as a golem), only the character who applied the oil can activate it.

No creature or object can have more than one delayed-effect potion or oil in effect at the same time. If a second delayed-effect potion or oil is consumed by the same creature or applied to the same object, the duration of the first *pending potion* infusion ends, and the potion or oil takes effect immediately.

Material Component: A handful of needles from an evergreen tree.

REINFORCE CONSTRUCT

Transmutation

Level: Artificer 2
Components: V, S
Casting Time: 1 standard action
Range: Touch
Target: Construct touched
Duration: 1 hour/level or until discharged; see text
Saving Throw: Will negates (harmless)
Spell Resistance: No

You bolster a construct's frame, making it better able to withstand blows. The construct gains temporary hit points equal to 1d6 + 1 per caster level (maximum +10). A warforged artificer who imbues himself with this infusion instead gains temporary hit points equal to 1d10 + 1 per caster level (maximum +10).

Special: A character with any Mark of Making dragonmark, or with the Favored in House feat (Cannith), casts this infusion at +1 caster level.

SCALDING TOUCH

Evocation [Fire]

Level: Sorcerer/wizard 7
Components: V, S
Casting Time: 1 standard action
Range: Touch
Targets: Up to one creature/level touched
Duration: Instantaneous
Saving Throw: Fortitude partial; see text
Spell Resistance: Yes

CHAPTER FIVE

MAGIC ITEMS AND EQUIPMENT

Throughout Eberron, arcane energy infuses the landscape and touches the lives of each of its inhabitants. Thanks to their residents' facility with magical craft, cities in Eberron contain soaring castles, elemental-powered craft, and a cornucopia of magic devices suitable for almost any purpose imaginable.

Each magic item differs from the next, but beyond that, the items belong to different classes. These classes are dependent on the tradition, knowledge, and materials of the items' creators, and are often recognizable as being of a particular magical vintage. For instance, bound-elemental items most often originate in Zilargo, while the horrific items of the daelkyr are usually found in Khyber.

ARTIFICER ITEMS

Even more than most other spellcasters, artificers are known for the items they create—some crafted for others; some created to fit their own specific needs. While some of the following items might pique the interest of characters of other classes, many are most effective when in the hands (or around the waist, head, and so on) of an artificer. Some provide bonuses to the artificer's infusions, while others are actually powered by infusions, becoming more powerful as magic is fed into them. Items powered by infusions become attuned to the artificer who powers them. While any character can make use of an artificer item's default functions while it is powered by an infusion, the specific functions so powered are available only to the artificer who cast the infusion.

In addition to the many specialty items introduced in this chapter, spell-storing minor schemas are common across Khorvaire and beyond.

Artificer Items	Price
Infinite scrollcase	2,800 gp
Ring of master artifice, least	5,000 gp
Spare hand	12,000 gp
Cannith goggles	13,000 gp
Ring of master artifice, lesser	25,000 gp
Wand bracelet	25,000 gp
Ring of master artifice, greater	61,000 gp

CANNITH GOGGLES

Cannith goggles enhance your vision.

Lore: Many ancient treasures and objects of lore are found in the depths of Khyber and the ruins of Xen'drik, most often in places where humans find it difficult to see (Knowledge [history] DC 10). The artificers of House Cannith were tasked to find a way to enhance human vision, and the result of their research is the *Cannith goggles* (Knowledge [history] DC 20).

Description: *Cannith goggles* are round, translucent lenses made of magically hardened glass stained a light shade of orange.

The goggles are mounted in a flexible metal frame that is affixed to your face by a soft leather strap that clasps behind your head.

Activation: *Cannith goggles* provide their most basic functions when worn by any character. In addition, if you are an artificer and wearing the goggles, you are able to use your infusions to power them, enhancing their vision-based benefits according to the level of the infusion used. Using an infusion to power the *Cannith goggles* requires 10 minutes and the expenditure of an infusion of the level indicated below. An infusion can power the goggles for 24 hours.

Effect: The goggles give you a +5 competence bonus on Search and Spot checks. If you power your *Cannith goggles* with a 1st-level infusion, the goggles allow you to see more clearly in dimly lit areas, as if you had low-light vision. If you power your *Cannith goggles* with a 2nd-level infusion, you gain low-light vision plus darkvision to a distance of 60 feet. A 3rd-level infusion used to power the goggles provides low-light vision and darkvision to a range of 120 feet.

Aura/Caster Level: Faint transmutation. CL 5th.

Construction: Requires Craft Wondrous Item, *hardening* spell or infusion, 6,500 gp, 520 XP, 13 days.

Variant: When powered by a 5th-level infusion, a few pairs of *Cannith goggles* grant *true seeing* (as the spell) with a range of 30 feet for 10 minutes. (Strong divination, CL 11th, +15,000 gp.)

Weight: 1/2 lb.

Price: 13,000 gp.

INFINITE SCROLLCASE

An *infinite scrollcase* allows you to store and easily retrieve many scrolls or other parchments in an extradimensional space.

Description: This elaborate mahogany tube has a slit that runs its length. A wooden dowel, capped on the ends with gold, fits against the slit, locking into place with jeweled clasps.

Activation: When you release the clasps and pull the dowel away from the main tube, the desired scroll is unfurled through the slit, ready to cast. Retrieving a scroll from the *infinite scrollcase* is a move action that does not provoke

Many artificers create items to fit their own needs

attacks of opportunity. If you have at least a +1 base attack bonus, you can retrieve a scroll from the *infinite scrollcase* as part of a move action, similar to drawing a weapon.

Effect: The *infinite scrollcase* holds up to fifty scrolls or other parchments, which can be placed within it or removed as with any normal scrollcase. Regardless of the number of scrolls within the scrollcase, the dowel always pulls the scroll you desire. When you cast a spell from a scroll unfurled from the *infinite scrollcase*, you gain a +4 competence bonus on Concentration checks made to cast that spell defensively.

Aura/Caster Level: Moderate conjuration. CL 9th.

Construction: Requires Craft Wondrous Item, 1,400 gp, 112 XP, 3 days.

Weight: 3 lb.

Price: 2,800 gp.

RING OF MASTER ARTIFICE

A *ring of master artifice* increases the number of infusions an artificer can imbue each day.

Description: An unassembled *ring of master artifice* appears to be several thin, interlocking rings made of different metals, including silver, adamantine, mithral, and platinum.

When twisted and turned the appropriate way, the interlocking rings can be combined into a single ring that appears much like a wire loop braided from the various metals.

Prerequisite: *The ring of master artifice* functions only for a character who can cast infusions.

Activation: Assembling the ring from its various components requires 5 minutes and a DC 22 Intelligence check, which you can attempt any number of times. Once assembled, a *ring of master artifice* must be worn for 24 hours for its magic to take effect. After that time, you gain the ring's benefit every time you concentrate to regain your daily allotment of infusions.

Effect: The ring increases the number of infusions you can cast daily, depending on the nature of the ring. A *least ring of master artifice* provides a bonus 1st-level and 2nd-level infusion, a *lesser ring of master artifice* provides a bonus 3rd-level and 4th-level infusion, and a *greater ring of master artifice* provides a bonus 5th-level and 6th-level infusion.

Aura/Caster Level: Moderate (least) or Strong (lesser, greater) no school. CL 12th (least), 14th (lesser), 16th (greater).

Construction: Requires Forge Ring, 2,500 gp, 200 XP, 5 days (least); 12,500 gp, 1,000 XP, 25 days (lesser); 30,500 gp, 2,440 XP, 61 days (greater).

Weight: —

Price: Least 5,000 gp, lesser 25,000 gp, greater 61,000 gp.

SPARE HAND

A *spare hand* can hold and manipulate objects for you.

Description: A *spare hand* is a magic animated arm and three-fingered claw, attached to a heavy leather belt reinforced with strips of metal.

When the belt is worn about your waist, the arm extends from your hip, obeying your mental commands. If not holding an item or performing a task, it occasionally mimics the motion of one of your arms.

Activation: While some features of the *spare hand* function continuously, this item is more effective when worn by an artificer. If you are an artificer, while wearing the belt, you can use your infusions to power the *spare hand*, enabling more complex functions. Using an infusion to power the *spare hand* requires 10 minutes and the expenditure of an infusion of the level indicated below. An infusion can power the hand for 24 hours. A *spare hand* is worn around the waist, and so is considered a belt.

Effect: As its most basic function, a *spare hand* can grasp or carry any object you could normally carry in one hand, freeing your normal hands for other tasks. A *spare hand* can hold magic items such as wands and rods for easy access, but you cannot activate those items while they are so held. Transferring an item to or from a *spare hand* is a free action.

Whenever the *spare hand* is not carrying an item, you gain a +2 competence bonus on Climb, Escape Artist, and grapple checks. Without further augmentation from an infusion (see below), the *spare hand* cannot do anything other than hold an item—it cannot wield a weapon, retrieve a stored item, or perform any other task.

If you power the *spare hand* with a 1st-level infusion, it gains additional animated qualities. Once per round, you can command the hand to stow an item or retrieve a stowed item (including a weapon) as a free action.

If you instead expend a 2nd-level infusion, your *spare hand* gains the above ability, and it can also hold a buckler or light shield for you, freeing your normal hand while still providing you the bonus to Armor Class from the shield. You still incur any armor check penalty or other drawbacks of holding the shield, and you are subject to normal penalties if you are not proficient with the shield.

If you expend a 3rd-level infusion, your *spare hand* gains all the above abilities, and it is also capable of wielding a light weapon. You can command the *spare hand* to make off-hand attacks with this weapon as if you were wielding it. The *spare hand* attacks using your normal attack modifier, plus any appropriate penalties for an off-hand attack.

Aura/Caster Level: Moderate transmutation. CL 11th.

Construction: Requires Craft Wondrous Item, 6,000 gp, 480 XP, 12 days.

Variant: Rare *spare hands* belts sport two hands instead of one. Each hand requires its own separate infusion each day to power it. (Strong transmutation, CL 16th, +10,000 gp.)

Weight: 5 lb.

Price: 12,000 gp.

WAND BRACELET

A *wand bracelet* holds a number of small items that you can retrieve quickly.

Lore: The name "*wand bracelet*" describes the most common use of the item. Originally designed to hold small keepsakes as charms, and crafted to be appropriate for formal gatherings, the *wand bracelet* has instead found popularity among Cannith wand adepts and artificers who favor spell trigger devices (Knowledge [arcana] DC 15). The bracelet is also sometimes known as the *assassin's charm*, because small weapons can easily be concealed within it (Knowledge [arcana] DC 20).

Description: This golden chain bracelet has a number of small metal objects hanging from it like charms. You typically wear the bracelet on the arm opposite the hand that actually uses the items stored within it.

Activation: A *wand bracelet* can store up to four items, which appear as charms along the bracelet. As a free action, you can grab one of the charms from the bracelet. If you have a small item in your hand, you can use a move action to store the item in the bracelet, or to switch the held item for a stored item by touching the item to the charm representing the stored item. Neither action provokes attacks of opportunity.

Effect: Grabbing a charm from the *wand bracelet* causes the item to appear in your hand. Storing an item causes it to shrink down and appear as a charm hanging from the bracelet. Any item to be stored can weigh no more than 3 pounds and must be able to be held in one hand, such as a wand or light weapon. Only the wearer of the bracelet is able to retrieve or store items.

Aura/Caster Level: Faint transmutation. CL 6th.

Construction: Requires Craft Wondrous Item, 12,500 gp, 1,000 XP, 25 days.

Weight: 0.25 lb.

Price: 25,000 gp.

DRAGONSHARD ITEMS

The great demand for dragonshards is driven by the multitude of items that can be constructed from them.

DRAGONSHARD ITEMS

Siberys Shard Items	Price
Fuel shard (least)	225 gp
Fuel shard (lesser)	350 gp
Fuel shard (greater)	800 gp
Image projector	1,200 gp
Fuel shard (Siberys)	1,800 gp
Reparation apparatus	3,000 gp
Dragonmark rod, Scribing	15,000 gp
Dragonmark rod, Detection	17,500 gp
Dragonmark rod, Handling	20,000 gp
Dragonmark rod, Finding	22,500 gp
Dragonmark rod, Making	22,500 gp
Dragonmark rod, Hospitality	25,000 gp
Dragonmark rod, Passage	25,000 gp
Dragonmark rod, Sentinel	25,000 gp
Dragonmark rod, Healing	27,500 gp
Dragonmark rod, Storm	27,500 gp
Dragonmark rod, Warding	27,500 gp
Dragonmark rod, Shadow	30,000 gp

Quori Embedded Shards	Price
Power repository (1st)	1,500 gp
Sustainer	2,500 gp
Combat instructor	3,000 gp
Power link	3,000 gp
Power repository (2nd)	6,000 gp
Power repository (3rd)	13,500 gp
Power repository (4th)	24,000 gp

Eberron Shard Items	Price
Empowered spellshard (1st)	1,500 gp
Empowered spellshard (2nd)	3,000 gp
Empowered spellshard (3rd)	6,000 gp
Truelight lantern	36,000 gp

Khyber Shard Items	Price
Rock boots	3,000 gp
Bracers of wind	10,000 gp
Ring of the stalker	15,500 gp
Water cloak	17,000 gp
Gloves of flame	19,000 gp
Water whip	30,301 gp
Earthplate armor	41,650 gp
Fiery tunic	48,000 gp

Elemental Vessels	Price
Earth sled	24,000 gp
Tumbler	200,000 gp

SIBERYS SHARD ITEMS

Siberys shards are commonly incorporated into items that enhance a wielder's dragonmark.

Blasting Chime

A *blasting chime* allows you to blast your foes with coherent beams of sonic force.

Lore: The first *blasting chime* was constructed for a special team of House Medani bodyguards, those selected to protect Barton Trelib D'Medani himself. Baron D'Medani controls the Warning Guild from an enclave in Wroat (Knowledge [history] DC 15).

While effective, the first prototype *blasting chimes* were quite small—the later, more recognizable version is larger and more powerful. One or two *blasting chimes* are said to be so large that they are not portable, but instead hang like conventional bells in tall steeples. However, these overlarge *blasting chimes* serve to provide more than warning in case of an attack on a fortified structure—they can blast away armies (Knowledge [history] DC 20).

Description: A *blasting chime* appears as a outsized hand bell with a grip so long that it more resembles a weapon haft. A *blasting chime* has a Siberys dragonshard suspended inside the bell, which acts as the clapper. When the chime is activated, a secondary bass tone resounds as the bell orifice releases a flash of concentrated sound so destructive it is visible as a line of white light.

Prerequisite: This item functions for any character, but characters with the Least Mark of Detection can use the chime one additional time per day.

Activation: Activating a *blasting chime* is a standard action, and requires you to make the appropriate hand motion to sound it, then aim the mouth of the bell at the area you want to affect.

Most characters (see Prerequisite, above) can activate a *blasting chime* three times per day.

Effect: Upon activation, a *blasting chime* releases a 120-foot line of sonic energy that deals 6d6 points of sonic damage to every creature in the area (Reflex DC 15 half). Sonic energy affects objects and ignores hardness, so it is useful in breaking down doors and other fortifications.

Variant (Thunderbolt Chime): A close relative of

DRAGONMARK RODS

Dragonmark	Spells
Detection	Least: *detect magic, detect poison*
	Lesser: *detect scrying, see invisibility*
	Greater: *true seeing**
Finding	Least: *identify*, know direction, locate object*
	Lesser: *helping hand, locate creature*
	Greater: *find the path*
Handling	Least: *calm animals, charm animal, speak with animals*
	Lesser: *dominate animal, greater magic fang*
	Greater: *animal growth, summon nature's ally V*
Healing	Least: *cure light wounds, lesser restoration*
	Lesser: *cure serious wounds, neutralize poison, remove disease, restoration**
	Greater: *heal*
Hospitality	Least: *purify food and drink, prestidigitation, unseen servant*
	Lesser: *create food and water, Leomund's secure shelter*
	Greater: *heroes' feast, Mordenkainen's magnificent mansion*
Making	Least: *make whole, mending, repair light damage*[E]
	Lesser: *minor creation, repair serious damage*[E]
	Greater: *fabricate, major creation*
Passage	Least: *expeditious retreat, mount, dimension leap*
	Lesser: *dimension door, phantom steed*
	Greater: *overland flight, teleport*
Scribing	Least: *arcane mark, comprehend languages, whispering wind*
	Lesser: *illusory script*, secret page, tongues*
	Greater: *sending*
Sentinel	Least: *mage armor, protection from arrows, shield of faith, shield other**
	Lesser: *protection from energy, lesser globe of invulnerability*
	Greater: *globe of invulnerability*
Shadow	Least: *darkness, disguise self, minor image*
	Lesser: *clairaudience/clairvoyance, shadow conjuration, scrying**
	Greater: *mislead, prying eyes, shadow walk*
Storm	Least: *endure elements, fog cloud, gust of wind*
	Lesser: *sleet storm, wind's favor, wind wall*
	Greater: *control weather, control winds*
Warding	Least: *alarm, arcane lock*, fire trap*, misdirection*
	Lesser: *explosive runes, glyph of warding*, nondetection**
	Greater: *Mordenkainen's faithful hound, greater glyph of warding*, guards and wards*

*Wielder must provide material component or arcane focus.
[E]See the EBERRON *Campaign Setting*.

the *blasting chime* is the *thunderbolt chime*. Instead of releasing a stroke of coherent sonic energy in a 120-foot line, a *thunderbolt chime* releases a stroke of electricity in a 120-foot line. This stroke of electricity deals 6d6 points of electricity damage to every creature in the area that fails a DC 17 Reflex save (on a successful save, targets take half damage). Against targets wearing metal armor, the check to overcome spell resistance is made as though the item's caster level is two higher.

Aura/Caster Level: Moderate evocation. CL 6th.

Construction: Requires Craft Wondrous Item, creator must have the Least Mark of Detection, 9,720 gp, 778 XP, 10 days.

Weight: 4 lb.

Price: 19,440 gp.

Dragonmark Rod

A *dragonmark rod* augments the magical power of a dragon-marked character.

Description: A *dragonmark rod* is a densewood quarterstaff with iron bands around both ends and a handgrip wrapped in black leather. Affixed to the top of the staff is a densewood carving of one of the twelve least dragonmarks, mounted directly above a Siberys dragonshard.

When activated, the dragonshard glows and energy plays along the length of the staff.

Prerequisite: This item functions only for characters with a dragonmark that matches the mark carved at the top of the rod. Furthermore, the abilities unlocked are limited by the level of dragonmark possessed by the bearer, with a character only able to use the powers of his own mark or lower. For example, a character with a lesser dragonmark can use the least and lesser abilities, but not the greater abilities. A character with a greater or Siberys mark can use all the powers of a *dragonmark rod*.

Activation: As a standard action, you call on the power of the *dragonmark rod*. You can use least abilities up to three times per day, lesser abilities two times per day, and a greater ability once per day. When you activate the *dragonmark rod*, you choose which power you wish to use.

Effect: All spell-like abilities associated with your dragonmark are available within the *dragonmark rod*. You use your effective dragonmark caster level (1, 6, or 10 + your levels in the dragonmark heir prestige class) to power each ability.

A *dragonmark rod* can generate any of the effects of least, lesser, or greater dragonmarks, but not of a Siberys dragonmark. For example, a Mark of Finding *dragonmark rod* contains the least abilities *identify*, *know direction*, and *locate object*; the lesser abilities *helping hand* and *locate creature*; and the greater ability *find the path*.

If the spell to be used has a costly material component or arcane focus, you must supply the component or focus. See the Dragonmark Rods table for details, and for a full list of the spells each rod can generate.

Aura/Caster Level: Moderate conjuration. CL 12th.

Construction: Requires Craft Rod, creator must have a greater or Siberys dragonmark of the type used by the staff, 30,000 gp, 2,400 XP, 60 days (shadow); 27,500 gp, 2,200 XP, 55 days (healing, storm, warding); 25,000 gp, 2,000 XP, 50 days (hospitality, passage, sentinel); 22,500 gp, 1,800 XP, 45 days (finding, making); 20,000 gp, 1,600 XP, 40 days (handling); 17,500 gp, 1,400 XP, 35 days (detection); 15,000 gp 1,200 XP, 30 days (scribing).

Weight: 2 lb.

Price: 60,000 gp (shadow), 55,000 gp (healing, storm, warding), 50,000 gp (hospitality, passage, sentinel), 45,000 gp (finding, making), 40,000 gp (handling), 35,000 gp (detection), 30,000 gp (scribing).

Image Projector

An *image projector* allows you to store an image inside it for replaying at a later time.

Lore: The *image projector* was first created at the behest of House Phiarlan, ostensibly to help aid performances by providing visual effects to complement actors and musicians (Knowledge [local] DC 15). However, these devices also serve a much more insidious purpose—allowing house agents to capture a magical record of a scene in its entirety, then play it back at a later time (Knowledge [local] DC 20). Rumors persist of even more powerful projectors, able to capture true conversation in addition to images and rough sounds (Knowledge [local] or Knowledge [arcana] DC 25).

Description: An *image projector* consists of a Siberys dragonshard suspended by metal wires inside a 1-foot-diameter hoop of silver.

The hoop floats in mid-air when activated, with barely perceptible lines of light expanding outward to create the image stored within the shard.

Prerequisite: This item functions only for a character with the *minor image* ability of the least Mark of Shadow.

Activation: Activating the *image projector* for either playback or recording is a standard action, and is used in conjunction with your *minor image* ability. The moving image created by the *image projector* can be up to 1 minute long. You can specify that the image replay once or set it to loop for a period of up to 10 minutes, beginning again when the end of the image duration is reached. You can also set a delay of up to 1 hour on the recording function, in which case the item records activity for 1 minute following the delay.

Effect: The *image projector* has two primary functions: recording and playback. You can record up to 1 minute of a scene, either an illusion you generate with your *minor image* ability, or all activity within 10 feet of the *image projector*.

A dragonmark rod can create any of the effects of least, lesser, or greater dragonmarks of its type

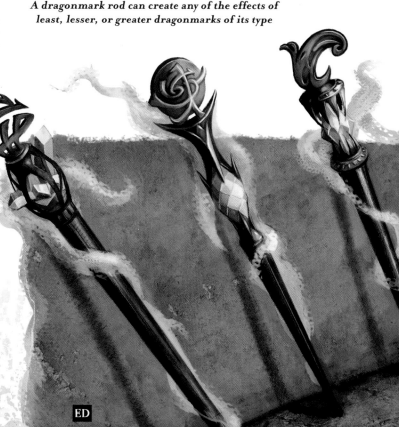

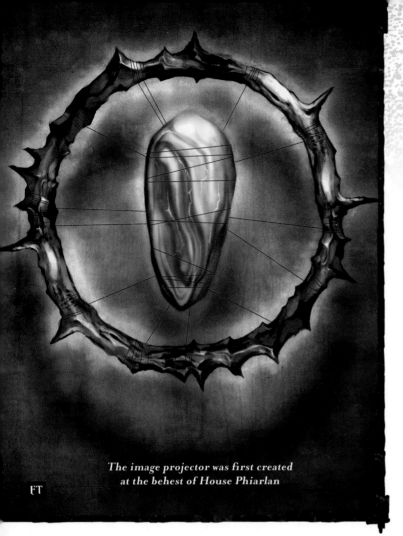

The image projector was first created at the behest of House Phiarlan

FT

When played back, the *image projector* replicates the scene stored within it, replaying the events as a *minor image* spell (see page 254 of the *Player's Handbook*). If the stored image was captured from the projector's surroundings, then the *minor image* shown during playback replicates any activity that took place during the time of the recording. Though some sound is replicated during playback, it is not clear enough to enable you to make out speech.

Aura/Caster Level: Moderate conjuration. CL 5th.

Construction: Requires Craft Wondrous Item, creator must have the least Mark of Shadow, 600 gp, 48 XP, 2 days.

Weight: 1 lb.

Price: 1,200 gp.

Reparation Apparatus

A *reparation apparatus* enhances your ability to repair objects and constructs.

Lore: Many years ago, a group of House Cannith scions and apprentices were traveling through hostile territory with a bodyguard of warforged. The party was attacked, and though they survived, many of their warforged were destroyed despite their best efforts to repair them with the powers of the Mark of Making (Knowledge [history] DC 15). Frustrated by their mark's lack of effectiveness, the Cannith crafters developed the *reparation apparatus* to make their repair magic more effective (Knowledge [history] DC 20).

Description: A *reparation apparatus* fits over your hand like a fingerless gauntlet, and numerous implements sprout from it. A golden Siberys dragonshard is mounted at the

wrist, and engravings on the metal of the gauntlet resemble the pattern within the shard.

When you activate the item, the implements spring to life, helping to repair any object you work on.

Prerequisite: This item only functions for a character with the *repair light damage* ability of the least Mark of Making, or the *repair serious damage* ability of the lesser Mark of Making.

Activation: This magic item is activated any time you use a *repair damage* spell, infusion, or spell-like ability, including any granted by your dragonmark.

Effect: When using any *repair damage* effect, the wielder's effective caster level is increased by 4. For example, the Mark of Making's *repair light damage* spell-like ability automatically repairs the maximum 1d8+5 points of damage, while a 5th-level artificer with an appropriate dragonmark will repair 2d8+9 points of damage using a *repair moderate damage* infusion.

Aura/Caster Level: Moderate transmutation. CL 7th.

Construction: Requires Craft Wondrous Item, creator must have the least Mark of Making, 1,500 gp, 120 XP, 3 days.

Weight: 1 lb.

Price: 3,000 gp.

Truth Chime

A *truth chime* allows you to remove veiling magical guises from all creatures not of House Medani in the area where the tone resonates.

Lore: According to some traditions, a bell's initial resonance when sounded denotes the awakened mind that is able to clearly delve into the nature of reality. The fading tone, then, is a symbol of the impermanence of reality, no matter how well perceived. Thus, the clear, brilliant sound of the bell symbolizes the emptiness, and therefore the openness of reality. This understanding gives a *truth chime* its power (Knowledge [history] DC 15).

Those of House Medani graced with the Mark of Detection prefer *truth chimes* to other, less refined means of getting to the bottom of a particular question—thus, the tones of tiny bells are sometimes heard wafting from the Tower of Inquisition in Wroat. The bells' pleasant sound is thus considered at odds with the techniques utilized within to extract the truth from detainees (Knowledge [history] DC 20).

Description: A *truth chime* appears as a small hand bell with an ornate grip and inscribed bell. A *truth chime* has no internal clapper—instead, it has a Siberys dragonshard imbedded in a small metallic "scepter" that is used to strike the bell. When the chime is activated, a sweet tone resonates and the bell momentarily gives off a rosy glow that permeates the air in all directions to a distance of 30 feet.

Prerequisite: This item functions for any character; however, against characters who possess the Least Mark of Detection, a *truth chime* is completely ineffective. Thus, a *truth chime* can never be used against one of House Medani.

Activation: Activating a *truth chime* is a standard action, and requires you to make the appropriate hand motion to sound it. A *truth chime* can be activated once per day.

Effect: Upon activation, a *truth chime* generates two effects simultaneously.

The first effect is an area *dispel magic* in a 30-foot radius with a dispel check of 1d20 +10 (which doesn't affect anyone who has the Least Mark of Detection).

Also, the wielder gains a momentary view of reality as if affected by a *true seeing* spell for 1 round (from the time the chime sounds to the last tone fades away) in a 30-foot-radius area. Again, this *true seeing* effect doesn't allow the bell wielder to see anything special about anyone in the area who has the Least Mark of Detection.

Variant (Recalling Chime): A variant of the *truth chime* is the *recalling chime*, which is visibly similar, but instead of ignoring all creatures in the area that have the Least Mark of Detection, a *recalling chime* affects those creatures and only those creatures.

When a *recalling chime* is activated, all dragonmarked members of House Medani within 30 feet of the wielder are affected as if by *word of recall* (up to six targets plus the wielder). The *word of recall* deposits all characters in a special reception room in the Warning Guild inside the Medani enclave in the city of Wroat.

Unlike a *truth chime*, a *recalling chime* is usable only once every two days.

Aura/Caster Level: Moderate divination. CL 10th.

Construction: Requires Craft Wondrous Item, creator must have the Least Mark of Detection, 18,000 gp, 1,440 XP, 18 days.

Weight: 4 lb.

Price: 36,000 gp.

Fuel Shard

A *fuel shard* provides a one-time boost to your dragonmark ability.

Description: A *fuel shard* is a small Siberys dragonshard attuned to your dragonmark. Inlaid in silver on the surface of the shard is a replica of your least mark.

When you activate the magic stored within the shard, it emits a brilliant golden glow and then crumbles into dust.

Prerequisite: This item only functions for a character with a least dragonmark.

Activation: You use this item by holding it in your hand when you use your least dragonmark ability. The magic of the *fuel shard* functions only once.

Effect: The *fuel shard* enhances the power of your dragonmark ability in one of three ways: You can choose to increase the variable numeric effects of your dragonmark ability's by one half, as if the mark's spell-like ability was under the effect of the Empower Spell feat; you can elect to double the duration of your ability, as if with the Extend Spell feat; or you can increase any DC associated by your ability by 2. You can select only one enhancement, and you can use only one *fuel shard* at a time to affect your dragonmark ability.

Aura/Caster Level: Strong conjuration. CL 12th.

Construction: Requires Craft Wondrous Item, creator must have a dragonmark of the type to which the *fuel shard* is attuned, 113 gp, 9 XP, 1 day.

Variant: Some *fuel shards* affect lesser, greater, and even Siberys dragonmark abilities. The Siberys shards used in their construction are more expensive, as is the process of creating such items (lesser +238 gp, strong conjuration, CL 14th; greater +688 gp, strong conjuration, CL 15th; Siberys +1,688 gp, strong conjuration, CL 17th).

Weight: 1 lb.

Price: 225 gp.

QUORI EMBEDDED SHARDS

In addition to being incorporated into items that enhance a wielder's dragonmark, Siberys shards are also used by the kalashtar and Inspired to create quori embedded shards.

Combat Instructor

A *combat instructor* draws on your quori spirit to grant you insight into the events unfolding in melee.

Description: Like all quori embedded shards, a *combat instructor* is a Siberys dragonshard implanted in your body.

The *combat instructor* glows a soft yellow when you use it.

Prerequisite: The user of a quori embedded shard must be a kalashtar or Inspired, and the shard must be implanted (see page 264 of the EBERRON *Campaign Setting*)

Activation: You can activate your *combat instructor* three times per day as a standard action by focusing on the power within the shard. When activated, it emits a brief flash of greenish-yellow light. The effect generated by the shard lasts 1 minute.

Effect: A *combat instructor* shard gives you the benefit of an *offensive precognition* effect (see page 124 of the *Expanded Psionics Handbook*), granting you a +1 insight bonus on attack rolls.

Aura/Manifester Level: Moderate clairsentience. ML 5th.

Construction: Requires Craft Universal Item, *offensive precognition* power, 1,500 gp, 120 XP, 3 days.

Weight: 1 lb.

Price: 3,000 gp.

Power Link

A *power link* taps the latent psionic power of your quori spirit.

Description: Like all quori embedded shards, a *power link* is a Siberys dragonshard implanted in your body.

The *power link* glows a soft yellow when you use it.

Prerequisite: The user of a quori embedded shard must be a kalashtar or Inspired, and the shard must be implanted (see page 264 of the EBERRON *Campaign Setting*)

Activation: You call upon the power of this shard as a free action while manifesting a psionic power, up to three times per day. If you have multiple embedded *power link* shards, you can draw from any number of them with a single action.

Effect: When you draw upon a *power link*, the power you manifest is augmented by 2 power points (beyond any augmentation you provide from your own power point reserve). This augmentation can result in more power points invested in the power than you have levels. Each additional implanted *power link* shard you draw on increases the augmentation by an additional 2 power points.

Aura/Manifester Level: Moderate psychokinesis. ML 5th.

Construction: Requires Craft Universal Item, *bestow power* power, 1,500 gp, 120 XP, 3 days.

Weight: 1 lb.

Price: 3,000 gp.

Sustainer

A *sustainer* eliminates your need for food and water.

Description: Like all quori embedded shards, a *sustainer* is a Siberys dragonshard implanted in your body.

A dim golden glow constantly emanates from the shard, though the light is easily blocked by covering the shard with clothing.

Prerequisite: The user of a quori embedded shard must be a kalashtar or Inspired, and the shard must be implanted (see page 264 of the EBERRON *Campaign Setting*)

Activation: Once implanted, a *sustainer* shard is continually active.

Effect: A *sustainer* embedded shard bestows a continual *sustenance* effect (see page 134 of the *Expanded Psionics Handbook*), allowing you to go without food and water.

Aura/Manifester Level: Moderate psychometabolism. ML 5th.

Construction: Requires Craft Universal Item, *sustenance* power, 1,250 gp, 100 XP, 3 days.

Weight: 1 lb.

Price: 2,500 gp.

Power Repository

A *power repository* stores a psionic power that you can exchange for one of your own powers.

Description: Like all quori embedded shards, a *power repository* is a Siberys dragonshard implanted in your body.

The *power repository* glows a soft yellow when you use it.

Prerequisite: The user of a quori embedded shard must be a kalashtar or Inspired, and the shard must be implanted (see page 264 of the EBERRON *Campaign Setting*)

Activation: Once per day, you can spend 1 hour in meditation to draw upon the *power repository*, exchanging a power you know for the power within the shard.

Effect: The *power repository* always has some power of up to 4th level stored within it. Once the shard is embedded in your body, you can swap a power that you know (of the same level) for the power stored within it. Once you have placed a power that you know within the shard, you can no longer manifest that power, but can manifest the power formerly stored within the shard instead.

You can meditate again to swap the powers back, or even swap a different power for the new power within the shard, as long as they are of equal level. In effect, you gain the versatility of an extra power known, but gain the ability to manifest that power only by giving up access to a power normally in your repertoire.

Aura/Manifester Level: Moderate telepathy. ML 7th.

Construction: Requires Craft Universal Item, *psychic reformation* power, 1,500 gp, 120 XP, 3 days (1st level); 6,000 gp, 480 XP, 12 days (2nd level); 13,500 gp, 1,080 XP, 27 days (3rd level); 24,000 gp, 1,920 XP, 3 days (4th level).

Weight: 1 lb.

Price: 3,000 gp (1st), 12,000 gp (2nd), 27,000 gp (3rd), 48,000 gp (4th).

EBERRON SHARD ITEMS

Eberron shards are keenly attuned to all types of magic, and are commonly used in items as a focus for specific spells. Creating an item that incorporates an Eberron shard requires first attuning the shard to the spell it will hold (see page 265 of the EBERRON *Campaign Setting*).

Empowered Spellshard

An *empowered spellshard* grants you an increased effect when you cast the spell to which the shard is attuned.

Lore: These shards were created during the Last War to assist battle mages on the front lines (Knowledge [history] DC 10). As a result, many *empowered spellshards* are keyed to destructive evocations (Knowledge [history] DC 15).

Description: An *empowered spellshard* is an Eberron dragonshard inscribed with arcane symbols, banded with mithral, and hanging from a small silver chain.

The crimson mark within the shard glows softly when you use it as a focus for a spell you cast.

Activation: An *empowered spellshard* is keyed to a specific spell of up to 3rd level. When you cast the attuned spell, you use the *empowered spellshard* as a focus in addition to the spell's normal components (if any). An *empowered spellshard* functions three times per day.

Effect: When you use an *empowered spellshard* as a focus, the attuned spell is empowered as though using the Empower Spell feat. All variable, numeric effects of the spell are increased by one-half. The markings on the shard reveal the spell to which it is attuned with a DC 30 Spellcraft check.

Aura/Caster Level: Moderate no school. CL 9th.

Construction: Requires Craft Wondrous Item and Empower Spell, the spell to which the shard is attuned, 750 gp, 60 XP, 2 days (1st level); 1,500 gp, 120 XP, 3 days (2nd level); 3,000 gp, 240 XP, 6 days (3rd level).

Weight: 0.25 lb.

Price: 1,500 gp (1st), 3,000 gp (2nd), 6,000 gp (3rd).

Truelight Lantern

A *truelight lantern* sheds revealing light that overcomes illusions.

Description: A *truelight lantern* is elaborately crafted from flametouched iron, burnished to a silvery hue. It shares the properties of an *everbright lantern* (see page 265 of the EBERRON *Campaign Setting*), shedding light as a bullseye lantern.

The flame that flickers inside the lantern is a translucent white, though it sheds no heat. When its other power is activated, the flame within the lantern becomes invisible, though its light continues to be shed.

Activation: While the *truelight lantern* continually emanates a bright light, its true powers can be activated as a standard action by speaking the word "reveal" in Celestial. The lantern can be activated in such a manner once per day, or can be activated additional times by having a *true seeing* spell cast into it (overriding the normal targeting restriction of the spell). In either case, the effect lasts for 10 minutes.

Effect: When activated, either by command word or by spell, the light of the *truelight lantern* provides clear illumination in a 60-foot cone and shadowy illumination in a 120-foot cone. Everything within the 60-foot cone of clear illumination can be seen as if all viewers were under the effect of a *true seeing* spell. This effect applies to all creatures, not just the bearer of the lantern.

Aura/Caster Level: Moderate divination. CL 11th.

Construction: Requires Craft Wondrous Item, *true seeing* spell, 18,000 gp, 1,440 XP, 36 days.

Weight: 3 lb.

Price: 36,000 gp.

KHYBER SHARD ITEMS

Like many items of elemental magic, Khyber shard items are primarily constructed in Zilargo. In recent years, some specialists in the field have begun experimenting with the binding of nontraditional elemental creatures or multiple elementals into items. Some of the following items are examples of this work.

Bracers of Wind

A Medium air elemental is bound within these bracers, churning the air around you and focusing your ranged attacks.

Description: *Bracers of wind* are silver plates attached to your forearms by ornate leather straps. Etching on the surface of the bracers is reminiscent of the swirl within the Khyber shards set into the plates just above your wrists.

A faint breeze surrounds you when you wear *bracers of wind*, occasionally billowing your cloak or hair. When the magic of the bracers is focused, an audible surge of air rushes around you.

Activation: *Bracers of wind* continuously provide protection from ranged weapons while worn. In addition, when you throw or fire a ranged weapon, the wind swirls around the weapon or projectile, increasing its accuracy. You can suppress the winds about you by uttering "calm" in Auran, though doing so also suppresses the benefits the bracers bestow. You reactivate the bracers by saying "zephyr" while focusing on the etchings of the silver plates as a standard action.

Effect: The winds around you swell and surge, causing ranged attacks made against you to take a −2 penalty on attack rolls, as if fired in a strong wind (see Table 3–24: Wind Effects, page 95 of the *Dungeon Master's Guide*). Siege weapons, thrown boulders, and the like are not affected. This effect does not stack if the wind force in the area is already strong or greater.

In addition, when you fire or throw a ranged weapon you gain a +1 competence bonus on the attack roll.

Aura/Caster Level: Moderate conjuration. CL 11th.

Construction: Requires Bind Elemental, *planar binding* spell, 5,000 gp, 400 XP, 10 days.

Weight: 1 lb.

Price: 10,000 gp.

Earthplate Armor

The Large earth elemental bound into this suit of full plate gives you the ability to shrug off damage that would drop ordinary folk. You can also sense the presence of your enemies when they draw close to you.

Description: At first glance, this suit of full plate armor looks filthy and ill kept. On closer examination, however, you can see that it is expertly crafted, and that what appears to be dirt is actually the color of the metal itself. A rare black Khyber dragonshard is set horizontally into the front of the armor across the abdomen, binding an earth elemental tightly within.

This suit of armor has significant weight, but with this weight comes protection. Runes in the Gnome language mark its greaves and gauntlets, and the aroma of fresh earth seems to emanate from the suit when you move in it quickly.

Activation: The enhancement bonus of the armor is always active, requiring no action on your part.

The armor's additional effects are activated together as a single standard action. The tremorsense and *stoneskin* effects last for 90 minutes or until the *stoneskin* effect has absorbed 90 points of damage. This power functions only once per day.

Effect: When activated, this *+2 full plate armor* grants you the benefit of a *stoneskin* spell (see page 284 of the *Player's Handbook*). As long as the *stoneskin* effect is active, you also benefit from tremorsense with a range of 5 feet (see page 316 of the *Monster Manual*).

Aura/Caster Level: Moderate abjuration. CL 9th.

Construction: Requires Bind Elemental, *planar binding* and *stoneskin* spells, 21,650 gp, 1,600 XP, 40 days.

Weight: 70 lb.

Price: 41,650 gp.

Elementals bound with Khyber shards empower potent abilities

AS

Fiery Tunic

This shirt gives you some of the elemental resistance of the Medium fire elemental bound within it. You can also cause a metallic weapon to ignite and protect yourself with a shield of fire.

Description: This eye-catching tunic looks like liquid flame running down your torso. The flame doesn't harm you, nor does it char or damage your other possessions. A Khyber shard burns a brilliant red in the middle of the chest, fused seamlessly with the cloth of the shirt.

When the shirt is activated to ignite a weapon or provide a fire shield, its flames roil into a turbulent inferno as the elemental surges in its bonds. If a fire shield is selected, a flowing aura of flame seems to surround you, just a few inches from your skin. If wielding a metallic melee weapon when you activate this item, the weapon bursts into flame.

Activation: The tunic's resistance to fire is always active and requires no action on your part. Activating the *fire shield* and igniting a weapon is a single swift action that does not provoke attacks of opportunity. Either effect can be deactivated as a swift action.

Effect: You gain resistance to fire 10 while you wear the *fiery tunic*. In addition, you can activate the shirt three times per day to produce two effects, each of which lasts for 5 rounds after activation. The first effect generates a *fire shield,* as the spell (warm shield effect only). The second effect is to ignite a metallic melee weapon you are currently holding. As long as you hold the weapon, it acts as a flaming weapon, dealing an extra 1d6 points of fire damage on a successful attack. If the weapon leaves your hands, the effect ends.

Aura/Caster Level: Moderate abjuration and evocation. CL 7th.

Construction: Requires Bind Elemental, *fire shield, planar binding,* and *resist energy* spells, 24,000 gp, 1,920 XP, 48 days.

Weight: 2 lb.

Price: 48,000 gp.

Gloves of Flame

The Medium fire elemental bound into *gloves of flame* allows you to strike at your foes with fiery blasts, and provides some protection against cold.

Description: *Gloves of flame* are blackened leather gloves with steel plates sewn onto the backs of each hand and finger. Small Khyber dragonshards are mounted on the back of each hand, both glowing an eerie orange that highlights the swirling mark within.

A faint smell of sulfur surrounds you when you don the gloves, and when you activate them, a torch-bright flame appears in one of your hands. If you hold an item in your hand, the flame flickers across the item, though neither you nor the item take damage.

Activation: The gloves provide continual protection against cold while you wear them. In addition, you can utter the word "burn" in Ignan (as a swift action) to generate flame in your hand up to five times per day. The flame can be used offensively as a melee touch attack, or you can release a sheet of fire at nearby enemies. You can extinguish your flame as a free action by uttering the word "rest" in Ignan.

Effect: While wearing the gloves, you are continually warmed, and gain the protection of *endure elements* (see page 226 of the *Player's Handbook*) when in cold environments. You also gain resistance to cold 5.

When a flame burns in your hand, you can make a melee touch attack to deal 1d6+5 points of fire damage. Alternatively, you can release the flames in an arc in front of you, as a *burning hands* spell (see page 207 of the *Player's Handbook*), dealing 5d4 points of fire damage to targets in a 15-foot cone (Reflex DC 11 half). Using either of these effects extinguishes the flame.

The flames you create are as bright as a torch, and persist for up to 10 minutes or until extinguished.

Aura/Caster Level: Moderate conjuration. CL 5th.

Construction: Requires Bind Elemental, *planar binding* spell, 9,500 gp, 760 XP, 19 days.

Weight: 1 lb.

Price: 19,000 gp.

Ring of the Stalker

This ring enables you to hunt your prey like the invisible stalker bound into it. You can track your prey more effectively, as well as disappear from its view.

Lore: The first *ring of the stalker* was developed by a pair of spellcasters—a ranger and a sorcerer (Knowledge [history] or Knowledge [arcana] DC 15). Both the original creators were gnomes of Zilargo who were hired to pursue industrial espionage agents in the elemental vessel industry (Knowledge [history] DC 20). The ranger's name was Gaanshana, a female gnome who lost her husband in a raid by a rival agent seeking to uncover some of the secrets of a group called the Power of Purity. She vowed revenge, which she achieved shortly after this ring was created. The sorcerer was her brother, Greeken. Both gnomes are rumored to still be alive in Zilargo (Knowledge [history] or Knowledge [local, Zilargo] DC 30).

Description: The *ring of the stalker* looks like a simple band of glass, so it almost escapes notice. However, closer inspection of the ring reveals that wisps of dark cloudstuff rage through its interior, the ring seeming to hum with the energy of the invisible stalker bound within it. The *ring of the stalker* is a small Khyber dragonshard shaped into ring form, so that the shard is the item, rather than simply being added to it.

Activation: The Survival bonus provided by the ring is always active if you are tracking the creature you have designated as your prey. Designating a creature as your prey is a full-round action that can be performed once per day, and the ring enables you to have only one such creature as your prey at a time. If you designate a new prey while invisible, you immediately become visible to your old prey and invisible to your new prey.

Activating and deactivating the invisibility property of the ring is a standard action that does not provoke attacks of opportunity. The invisibility effect lasts for 10 minutes each use, and is subject to the normal conditions of the spell (it is no longer effective when you make an attack, for example). You can use the invisibility effect three times per day.

Effect: You can designate one creature as your prey, gaining a +5 competence bonus on Listen, Search, Spot, and Survival checks made to locate or find that creature.

In addition, three times per day, you can make yourself invisible to your prey (though any other creatures in the vicinity can still see you). This effect otherwise functions as the *invisibility* spell (see page 245 of the *Player's Handbook*).

Aura/Caster Level: Moderate illusion. CL 10th.

Construction: Requires Bind Elemental, *invisibility* and *planar binding* spells, 7,750 gp, 620 XP, 16 days.

Weight: —

Price: 15,500 gp.

Rock Boots

When wearing these boots, you can move through any terrain with ease, as well as knock down your opponents with a mighty shockwave, all powered by the Medium earth elemental bound within.

Description: *Rock boots* are made from heavy leather, and have solid iron plating along the toes and ankles. A smoky Khyber dragonshard is set into the back of each boot, a few inches above the heel.

The boots feel very solid, though they do not significantly impede your movement. When you step, the boots make a sound like rock on rock, and when you activate their movement powers, the air fills with the scent of freshly dug soil.

Activation: The stability that *rock boots* grant you is always active, provided you have contact with the ground. As a free action, you can draw on the power of the earth elemental within the boots to allow you to move more easily through difficult terrain for up to 10 rounds each day. You can also stomp your foot down violently upon the ground as a standard action up to three times per day, releasing a shockwave that travels through the ground and can knock creatures prone.

Effect: While wearing *rock boots*, you gain a +4 bonus on Strength checks made to resist being bull rushed or tripped when standing on the ground.

When you activate the movement powers of the *rock boots*, you take no movement penalties for moving over difficult terrain for that round.

The stomp ability creates a shockwave that travels in a 20-foot cone away from you. Creatures on the ground in the area must make DC 13 Reflex saves or fall prone.

A character wearing *rock boots* takes a −2 penalty on Move Silently checks.

Aura/Caster Level: Moderate conjuration. CL 11th.

Construction: Requires Bind Elemental, *planar binding* spell, 1,500 gp, 120 XP, 3 days.

Weight: 1 lb.

Price: 3,000 gp.

Water Cloak

The Medium water elemental bound to this cloak protects you from fire attacks.

Description: A *water cloak* is made from sailcloth, with elaborate embroidery that evokes the waves of the sea. Within the pattern of waves, a repeating swirl of thread matches the symbol writhing within the Khyber dragonshard that forms the clasp at the neck of the cloak.

Though the outer surface of the cloak feels damp to the touch and the lower edge appears soaked in water, you feel completely dry when wrapped within it, even when standing in pouring rain.

Activation: A *water cloak* protects you any time you might be damaged by a fire attack. Using the cloak to extinguish flames is a standard action, and it can be used five times per day. You can also counter any spell with the fire descriptor, which typically requires a readied action (see Counterspells,

page 170 of the *Player's Handbook*). This function of the cloak has no daily limit.

Effect: You gain a +5 bonus on Reflex saving throws against any effect that deals fire damage, including spells and breath weapons. You also gain the ability to avoid fire damage as if you had evasion. Whenever you make a successful Reflex saving throw against any fire effect that deals half damage on a successful save, you instead take no damage.

Five times per day, you can extinguish all nonmagical fires within 30 feet of you. Doing this has no effect on fire creatures or on magical fire effects.

At will, you can use the cloak's power to counterspell any spell with the fire descriptor. You must succeed on a dispel check (1d20 + the cloak's caster level) against the caster level of the spell to successfully counterspell the fire spell.

Aura/Caster Level: Moderate conjuration. CL 10th.

Construction: Requires Bind Elemental, *planar binding* spell, 8,500 gp, 680 XP, 17 days.

Weight: 1 lb.

Price: 17,000 gp.

Water Whip

The *water whip* is a potent weapon that allows you to deal extra energy damage to an opponent, depending on whether you desire the whip to be scalding hot or icy cold. The whip is also nearly impossible to remove from your hand, always seeming to find its way back to your grip.

Lore: The first *water whip* was created by a sahuagin druid (Knowledge [history] DC 15). The sahuagin's name was Ak'ash'eck, and he roamed the northwestern fringe of Shargon's Teeth years ago (Knowledge [history] DC 20). Ak'ash'eck enjoyed preying on unwary folk sailing south to trade with his fellows. He was famous in his day for the trick of ensnaring a victim near the railing of a ship passing at night, then pulling the victim overboard before an alarm could be raised (Knowledge [history] DC 30).

Description: This weapon looks less like a traditional whip than a tube of water, tapering along its length to icicle sharpness at one end. The very base of the *water whip*'s handle is made of a small, faintly blue Khyber dragonshard. The whip shimmers and undulates with deceptive grace as you twist it through the air.

Despite its appearance, the whip is firm to your grasp. When the scalding property is activated, the handle grows warm and slightly tacky, and it hisses and steams as it snakes through the air. While in its cold state, the handle is cool and slick (although you have no trouble maintaining your grip), cracking like breaking ice when you wield it.

Activation: Activating or deactivating the scalding or icy property of the whip is a standard action that does not provoke attacks of opportunity. Switching back and forth between the two energy types can be done as often as you wish, although doing so requires another standard action. Each energy effect lasts until you deactivate it.

Effect: Both a water elemental and a fire elemental have been bound within the *water whip*, allowing it to emanate two distinct energy properties. Water works well with fire in this case, making this +1 whip more potent than it appears. The whip deals 1d6 points of lethal damage (as opposed to 1d3 points of nonlethal damage for a standard whip) adjusted by your Strength modifier and the whip's enhancement bonus (base +1, although more potent versions of the whip can be found). By making the *water whip*

Loading
Ramp

Cargo Area

Passenger Cabin

Cabin
Window

Pilot's
Podium

≈1 FOOT

scalding hot, you can deal an extra 1d6 points of fire damage. Alternatively, the whip can be made icy cold, dealing an extra 1d6 points of cold damage with each successful attack. You cannot activate both the icy and scalding properties at the same time.

A creature armed with the *water whip* is difficult to disarm. If someone knocks it from your grasp, the *water whip* flows immediately back to your hand at the beginning of your next turn (even if it is within someone else's grasp) as long as it is within 30 feet of you. Doing this requires no action on your part. Drawing a *water whip* is always a free action.

Aura/Caster Level: Moderate transmutation. CL 8th.

Construction: Requires Bind Elemental, *planar binding* spell, 15,301 gp, 1,200 XP, 31 days.

Weight: 2 lb.

Price: 30,301 gp.

ELEMENTAL VESSELS

Khyber shards and their elemental binding properties power an ever-increasing range of elemental vehicles and vessels across Eberron.

Earth Sled

An earth sled uses the power of a bound earth elemental to move effortlessly along the ground, even where no road is present.

Lore: During the Last War, it became necessary for troops in Breland to hold mountain passes and other remote locations against the forces of Droaam. Defensible

positions within the mountains were plentiful, but the lack of roads made occupying those locations difficult. Hostile forces could more easily lay siege to remote outposts, which would quickly starve without supplies. In response, House Cannith and House Orien utilized the same techniques used in the development of airships and elemental galleons, creating a skiff that could traverse nearly any terrain courtesy of the Huge earth elemental bound within it (Knowledge [history] DC 15).

Since the Last War, earth sleds have continued to find service supplying remote locations across Khorvaire, and some have found their way into the hands of explorers wanting relatively fast movement across trackless terrain (Knowledge [history] or Knowledge [local] DC 20).

House Orien provides earth sled travel to remote locations for a rate of 3 sp per mile (Knowledge [local] or Gather Information DC 10).

Description: An earth sled looks like a small barge, approximately 30 feet long and 15 feet wide at its center. A short railing surrounds the open front of the vessel, and a small enclosure in the back provides some shelter from the elements. A podium at the fore of the craft sports two handles, which the driver uses to communicate with the elemental bound into the vessel.

Though an earth sled can carry up to twenty Medium creatures, most are outfitted to carry eight to ten creatures, with the rest of the space devoted to cargo. It has a total capacity of 5,600 pounds including passengers and cargo.

The elemental moves through the very ground beneath the sled, carrying it a foot or two above the surface. In motion, the earth sled appears to float along the ground, only a slight furrow marking its passage.

An earth sled can traverse shallow water and bogs up to 4 feet deep with ease. Deeper water can also be navigated, though passengers and cargo run the risk of becoming wet. In theory, so long as the driver could somehow breathe, an earth sled could continue to skim along the bottom of a river, lake, or even the ocean.

The earth sled can also climb up natural sheer surfaces, but not worked stone walls or similar construction.

Activation: A character with any Mark of Passage dragonmark can direct an earth sled by grasping the handles at the steering podium. The vessel can move at a constant speed of 6 miles per hour, regardless of the terrain through which it passes.

Aura/Caster Level: Strong conjuration. CL 12th.

Construction: Requires Bind Elemental, *planar binding* spell, 12,000 gp, 960 XP, 24 days.

Weight: 1 lb.

Price: 24,000 gp.

Tumbler

This unique vessel can travel through the ground as easily as the Huge earth elemental bound within it, carrying its passengers to hidden caverns or remote veins of precious metals. Large enough to hold a dozen humanoids, it can easily reach places few other vessels can. A second bound elemental (this one a Small air elemental) keeps the air within the tumbler refreshed.

Lore: The tumbler was initially developed by the gnomes of Zilargo to aid in mining expeditions (Knowledge [arcana] or Gather Information DC 15). Rumor has it that the gnomes have since begun selling the vessel in limited numbers to various governments across Khorvaire for use in espionage, because its burrowing power makes it easy for spies or squads of elite troops to sneak into places they shouldn't (Knowledge [local] or Gather Information DC 25).

Description: A tumbler is an odd vehicle. It looks like a large sphere of rough-hewn rock, with a seam that breaks a surface covered in dull stony spines. When a tumbler is open to accept or debark passengers, one can see seats within for up to twelve human-sized or smaller creatures.

The tumbler rolls when in motion across the ground, but a magic stabilization device built into the vessel keeps its occupants level as it goes. In addition, a ring of clear crystal windows are set into the sides of the sphere, fixed according to the perspective of the passengers. These windows prevent disorientation, allows the pilot of the vessel to see out, and lets passengers know where they are.

Activation: A pilot can operate a tumbler aboveground with a successful DC 20 Profession (pilot) check, but piloting the vessel beneath the surface requires even greater expertise. A pilot must make a DC 25 Profession (pilot) check to activate the vessel's earth glide mode. The pilot navigates by means of instruments inside the vessel, and knowing how to decipher these devices is quite difficult.

Effect: A tumbler can move at a constant speed of 10 miles per hour across level ground, even that considered difficult terrain. However, the vessel's most unique power is its ability to move through the earth like the earth elemental bound into it. The tumbler in this mode can glide through stone or dirt (though not metal) as easily as a fish swims through water, at a speed of 2 miles per hour. The vessel's burrowing leaves behind no tunnel or hole, nor does it create any ripple or other signs of its presence. A tumbler can carry twelve Medium or smaller creatures, including the pilot. The passengers sit in a stacked row of seats, six on the bottom and six on the top (the pilot sits in the upper row).

The tumbler magically refreshes the air supply within it, allowing twelve Medium creatures to breathe comfortably for ten days (see Suffocation, page 304 of the *Dungeon Master's Guide*). If the tumbler spends at least 1 hour in the open air (whether aboveground or in a large cavern), this time limit is reset.

A *move earth* spell cast on an area containing a tumbler flings it back 30 feet, deals 4d6 points of damage to those inside (no save), and renders the craft powerless for 1 minute.

A tumbler can carry passengers through the earth as easily as an earth elemental moves

Aura/Caster Level: Moderate transmutation. CL 17th.

Construction: Requires Bind Elemental, *greater planar binding* spell, 100,000 gp, 8,000 XP, 200 days.

Price: 200,000 gp.

MINOR SCHEMAS

Schemas are the magic of Eberron in recorded form. Dating back to the time of the Giants, schemas have been used to pass magical knowledge through the generations. An individual schema might be a few sigils carved into a stone tablet, or an elaborate scripted presentation on the torso of a warforged titan.

In most cases, an individual schema represents a specific magical building block. These blocks can be combined into magical patterns, storing power ranging from simple cantrips to world-shaking destruction. A House Cannith magewright might use a simple pattern to quickly create hundreds of *continual flame* stones for use in street lamps, even as agents of the Emerald Claw seek to build a pattern that can replicate the destruction of Cyre.

Some schemas are representations of spells or infusions, which in knowledgeable hands can be used to replicate the casting of those spells. Such items are commonly called minor schemas. A minor schema stores a single spell or infusion of up to 6th level, and can be used once per day. It can be crafted with the Etch Schema feat (see page 47).

Spells or infusions with a costly material component, a costly focus, or an XP cost cannot be stored in a minor schema.

MINOR SCHEMAS

Spell/Infusion Level	Price
1st level	400 gp
2nd level	2,400 gp
3rd level	6,000 gp
4th level	11,200 gp
5th level	18,000 gp
6th level	26,400 gp

Description: A minor schema is usually a flat strip of some durable material (commonly metal or wood) approximately 2 inches wide and a foot or more long, with carved or etched symbols and sigils covering its face.

A minor schema that stores a low-level spell or infusion might appear fairly simple, whereas a schema with a

Schemas pass on magical knowledge through the generations

higher-level spell might have hundreds of components incorporated within its mystical diagram. A typical minor schema weighs approximately 1 pound. Minor schemas are never constructed of parchment or other frail materials.

Prerequisite: To use a minor schema, the spell or infusion contained within the item must be on your class spell list.

Activation: Determining what spell or infusion is recorded on a minor schema requires a Spellcraft check (DC 20 + the level of the spell or infusion). *Read magic* does not decipher a minor schema, though *identify* and similar spells will.

If the spell or infusion contained within a minor schema is on your class list, then you can activate that minor schema as a spell completion item (much like activating a scroll) once per day. Schemas have no arcane or divine designation; they are usable by any character with the spell on his spell list regardless of the type of spells he casts. Unlike a scroll, no minimum ability score is required to use a minor schema.

If your caster level is lower than the minor schema's caster level, you must make a caster level check (DC equal to the schema's caster level +1) to use the device successfully. If you fail, the schema becomes dormant and does not function for 1d6 days, but no other mishap occurs due to failure.

If the spell or infusion on a schema is not on your class list, you must instead succeed on a Use Magic Device check (DC 20 + the caster level of the spell or infusion) to activate a minor schema. (As with other spell completion items, artificers must make a Use Magic Device check to use minor schemas, even if a schema's spell or infusion appears on their class list.) Failure renders the minor schema dormant for 1d6 days, as noted above.

In any case, you must be able to see and read the pattern on a minor schema to activate it.

Activating a minor schema provokes attacks of opportunity, and it is subject to disruption just as casting a spell would be. Unlike reading a scroll, a chance for arcane spell failure does not apply when activating a minor schema.

Aura/Caster Level: Faint (1st-level to 3rd-level spell or infusion) or moderate (4th-level to 6th-level spell or infusion) varied. CL minimum required to cast the spell or infusion stored in the item.

Construction: Requires Etch Schema, the spell contained in the item, 200 gp, 16 XP, 1 day (1st); 1,200 gp, 96 XP, 3 days (2nd); 3,000 gp, 240 XP, 6 days (3rd); 5,600 gp, 448 XP, 12 days (4th); 9,000 gp, 720 XP, 18 days (5th); 13,200 gp, 1,056 XP, 27 days (6th).

Weight: —

Price: 400 gp (1st), 2,400 gp (2nd), 6,000 gp (3rd), 11,200 gp (4th), 18,000 gp (5th), 26,400 gp (6th).

DAELKYR ITEMS

The daelkyr and their minions utilize a terrible arcano-science. The tools of these pursuits are insanely difficult to use, though, and they might actually imperil the natural order of the multiverse. Each time a wholly new symbiont, minion, or other corruption is crafted, a localized reality is "spun up" from unstable astral material, then filtered for the desired monstrosity before the reality is allowed to collapse again. The *husk of infinite worlds* (used with a *monocle of tolerance*) is the preferred tool for the pursuit of such mad craft.

In addition to banes created specifically for daelkyr needs, other items rumored to be originally of daelkyr manufacture include the *shirt of the leech* and the *truth lens*.

HUSK OF INFINITE WORLDS

A *husk of infinite worlds* allows a daelkyr or its servants to breed corruption from mad fancy. When a creature is placed within the item, it is exposed to random, alternating pseudo-realities of such crazed extremes that the creature is horribly changed (assuming it survives the experience).

Description: This egglike mass is 10 feet in diameter, translucent, and riddled with dark spots. A slender, wet flap allows passage into or out of the dark interior.

When activated, the husk blazes from within, projecting a kaleidoscope of colors and insane half-imagined images on any nearby walls. A wail like that of a creature screaming in agony accompanies the show of lights, and odd scents come and go at random.

Lore: The husks are created from the quiescent forms of the daelkyr (Knowledge [arcana] DC 35). The proper method of activating a husk requires a DC 45 Knowledge (arcana) check, so improper activation is relatively easy.

Activation: A single Large or smaller "seed" creature placed within the egglike mass of the husk will begin the activation process. Though often placed there by force, creatures unfamiliar with the husk sometimes unknowingly enter to investigate. Once activated by entry, light and sound emanate from the husk as its interior begins to change phase, literally "spinning up" a series of localized realities from unstable astral material. Each reality lasts only tenths of a second before being replaced by the next probability of sick nightmare.

Effect: When properly controlled by pressing the series of black dots on the husk's surface in the correct order and cadence (a DC 45 Knowledge [arcana] check), the evolution

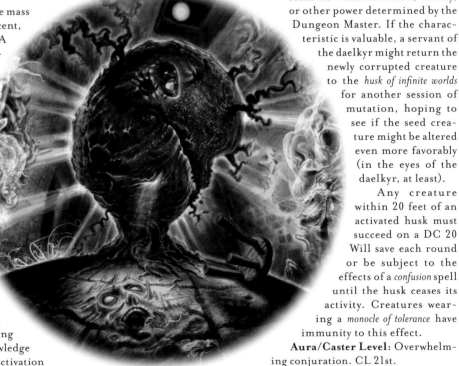

With a husk of infinite worlds, the daelkyr can create new terrifying abominations

of probabilities can be partially guided and the results filtered. When improperly activated (either by the unexpected appearance of a seed creature or a failed check), the husk spins rapidly out of control.

A seed creature must succeed on a DC 26 Will save each round or be stunned for that round by the spinning realities growing and dying all around it. An unrestrained creature that is not stunned can attempt a successful DC 20 Intelligence check to negotiate the husk's artificial realities and escape through the exit flap, but allies outside the husk cannot stop its activation or otherwise assist the trapped creature. A trapped creature can spend 1d10 rounds within an out-of-control husk before devolving into clear protoplasm that runs out of the husk like water, causing it to deactivate.

If the *husk of infinite worlds* is properly controlled, the seed creature within it automatically emerges in a state of abysmal corruption. However, only 1% of such creatures will have evolved into a form that can survive for more than 1d4 rounds. These creatures that survive the *husk of infinite worlds* all sport some new characteristic, ability, or other power determined by the Dungeon Master. If the characteristic is valuable, a servant of the daelkyr might return the newly corrupted creature to the *husk of infinite worlds* for another session of mutation, hoping to see if the seed creature might be altered even more favorably (in the eyes of the daelkyr, at least).

Any creature within 20 feet of an activated husk must succeed on a DC 20 Will save each round or be subject to the effects of a *confusion* spell until the husk ceases its activity. Creatures wearing a *monocle of tolerance* have immunity to this effect.

Aura/Caster Level: Overwhelming conjuration. CL 21st.

Construction: Requires Craft Wondrous Item, *wish* spell, 1 year; requires unconscious form of a daelkyr to serve as the basis of the husk.

Weight: 2,000 lb.

Price: Artifact-level item.

MONOCLE OF TOLERANCE

A *monocle of tolerance* allows you to withstand the external effects of a *husk of infinite worlds*.

Description: This monocle's glass has a slightly yellowish tint, and the frame is carved of a purplish quartz. When activated, the glass turns completely black.

Activation: As part of a move action, you fit the monocle to one of your eyes, which causes it to activate.

Effect: If you are not within 60 feet of a *husk of infinite worlds*, it is impossible to see through the opaque glass of an activated *monocle of tolerance*. If within 60 feet of a husk and wearing the monocle, you can see normally, and you can see in both regular and magical darkness to a distance of 20 feet. The monocle also allows you to ignore the external *confusion* effects of an activated husk (see *husk of infinite worlds*, above).

Aura/Caster Level: Moderate divination. CL 9th.

Construction: Requires Craft Wondrous Item, *true seeing* spell, 1,750 gp, 140 XP, 4 days.

Weight: —

Price: 3,500 gp.

SHIRT OF THE LEECH

A *shirt of the leech* enables you to benefit from healing magic even if you are not the intended recipient. You can gain small portions of magical healing at a distance when a friendly healer casts a *cure* spell, or you can attempt to steal the healing intended for an enemy.

Description: The *shirt of the leech* is dark red silk the color of dried blood. When donned, it becomes almost uncomfortably tight, fitting you like a second skin.

When the shirt is activated, it vibrates almost imperceptibly with a faint purring sound. The shirt also grows noticeably tighter still, although it does not impede your ability to move or function physically.

Activation: The *shirt of the leech* can be activated as an immediate action three times per day.

Effect: Whenever a conjuration (healing) spell of 4th level or lower is cast within 30 feet of you, you recognize that the spell is being cast (but not specifically which spell it is) and can activate the *shirt of the leech* in response. You must have line of sight to the caster for the shirt to function.

When activating the shirt, you must make a saving throw against the healing spell being cast. If you succeed, you gain the full effect of the spell instead of its intended target. If you fail, you gain half the effect (round down) and the intended target gains the remainder.

If the healing spell would affect more than one creature, you automatically succeed on the saving throw and gain the benefit of the spell, but none of the intended targets loses any benefit.

Aura/Caster Level: Moderate conjuration. CL 9th.

Construction: Requires Craft Wondrous Item, *mass cure light wounds* spell, 10,000 gp, 800 XP, 20 days.

Weight: —.

Price: 20,000 gp.

TRUTH LENS

This magic lens does not reveal the truth in the manner of *zone of truth* or similar spells, but the divination powers it possesses enable you to seek answers. With the proper question in mind, you can uncover any truth you desire.

Description: This simple crystal lens has a slight blue tint. When placed into either eye, it glimmers slightly, then gives the eye in which it is worn a white, blind appearance.

When the *truth lens* is activated, your gaze is compelled to turn in the direction of a creature you seek.

Activation: Activating the lens requires you to will the lens to work as you think of a question you want answered (a standard action). The lens can be activated once per week, but only functions if a creature with the answer you seek is within 500 feet. The lens automatically turns off once you step within 5 feet of the creature you seek, or after 5 minutes (whichever comes first).

Effect: The *truth lens* allows you to seek out the answer to a single question, which you must visualize clearly in your mind in a language you speak. You then activate the lens, which immediately provides you with the direction to the nearest sentient creature that knows the answer to your question.

The lens does not provide you with the identity of the creature until you come within 5 feet of it, at which point you know that this is the creature you seek. Even if the creature you seek is behind several walls or on another floor of a multistory building, you still know the direction to it (although in the case of a creature you cannot see, you are not provided with instruction on how to reach it).

If no creature with the answer you seek is within range, you know this immediately, and the lens provides no further direction. If multiple creatures that know the answer are within range, the lens points you in the direction of the closest one. You do not gain any other information about the creature, any special ability to communicate with it, or any ability to compel the creature to actually answer your question. You know only that the creature is capable of answering the question you visualize.

Aura/Caster Level: Moderate divination. CL 11th.

Construction: Requires Craft Wondrous Item, *find the path* spell, 6,500 gp, 520 XP, 13 days.

Weight: —.

Price: 13,000 gp.

PSIONIC ITEMS

Psionic artisans are just as industrious as their magically inclined brethren. In addition to new types of quori embedded shards (see page 115), the following new items can benefit psionic characters. Warforged have psionic component items they can attach to themselves as well, enhancing their psionic ability.

Psionic Items	Price
Galvanic crysteel blade	+1 bonus
Amulet of enemy detection	18,000 gp

Warforged Components	Price
Power crystal (1st)	400 gp
Power crystal (2nd)	1,600 gp
Psychic generator	2,500 gp
Power crystal (3rd)	3,600 gp
Power crystal (4th)	6,400 gp
Power crystal (5th)	10,000 gp
Power crystal (6th)	14,400 gp
Expanded reservoir	18,000 gp
Power crystal (7th)	19,200 gp
Power crystal (8th)	25,600 gp
Power crystal (9th)	32,400 gp

AMULET OF ENEMY DETECTION

An *amulet of enemy detection* warns you when those nearby wish to do you harm.

Description: An *amulet of enemy detection* is an intricately sculpted Riedran crysteel amulet, inlaid with gold and splinters of crystal gathered from the shells of Eberron shards. It is worn about the neck on a heavy gold chain.

Activation: Once you don the amulet, you must spend 1 hour in meditation with it, focusing your personality and psyche into the item. Thereafter, the item is attuned to you unless it leaves your possession for more than one week, or unless another creature attunes the item to itself.

Effect: The *amulet of enemy detection* bestows on you a continual *detect hostile intent* power (see page 91 of the *Expanded Psionics Handbook*). You become aware of the presence of any creatures within 30 feet that intend you harm. You also detect their direction from you, but not their exact distance or location.

While wearing an attuned *amulet of enemy detection,* you cannot be surprised or caught flat-footed by creatures that are within 30 feet and susceptible to mind-affecting powers. You can also make a Sense Motive check as a free action against any creature within 30 feet of you.

Aura/Manifester Level: Moderate telepathy. ML 5th.

Construction: Requires Craft Universal Item*, *detect hostile intent* power, 9,000 gp, 720 XP, 18 days.

Weight: 1/4 lb.

Price: 18,000 gp.

*See the *Expanded Psionics Handbook.*

GALVANIC CRYSTEEL BLADE

A *galvanic* weapon has a blade of Riedran crysteel that can be charged with additional psionic power.

Description: Most *galvanic crysteel blades* are finely crafted daggers, scimitars, or longswords. These Riedran crysteel blades have a purplish hue, and small crystals and Siberys dragonshards mounted about the pommel and crossbar glint with an inner light.

If psionically charged, these weapons emit a faint amethyst glow when wielded.

Activation: Once per day as a standard action, you can charge a *galvanic crysteel blade* by touching it and focusing your psychic energy into it by allocating 1 or more power points to the blade. These points are treated as if they had been spent to manifest a power and can be regained normally.

Effect: The Riedran crysteel used in the construction of the weapon increases its enhancement bonus on damage rolls by 1 if you have at least 1 power point. In addition, when the blade is charged, you can allocate up to 5 power points stored within it as part of a melee attack, adding a bonus on damage rolls with the weapon equal to the power points allocated. The decision to allocate power points to damage is made before the attack is rolled. If the attack misses, the points are lost.

A *galvanic crysteel blade* has the capacity to store 20 power points. Power points allocated to a *galvanic* weapon remain until expended. Once the power points are drained from the weapon, it loses its *galvanic* properties until charged again, though it retains the properties of Riedran crysteel (see page 127 of the EBERRON *Campaign Setting*).

Aura/Manifester Level: Moderate clairsentience. ML 8th.

Construction: Requires Craft Psionic Arms and Armor*, *offensive precognition* power, Riedran crysteel weapon (+1,500 gp).

Weight: As weapon.

Price: +1 bonus.

*See the *Expanded Psionics Handbook.*

WARFORGED COMPONENTS

Most of these components can be utilized by any warforged with psionic abilities, though they are particularly useful to those with the Psiforged Body feat (see page 51).

EXPANDED RESERVOIR

An *expanded reservoir* increases the number of power points you can store within the crystals of your body.

Description: An *expanded reservoir* is a crystal shard that pulses with faint psychic energy.

When embedded and utilized, its pulse becomes steadier.

Prerequisite: Only a character with the Psiforged Body feat can benefit from this item.

Activation: You embed the *expanded reservoir* in your chest or skull (your option), taking up an amulet or headband body slot, respectively. Once installed, you transfer power points to your body as normal.

Effect: An *expanded reservoir* increases the storage capacity of your psiforged body by 6 power points.

Aura/Manifester Level: Moderate psychokinesis. ML 12th.

Construction: Requires Craft Cognizance Crystal*, 9,000 gp, 720 XP, 18 days.

Psionic warforged components are attached to or embedded within a warforged character

ED

Weight: 1 lb.

Price: 18,000 gp.

*See page 44 of the *Expanded Psionics Handbook*.

POWER CRYSTAL

A *power crystal* grants the limited use of a psionic power.

Description: A *power crystal* is constructed from a psionically resonant crystal and an Eberron dragonshard. It is attached to the chest, head, or hand of a warforged, and so occupies the amulet, headband, or gloves body slot, respectively.

Activation: A *power crystal* stores the imprint of a psionic power. Once per day, you can use the *power crystal* to manifest that psionic power, using your own power point reserve or any power points stored within your body, if you are a psiforged (see the Psiforged Body feat, page 51).

Effect: The power imprinted in the crystal is manifested using power points supplied by you, and the specific effect depends on the power used. However, you cannot augment this power or enhance it with metapsionic feats. This power is treated as a normally manifested power, with all the attendant effects.

If you do not possess enough power points to manifest the power stored within a particular *power crystal*, you gain no benefit from it.

Aura: Faint (1st-level to 3rd-level power), moderate (4th-level to 6th-level power), strong (7th-level to 9th-level power) varied. ML minimum required to manifest the power stored in the item.

Construction: Requires Craft Universal Item* and Imprint Stone*, the power stored in the item, 200 gp, 16 XP, 1 day (1st); 800 gp, 64 XP, 2 days (2nd); 1,800 gp, 144 XP, 4 days (3rd); 3,200 gp, 256 XP, 7 days (4th); 5,000 gp, 400 XP, 10 days (5th); 7,200 gp, 576 XP, 15 days (6th); 9,600 gp, 768 XP, 20 days (7th); 12,800 gp, 1,024 XP, 26 days (8th); 16,200 gp, 1,296 XP, 33 days (9th).

Weight: 1/4 lb.

Price: 400 gp (1st), 1,600 gp (2nd), 3,600 gp (3rd), 6,400 gp (4th), 10,000 gp (5th), 14,400 gp (6th), 19,200 gp (7th), 25,600 gp (8th), 32,400 gp (9th).

*See Chapter 3 of the *Expanded Psionics Handbook*.

PSYCHIC GENERATOR

A *psychic generator* creates psychic energy that you can use to fuel your psionic powers.

Description: A *psychic generator* is a cluster of crystals that resonate with psionic energy.

Activation: The crystal cluster is embedded into your upper torso. Doing so does not take up a body slot. The *psychic generator* begins providing power points 24 hours after installation.

Effect: The *psychic generator* increases your daily power point reserve by 1 power point. This extra power point can be spent normally, stored in your body if you're psiforged, or stored in a cognizance crystal.

Aura/Manifester Level: Faint psychokinesis. ML 5th.

Construction: Requires Craft Universal Item, 1,250 gp, 100 XP, 3 days.

Weight: 1 lb.

Price: 2,500 gp.

GRAFTS

The idea of magically modifying one's body is not new, as demonstrated by the daelkyr's experiments with symbionts. However, a few years before the end of the last war, factions across Khorvaire began a new type of magical experimentation and research. Similar only peripherally to symbionts, grafts were viewed as a safer way to grant an individual greater inherent magical power.

Grafts involve taking a portion of an existing creature and transplanting it into or onto the body of another living creature. Grafting is a complex and, for the most part, new method of item creation, and its many benefits are still being fully explored. Bearers of grafts can gain the powers of many types of magic item without actually wearing those items. Many grafts are difficult to spot under casual observation, allowing their bearers greater opportunities for stealth.

Many different types of grafts have come into use since their initial discovery. Even so, the new magic of grafts has yet to spread beyond a few select nations. This section contains information on grafts representative of a few of the different cultures discussed in *Magic of Eberron*. (The rules presented here might deviate from those of the grafts presented in other books. These rules apply only to the grafts in this book, and not to any other form of graft previously introduced.)

Regardless of origin, all grafts in this book have the following rules in common.

Grafts can be created and applied only by someone with the appropriate feat. While the creation and application of a graft is similar in theory to the principles involved in the creation of wondrous items, grafts involve the magical manipulation of biological processes and structures, and the grafter must be able to manipulate life energy on a minute scale. *Magic of Eberron* includes three such feats: Deathless Fleshgrafter, Eldeen Plantgrafter, and Elemental Grafter, all of which are described in Chapter 2.

An individual can have a total of only five grafts grown on his body, and all such grafts must be of the same kind. A single body can only support so many augmentations before it is overwhelmed with competing biomagical signals, resulting in death or (more often) madness. No portion of the body (head, skin, flesh, legs, and arms) can have more than one graft. Furthermore, two different kinds of grafts (such as elemental grafts and plant grafts) cannot be applied to the same character (though a character can have multiple varieties of elemental graft, such as air elemental grafts and fire elemental grafts). Rumors of individuals who have attempted to bypass these biological limits abound, but such monstrosities—for that is what such creatures become—rarely live long.

Using a graft requires a sacrifice from the host. The grafts presented in this book take a toll on a creature's body. In most cases, a graft simply applies a permanent reduction to the character's hit point total (though this reduction is not damage and cannot be healed). Other grafts might cause a permanent reduction to an ability score or a permanent penalty on certain checks or saves. A creature with a graft cannot get rid of the penalties or other costs of a graft unless the graft is removed. The specific penalties of a graft are provided under the Graft Sacrifice entry of each graft's description.

All grafts come from a donor creature, or are grown from tissues taken from one or more creatures. As a result, each graft has a Graft Donor entry that describes where the graft originates. If taken from a donor creature, the graft tissues must be no more than seven days old when creation of the graft begins.

Grafts are difficult to remove. Grafts have no statistics of their own and cannot be attacked or damaged separately from the creature to which they are grafted. A character with the appropriate graft creation feat can remove a graft safely from a living creature, but doing so requires 8 hours of work in a quiet setting (similar to creating a graft; see below). A graft safely removed from one character can be applied to another, though this must take place within 24 hours of removal and deals 4d6 points of Constitution damage to the character receiving the used graft.

Without the proper feat, a graft can only be removed if the body part to which it is grafted is removed, but such grafts die instantly and cannot be reused. Likewise, any grafts on a creature that dies are killed at the same time, and they cannot be harvested or reused—which means that an NPC's grafts typically can't be recovered as treasure (for tips on dealing with this, consult the Symbionts and Grafts as Treasure sidebar, page 154). Grafts should, however, be treated as part of a creature for the purpose of being brought back from the dead, so a character with grafts who is killed and resurrected returns with her grafts intact.

A graft is not a magic item. It does not radiate magic once completed (although a graft might require the casting of specific spells as part of the construction process), and it does not take up a body slot like a magic item would. A graft cannot be suppressed with *dispel magic*, nor is it affected by an *antimagic field* or similar effects.

CREATING A GRAFT

The creation of a graft must take place in a quiet and comfortable setting, and requires a supply of materials (including the donated body part; see below). The cost of materials is covered in the cost of creating the graft. Creating a graft otherwise works exactly like crafting a wondrous item, including the cost to create, time required, preparation of spells, and expenditure of components, focuses, or experience points required by those spells (except as noted below). If a graft incurs extra costs in material components or experience points (as noted in its description), these costs are in addition to those derived from the graft's base price.

Unlike normal magic items, grafts need not be created over consecutive days. A crafter can spend a day here and there tending a growing graft, but it is not functional until the total time necessary to complete the graft has been spent. In addition, a character cannot spend more than a week between the days that he works on an incomplete graft. Doing so means the incomplete graft dies, and the crafter loses a portion of the gp cost involved in the graft's creation equal to the amount of time spent working on it. However, the grafter does not lose any experience points until the graft is completed.

A grafter must devote 8 hours to the grafting process on days during which he works on a graft. Failure to do so means the day's work is wasted, but no gp or XP costs are incurred.

The recipient of a graft does not incur any of the penalties involved with acquiring a graft (typically permanent hit point loss, but sometimes permanent skill or ability penalties) until the graft is attached in the second phase of the procedure. A graft is grown apart from its intended host until complete, much like any magic item. It is then attached in an 8-hour procedure, during which time both grafter and recipient must be present. Once a graft is fully completed, it continues to require care from the creator until it is attached. A completed graft outside a host body requires 1 hour of care each day or it will die.

GRAFTS

Deathless Grafts	Price
Legs of the undying marcher	6,000 gp
Arm of the ancestor	8,500 gp
Bone plating	9,000 gp
Deathless visage	32,000 gp
Deathless flesh	33,000 gp

Elemental Grafts	Price
Stony plating	2,800 gp
Tremor graft	6,000 gp
Dust form	7,000 gp
Scorching gaze	7,000 gp
Oceanic adaptation	8,000 gp
Breath of the waves	9,000 gp
Aqueous body	13,000 gp
Buffeting fists	13,000 gp
Hands of flame	13,000 gp
Incendiary skin	17,000 gp
Elemental flesh	31,000 gp
Whirlwind form	58,000 gp
Earth glider	113,000 gp

Plant Grafts	Price
Treebark carapace	3,200 gp
Perception seed	4,000 gp
Grappling vine	7,000 gp
Rootlegs	7,000 gp
Fatigue spores	12,000 gp
Darkwood flesh	19,000 gp
Healing nodules	21,000 gp

DEATHLESS GRAFTS

The elves of Aerenal are the only group on Eberron known to have dabbled in the construction of grafts well in advance of the more recent developments in the art. Deathless grafts, where the flesh of a revered undying is grafted onto a worthy elf hero, have been a part of Aerenal culture for centuries (albeit an uncommon part).

Deathless grafts were conceived for two main purposes. The undying guardians of Aerenal hoped to discover whether particular elves were worthy of the power and responsibilities of the deathless, and allowing these would-be guardians deathless grafts was seen as a sort of test. Deathless grafts were also often bestowed as badges of honor to a few fortunate elves who fought admirably for their nation.

These restrictions meant that deathless grafts remained rare for some time. Recently, however, they have seen more common use, and Aereni with the right connections, or those who have showed dedication to the protection of the island nation, are sometimes given the opportunity to receive a deathless graft.

The elves of Aerenal create grafts using the voluntarily donated flesh and tissues of the deathless, although secret cabals are known to grow deathless flesh and bone for their own grafting purposes.

Deathless grafts follow the same general rules for grafts described above. Adding a deathless graft requires access to a character with the Deathless Fleshgrafter feat (see page 46).

A character with at least two deathless grafts gains a bonus on Fortitude saves to resist poison and disease equal to the number of deathless grafts he has.

Arm of the Ancestor

The flesh from the arm of an undying ancestor has been grafted over your own arm. You gain the benefit of its great strength, as well as the ability to channel positive energy to either beneficial or harmful ends.

Graft Location: Arms.

Description: One of your arms is incongruous with the rest of your appearance, sheathed in the deathless flesh of an undying ancestor.

Now taut and a corpse-white in color, the flesh of the arm of the ancestor is withered and dry to the touch, but this appearance conceals great strength. Your fingers are long and nearly skeletal, and the arm smells of the dry and dusty tomb.

Activation: The arm of the ancestor can channel positive energy as a standard action that does not provoke attacks of opportunity. Its ability to damage undead is made as a melee touch attack.

Effect: The physical might of the arm of the ancestor grants you a +1 bonus on Climb and Swim checks, a +1 bonus on grapple checks, and a +1 bonus on damage rolls with any melee weapon wielded by the arm.

In addition, you can channel positive energy through the arm, touching a creature to bestow a beneficial or harmful effect. Living creatures you touch gain fast healing 3, while undead you touch take 3 points of damage per round. The fast healing or ongoing damage delivered by the arm lasts for a number of rounds equal to one-half your Hit Dice (minimum 1 round). You can use this ability once per hour.

Adding this graft takes a physical toll, numbing your sense of touch and making your arm slightly less nimble. As a result, you take a −2 penalty to Dexterity.

Construction: Requires Deathless Fleshgrafter, *bull's strength* spell, ability to turn undead, 4,250 gp, 340 XP, 9 days.

Graft Donor: Flesh from the arm of a deathless creature.

Graft Sacrifice: 4 hp, −2 Dexterity.

Price: 8,500 gp.

Bone Plating

Your skin is hardened with pieces of bone grown from samples taken from one of the honored deathless. As a result, your vulnerable areas are now covered with a protective bony layer.

Graft Location: Skin.

Description: Thin, strong layers of bone cover your skin. The bone is pale white, stretching over every vulnerable area from your collarbone to your ankles.

The bone plating is smooth to the touch, and it moves as you do, not hindering your movements in the least. The

plating and your skin are one featureless surface; no one can tell where one ends and the other begins.

Activation: Bone plating is always active once the graft is installed. Using it requires no action on your part.

Effect: Your natural armor bonus to AC improves by 1. Creatures without natural armor have an effective natural armor bonus of +0. Because the graft improves your natural armor, effects that provide an enhancement bonus to natural armor (such as a *barkskin* spell) stack with bone plating.

Bone plating also provides resistance to cold 5, or increases a character's existing resistance to cold (regardless of its origin) by 5 points.

Construction: Requires Deathless Fleshgrafter, 4,500 gp, 360 XP, 9 days.

Graft Donor: A piece of bone from a deathless creature.

Graft Sacrifice: 4 hp.

Price: 9,000 gp.

Deathless Flesh

This graft fuses to the muscles and subdermal tissues of your entire body, giving your flesh the resilience of the deathless. You become more resistant to damage, and you can shrug off blows that would normally drop a creature of your size.

Graft Location: Flesh.

Description: Deathless flesh makes your body look slighter, even frail. Your muscles appear almost shrunken beneath your skin, which takes on a deathly pallor.

Looks are deceiving, however, and despite your appearance, you are stronger and more able than ever.

Activation: Deathless flesh is always active once the graft is installed. Using it requires no action on your part.

Effect: You gain a benefit similar to the fortification armor quality. Any time that you are subjected to a critical hit or sneak attack, there is a 50% chance that you ignore the extra damage from that critical hit or sneak attack. In addition, any time you are subjected to a death effect, there is a 50% chance that you can ignore the effect as if you were immune.

Unfortunately, this graft takes a heavy toll on your physical health, and you take a permanent −2 penalty to your Constitution score.

Construction: Requires Deathless Fleshgrafter, *limited wish* or *miracle* spell, 16,500 gp, 1,320 XP, 33 days.

Graft Donor: A piece of muscle cut from a deathless creature.

Graft Sacrifice: −2 Constitution.

Price: 33,000 gp.

Deathless Visage

This graft provides a shred of insight into the long-term mindset and wisdom of the undying councilors of Aerenal. The foresight and patience of immortals is terrifying to any mortal creature, and this item can invoke that terror with but a glance. You can also call upon the knowledge of the ancient elves for aid when necessary, but you also feel the weight of the elven nation resting on your shoulders, interfering with your social interactions.

Graft Location: Head.

Description: This graft is grown over the upper portion of your face. While it does not affect your appearance much, your features tighten slightly, giving your face a gaunter, skull-like visage. Your brow seems weighed down with great concerns.

The graft doesn't just cover your face, however, but fuses with the flesh on your head, extending through your skull and into portions of your brain. There, it allows you access to the ancestral memory of the Aereni.

When you activate your terrifying glare, your eyes flash black with eternal darkness, and those whom you gaze upon are terrified at the immortality you seem to represent.

Prerequisite: This graft can only be given to a creature with a maximum life span of at least two hundred years.

Activation: Activating the glare attack of this graft is a standard action that does not provoke attacks of opportunity. The Knowledge check bonus of the graft is activated as part of a Knowledge check and can be used at will.

Effect: When the deathless visage graft is activated, you can fix your glare upon a single creature within 30 feet that can see you (and be seen by you). This effect is similar to a gaze attack used actively (see page 309 of the *Monster Manual*), but it does not affect creatures on their turns as a gaze attack can. The creature you target becomes frightened for 1d4 rounds unless it succeeds on a Will save (DC 10 +1/2 your HD + your Cha modifier). Even if the creature succeeds on the save, it is shaken for 1 round. This is a mind-affecting fear ability. A creature that successfully saves against this effect is immune to it for 24 hours.

The secondary power of the graft allows you to tap into the long memory of the elves. You gain a +2 insight bonus on all Knowledge checks.

The drawback to this graft is the heavy psychological burden it places upon your mind and soul, making you somewhat less socially capable. You take a −2 penalty on Bluff, Diplomacy, Gather Information, and Intimidate checks made against any creature other than an Aerenal elf or a deathless creature.

Construction: Requires Deathless Fleshgrafter, *cause fear, glimpse of eternity*,* 16,000 gp, 1,280 XP, 32 days.

Graft Donor: Flesh from the scalp of a deathless creature.

Graft Sacrifice: 6 hp, −2 penalty on Bluff, Diplomacy, Gather Information, and Intimidate checks against all but Aereni and deathless creatures.

Price: 32,000 gp.

*New spell described on page 96.

Legs of the Undying Marcher

Flesh from the legs of an undying donor has been fused to your own legs. You now have the endurance of the deathless, and a memory of past conflicts that grants you better stability and reflexes in battle.

Graft Location: Legs.

Description: Flesh from the legs of one of the undying has been fused to your own legs, completely replacing your natural flesh.

Your new limbs are gaunt and seemingly devoid of muscle. Their skin is corpse-white and shriveled like that of the undying, but despite their appearance, they are stronger and sturdier than ever. At times, you even feel your movement guided by your deathless donor.

Activation: Legs of the undying marcher are always active once the graft is installed. Using them requires no action on your part.

Effect: Your legs never tire while walking, and so you need never make Constitution checks to avoid non-lethal damage or fatigue while making a forced march.

Your legs also hold the accumulated experiences of their deathless donor, resulting in feelings of premonition that grant you a +2 bonus on all Reflex saves. Finally, the durability of the legs gives you increased stability, resulting in a +4 bonus on checks to resist being bull rushed or tripped.

Construction: Requires Deathless Fleshgrafter, *lesser restoration* spell, 3,000 gp, 240 XP, 6 days.

Graft Donor: Flesh from the legs of a deathless creature.

Graft Sacrifice: 2 hp.

Price: 6,000 gp.

ELEMENTAL GRAFTS

Among the groups most heavily invested in early graft research were the gnomes of Zilargo, who long sought new ways to keep their land safe from the ravages of the Last War (as well as new ways to profit off that war as it raged in other parts of the continent). Groups of elemental specialists in Zilargo, including the Power of Purity (see page 34), hoped to better understand elemental magic by fusing portions of elemental essence to their own bodies. While many elemental grafts grant their wielders the powers of the elementals, others build on more spiritual connections to the elements, granting their bearers surprising and unique abilities.

Elemental grafts began growing fashionable about five years ago. More prevalent than other types of grafts, they are especially common among members of House Lyrandar and House Orien. In addition, the elemental scions of Zilargo (see page 68) all have elemental grafts that grow and transform as they gain levels in that prestige class.

Fear lives in the gaze of the deathless visage

Elemental grafts typically give the creatures that bear them an alien look. While not all such creatures have overt physical characteristics that identify them as the recipients of grafts, the process of binding a portion of a creature from another plane to one's own flesh always has interesting side effects.

The creatures that become elemental graft donors must be called. Some are willing (such as those that agree to aid the Power of Purity organization, and their subsect, the Inmost) but others are specifically harvested for their ability to create grafts. Graft materials taken from summoned creatures vanish with the creatures they were taken from when the summoning spell's duration ends.

Elemental grafts follow the same general rules for grafts described on page 126. Adding elemental grafts requires access to a character with the Elemental Grafter feat (see page 47).

A character with at least two elemental grafts of the same variety (air, earth, fire, or water) gains a particular benefit as follows, but only as long as he has no elemental grafts of the opposing variety.

- A character with at least two air grafts (and no earth grafts) gains a bonus to his land speed equal to 5 feet per air graft beyond the first, but only when wearing light or no armor and carrying no more than a light load.
- A character with at least two earth grafts (and no air grafts) gains damage reduction equal to the

number of earth grafts beyond the first (so that a character with three earth grafts would have damage reduction 2/—). This benefit stacks with any other damage reduction of the same kind (such as from barbarian levels).

- A character with at least two fire grafts (and no water grafts) gains a +2 bonus on Reflex saves and initiative checks per fire graft beyond the first.
- A character with at least two water grafts (and no fire grafts) gains a Swim speed equal to 20 feet plus 10 feet per water graft beyond the first. (If the character already has a swim speed greater than this, he instead gains a +5-foot bonus to his swim speed per water graft).

A creature with a swim speed can move through water at its swim speed without making Swim checks. It has a +8 racial bonus on any Swim check to perform some special action or avoid a hazard. The creature can always choose to take 10 on a Swim check, even if distracted or endangered. The creature can use the run action while swimming, provided it swims in a straight line.

Aqueous Body [Water]

The essential substance of a water elemental has been grafted to your own body, allowing you to move through the water as if born there. In addition, you can call upon your natural fluidity to make you more evasive in underwater combat, leading your opponents to sometimes miss you when their blows would otherwise land.

Graft Location: Flesh.

Description: Your flesh has a faint blue cast, and your veins seem to stand out starkly against your skin.

While underwater, your flesh turns nearly translucent and your outline becomes difficult to distinguish.

Activation: The miss chance granted by the graft is always active when you are within the water, requiring no action on your part.

Effect: While you are underwater, you gain concealment (attacks directed against you have a 20% miss chance), and you can use the Hide skill without needing cover or concealment. Furthermore, you can breathe underwater for any length of time, as if under the effect of a permanent *water breathing* spell.

This graft reduces your overall agility, resulting in a permanent −2 penalty to your Dexterity score.

Construction: Requires Elemental Grafter, *blur* and *water breathing* spells, 6,500 gp, 520 XP, 13 days.

Graft Donor: Any portion of a water elemental.

Graft Sacrifice: 6 hp, −2 Dexterity.

Price: 13,000 gp.

Breath of the Waves [Water]

You channel the healthy vitality of water in your veins, and can breathe its magically enhanced restorative properties onto yourself or your companions. You also never need to fear dying of thirst, because the water flowing through you keeps your body endlessly hydrated.

Graft Location: Head.

Description: The inside of your mouth, including your tongue and throat, have been replaced with the substance of a water elemental. Water laps gently around the inside of your mouth, and your tongue seems to be made of water. Your teeth are still present, but are as translucent as ice.

The "flesh" of an earth elemental can be a graft

Those near you can hear the lapping of gentle waves behind every word you speak. You also sound full of vitality, even when death threatens or you are beset by sadness or illness. Your breath always smells fresh and pure.

Activation: The ability to avoid dehydration is always active and requires no action on your part. The ability to remove negative conditions through your breath can be activated once per hour as a standard action.

Effect: You have immunity to all effects that cause dehydration, including the *horrid wilting* spell. You also need never drink any water to avoid dehydration, because your graft provides you with all the water your body needs.

In addition, your breath can give an adjacent creature (or yourself) the benefit of revitalizing water, magically charged by your graft. When you breathe on a creature, any or all of the following conditions are instantly negated: exhausted, fatigued, nauseated, paralyzed, sickened, or stunned. If the creature you breathe on is dying (−1 to −9 hit points), it automatically stabilizes at its current hit point total.

Construction: Requires Elemental Grafter, *cure moderate wounds* spell, 4,500 gp, 360 XP, 9 days.

Graft Donor: Any portion of a water elemental.

Graft Sacrifice: 4 hp.

Price: 9,000 gp.

Buffeting Fists [Air]

A portion of an air elemental has been bound into your hands, allowing you to protect yourself from ranged attacks more effectively. You can also buffet your foes by slamming your fists together, forcing them away from you.

Graft Location: Arms.

Description: Your hands are nearly invisible at times, their flesh swirling as if stirred from within by strong winds.

When you move your hands rapidly, you produce a noticeably strong current of air. In battle, you seem to be surrounded by a strong breeze that emanates from your hands, and the roaring of strong winds surrounds you when you buffet your foes.

Activation: Your ability to deflect arrows is always active. Your buffet ability can be activated once per day as a standard action that does not provoke attacks of opportunity.

Effect: You gain the ability to deflect ranged attacks as if you had the Deflect Arrows feat, except that you can deflect a number of attacks per round equal to 1 + your Dexterity modifier (minimum one).

In addition, once per day you can strike your fists together to buffet any foes near you with a strong blast of wind. Any enemies within 10 feet of you are treated as subjects of a bull rush attack from the wind, which has a Strength score equal to your own + 10. The wind is treated as a Large creature (or as a creature of your size, if larger), and gains the appropriate bonus on its bull rush checks (see page 154 of the *Player's Handbook* for information on bull rush attacks). Creatures in the area can be pushed back a maximum of 5 feet, but you are not pushed back on a failed check.

Construction: Requires Elemental Grafter, *protection from arrows* spell, 6,500 gp, 520 XP, 13 days.

Graft Donor: Any portion of an air elemental.

Graft Sacrifice: 4 hp.

Price: 13,000 gp.

Dust Form [Air]

You can cause the lower part of your body to assume the form of a whirlwind, allowing you to stir up tremendous amounts of dust and debris that blind and irritate your foes.

Graft Location: Legs.

Description: This elemental air graft causes your legs to grow thin and turn a pale blue. You also grow about 1 inch taller.

When you activate the graft, your legs vanish momentarily and are replaced with a swirling whirlwind that stirs up dust and debris.

Activation: Activating the graft is a move action that does not provoke attacks of opportunity. You can activate this graft once per minute.

Effect: Once activated, a swirling vortex of wind surrounds you for a moment, stirring up a cloud of dust and debris. When you activate the power, all living creatures adjacent to you must succeed on a Fortitude save (DC 10 + 1/2 your HD + your Con modifier) or be blinded for 1 round.

The graft slightly weakens the strength of your legs, resulting in a permanent −2 penalty on Climb, Jump, and Swim checks.

The graft does not function underwater.

Construction: Requires Elemental Grafter, *gust of wind* spell, 3,500 gp, 280 XP, 7 days.

Graft Donor: Any portion of an air elemental taken while it was in whirlwind form.

Graft Sacrifice: 4 hp, −2 penalty on Climb, Jump, and Swim checks.

Price: 7,000 gp.

Earth Glider [Earth]

You can glide through the earth with the utmost ease, and for miles at a time. Only veins of metal ore impede your underground progress.

Graft Location: Arms.

Description: This graft transforms your arms, hands, and fingers into tough burrowing tools. Your fingers have blunt ends and no fingernails. Your forearms, hands, and fingers are thicker than normal, and covered in the earthy, fractured skin common to earth elementals.

When you move your arms rapidly (while wielding a weapon in combat, for example), your movements make the faint thudding sound of rock on soil. While using the graft, your hands and arms glow a pale green.

Activation: Activating the graft requires a full-round action as you attune your arms with the earth.

Effect: You gain the ability to slip through solid earth as effortlessly as an earth elemental. You can glide at your normal land speed through stone, dirt, or almost any other sort of earth (except metal) as easily as a fish swims through water. Your burrowing leaves behind no tunnel or hole, nor does it create any ripple or other signs of its presence. You cannot bring any other creatures along with you while gliding through the earth in this manner.

You can remain in solid earth for a maximum number of consecutive rounds equal to one-third your HD (minimum 1 round). If still within a solid object when the effect ends, you are shunted to the nearest open space and take 1d6 points of damage per 5 feet that you so travel. Certain spells, if cast upon the earth or stone that you are occupying, can harm you; see the *meld into stone* spell (page 252 of the *Player's Handbook*) for details.

Your heavy arms reduce your agility, resulting in a permanent −2 penalty to your Dexterity score.

Construction: Requires Elemental Grafter, *meld into stone* spell, 56,500 gp, 4,520 XP, 113 days.

Graft Donor: Any portion of an earth elemental.

Graft Sacrifice: 6 hp, −2 Dexterity.

Price: 113,000 gp.

Elemental Flesh [Any]

Elemental essence courses through your body, granting you incredible resilience. Your flesh and vital organs strengthen, giving you the ability to ignore potentially crippling blows.

Graft Location: Flesh.

Description: Your body undergoes an elemental change, and you are surrounded by an otherworldly aura. You don't seem completely part of this plane, and you share some of the traits of the elemental donor that gave you this graft.

If your elemental donor was an air elemental, your skin is pale and partially translucent. On closer examination, your flesh seems to almost move of its own accord, as if currents of air flowed within your body. If your donor was an earth elemental, your eyes resemble chips of volcanic rock, and your skin and hair are the color of dark, healthy soil. If your donor was a fire elemental, your skin has a ruddy hue, your eyes dance with flickering light from time to time, and your body emanates a feverish heat. If your donor was a water elemental, your movements seem overly fluid and graceful, and your skin has a faint blue cast.

Prerequisite: You must have at least one other elemental graft before you can gain elemental flesh.

Activation: Elemental flesh is always active once the graft is installed. Using it requires no action on your part.

Effect: Many of the bodily processes performed by your more vital organs are now performed by the graft, making injuries to those organs less threatening. As such, you have a 50% chance to ignore the extra damage dealt by critical hits and sneak attacks (though you still take the normal damage dealt by those attacks).

You also have a 50% chance to resist any effect that stuns you, though you do not have immunity to any additional effects that might accompany the stunning (such as the damage dealt by a *sound burst* spell).

When you take this graft, you choose which type of elemental donated it. The graft then counts as an elemental graft of that type.

Construction: Requires Elemental Grafter, *limited wish* or *miracle* spell, 15,500 gp, 1,240 XP, 31 days.

Graft Donor: Any portion of a living elemental weighing at least 3 pounds.

Graft Sacrifice: 8 hp.

Price: 31,000 gp.

Hands of Flame [Fire]

Your hands become limned with flame, allowing you to heat your metallic weapons and deal fire damage with them. Your mere touch can cause flammable objects to ignite.

Graft Location: Arms.

Description: Your hands glow faintly with orange flame. While never actually alight, the skin of your hands and forearms seems to hold liquid fire, pulsing slightly as it races through your body.

When you activate the graft, its glow becomes almost white, and a shimmer of heat can be seen rising from your hands. Their flesh grows almost translucent, allowing anyone looking at them to see the tracings of fiery veins and white-hot bones beneath the skin. With the graft active, you can hear the crackling of flame as your hands move through the air.

Activation: Activating the graft is a swift action that does not provoke attacks of opportunity.

Effect: Each time you activate the graft, your hands grow white hot for 1 round. You generate so much heat that your mere touch deals 1d6 points of fire damage, and you set fire to any flammable objects your hands touch. (Your own clothing and gear are unaffected.) Your metallic weapons also conduct this heat, and while the graft is active, attacks with such weapons deal an extra 1d6 points of fire damage. If you drop the weapon or it is taken from you, the flames die immediately (although anyone taking the weapon from you takes 1d6 points of fire damage for doing so).

Construction: Requires Elemental Grafter, *flame blade* spell, 6,500 gp, 520 XP, 13 days.

Graft Donor: A piece of the body of a fire elemental.

Graft Sacrifice: 4 hp.

Variants: A number of Power of Purity spellcasters (see page 34) have recently undertaken attempts to construct similar grafts for other energy types. While they have yet to show any results (for some reason, fire seems easier to harness for this graft), similar grafts that deal other types of energy damage—acid, electricity, or cold—are probably not far off.

Price: 13,000 gp.

Incendiary Skin [Fire]

The essence of a fire elemental lives beneath your skin, injuring those who touch you while simultaneously granting you resistance to fire.

Graft Location: Skin.

Description: Your skin has a ruddy cast, and is warmer to the touch than normal. Up close, rivers of fire seem to course just beneath its surface, and it appears nearly luminescent when you are excited.

When you are angry, your skin blazes white-hot and gives off the faint odor of charred wood.

Activation: You can activate your incendiary skin's blazing effect as an immediate action. If activated in response to an attack, its effect applies to that attack as well as any other attacks made against you while the effect lasts.

The resistance to fire granted by this graft is always active. Using it requires no action on your part.

Effect: Your incendiary skin gives you resistance to fire 5. When you activate your skin's blazing effect, you become dangerously hot to the touch until the start of your next turn. Anyone striking you with a natural weapon or unarmed strike while your incendiary skin blazes takes 1d6 points of fire damage (Reflex negates; DC 10 + 1/2 your HD + your Con modifier). Your own clothing and gear are unaffected, but activating this effect is physically draining, and you take 1 point of damage each time you do so.

Construction: Requires Elemental Grafter, *fire shield* and *resist energy* spells, 8,500 gp, 680 XP, 17 days.

Graft Donor: Any portion of a fire elemental.

Graft Sacrifice: 4 hp.

Price: 17,000 gp.

Oceanic Adaptation [Water]

You graft elemental water to your arms, granting you the ability to move as freely in water as on land.

    Graft Location: Arms.

    Description: Two long patches of bright blue flesh have been grown along your arms. The patches always look wet, and are the brilliant hue of the water of a tropical reef.

    When actually immersed in water, the patches shimmer like quicksilver.

    Activation: The graft functions automatically while you are underwater. Using it requires no action on your part.

    Effect: You can move about in water as if under the effect of a *freedom of movement* spell (see Table 3–22: Combat Adjustments Underwater, page 92 of the *Dungeon Master's Guide*). Even moving through standing water (such as a shallow river or deep bog) does not affect your movement.

    You also gain a +2 bonus on weapon damage rolls if both you and your opponent are immersed in (not just touching) water at least 1 foot deep.

    Construction: Requires Elemental Grafter, *freedom of movement* spell, 4,000 gp, 320 XP, 8 days.

    Graft Donor: A piece of the body of a water elemental.

    Graft Sacrifice: 4 hp.

    Price: 8,000 gp.

Scorching Gaze [Fire]

Your eyes burn with the fire of your elemental graft donor. You can start flames crackling with a mere glance, and scorch your foes.

    Graft Location: Head.

    Description: Your eyes smolder with fire, which seems to lick up from your eye sockets toward your brow. The flames grow fiercer when you become angry.

    Your gaze can start fires, and you are surrounded by the faint smell of ash and coal. Some might assume you to have fiendish blood, but a fire elemental was the source of your gift.

    Activation: You can suppress or resume the effect of your gaze as a free action. Directing your gaze at a creature is a standard action. Focusing your gaze on an object to set it on fire is a full-round action.

    Effect: Your eyes give you a gaze attack that functions as described on page 309 of the *Monster Manual*. Your gaze has a range of 30 feet and deals 1d6 points of fire damage. A successful Fortitude save negates the damage (DC 10 + 1/2 your HD + your Con modifier).

    As a full-round action, you can direct your gaze upon a combustible item within 30 feet to set it on fire. Attended or magic items you focus on can attempt a DC 15 Reflex save to avoid being set ablaze. Items set on fire take 1d6 points of fire damage per round.

    Unfortunately, your fiery gaze makes you slightly less observant than normal, and you take a −2 penalty on Search and Spot checks.

    Construction: Requires Elemental Grafter, *scorching ray* spell, 3,500 gp, 280 XP, 7 days.

    Graft Donor: The eyes of a fire elemental.

    Graft Sacrifice: 4 hp, −2 penalty on Search and Spot checks.

    Price: 7,000 gp.

Stony Plating [Earth]

Your skin becomes hardened like an earth elemental's. Stony hide has been fused to key areas of your body, giving you greater protection against physical damage.

    Graft Location: Skin.

    Description: Portions of your skin have a rocky, craggy appearance, such that you look like you are partially formed of rock. Your skin pigmentation is slightly darker then normal—the color of rich earth—at these rough spots. The normal skin on your body merges seamlessly with the graft.

    The aroma of freshly turned earth surrounds you whenever you are struck in battle.

    Activation: Stony plating is always active once the graft is installed. Using it requires no action on your part.

    Effect: Your natural armor bonus to AC improves by 1. Creatures without natural armor have an effective natural armor bonus of +0. Because the graft improves your natural armor, effects that provide an enhancement bonus to natural armor (such as a *barkskin* spell) stack with stony plating.

    Construction: Requires Elemental Grafter, *stoneskin* spell, 1,400 gp, 112 XP, 3 days.

    Graft Donor: A piece of stone from the body of an earth elemental of at least Large size.

    Graft Sacrifice: 4 hp.

    Price: 2,800 gp.

Tremor Graft [Earth]

This graft grants you a connection with the earth, allowing you to feel the tread of those who pass near you. You can sense others through their steps, and you know the exact location of creatures near you even if you can't see them.

    Graft Location: Legs.

    Description: This graft is grown along the sides of your lower torso and down your legs. This skin is the color of slate and rough to the touch, like coarse sand.

    The skin along your sides seems to hum slightly, and even the smallest movements along the ground within the range of your ability is detected by the graft and transmitted to you.

    Activation: The graft requires a move action to activate. Its effect is instantaneous.

    Effect: As long as you are touching the ground, you can take a move action to activate your graft, sensing the number and location of all creatures within 20 feet. You know the exact location of creatures within range when you activate this ability, but unless you can also see them, this knowledge can quickly become moot as those creatures move.

    Your bulky legs make your movement slower and more ponderous. As a result, your land speed decreases by 5 feet.

    Construction: Requires Elemental Grafter, *meld into stone* spell, 3,000 gp, 240 XP, 6 days.

    Graft Donor: A piece of the body of an earth elemental.

    Graft Sacrifice: 2 hp, −5-ft. penalty to land speed.

    Price: 6,000 gp.

Whirlwind Form [Air]

You can wreathe yourself in a whirlwind, allowing you to move through the air with great ease.

    Graft Location: Skin.

    Description: Your body courses with pale blue vein-like structures that seem to move beneath the surface of your skin.

When the graft is activated, your entire body is wreathed in a churning whirlwind. You can race across the land at great speed, leaving a plume of dust in your wake.

Activation: Activating or deactivating the graft is a standard action.

Effect: When the graft is activated, a swirling vortex of air forms around you, allowing you to fly with the faultless control of an air elemental. While the graft is active, you gain a fly speed of 20 feet with perfect maneuverability.

However, the wind around you reduces your visibility and hearing, and you take a −4 penalty on Listen, Search, and Spot checks. The noise of the wind also makes stealth difficult, and you take a −4 penalty on your Hide and Move Silently checks.

This graft also puts a strain on your health, resulting in a permanent −2 penalty to your Constitution score.

The graft does not function underwater.

Construction: Requires Elemental Grafter, *overland flight* spell, 29,000 gp, 2,320 XP, 58 days.

Graft Donor: Any portion of an air elemental taken while it was in whirlwind form.

Graft Sacrifice: −2 Con.

Price: 58,000 gp.

PLANT GRAFTS

The druids of the Eldeen Reaches (specifically the Wardens of the Wood and the Gatekeepers) engaged in the research of grafts independently of similar efforts elsewhere. The Gatekeepers established grafts focused on protection, hoping to grow closer to the natural world by allowing plant flesh to merge with their own, even as they sought to become better guardians against the horrors of the Dragon Below.

Unlike the Zil, the Gatekeepers will adamantly deny any similarity between their natural plant grafts and the abominations of the hated daelkyr, pointing out that their grafts are given willingly by their allies of the land. Some Wardens of the Wood view plant grafts as an expression of utter sacrifice to the power of nature, and grafts among druids of that group have grown much more common over time.

Plant grafts follow the same general rules for grafts described on page 126. Adding plant grafts requires access to a character with the Eldeen Plantgrafter feat (see page 47).

A character with at least two plant grafts gains a bonus on Will saves against mind-affecting effects equal to the number of plant grafts he has.

Healing Nodules

Nodules of a curative fungus sprout from your body. These nodules can be broken off and consumed by you or other creatures, healing wounds or providing other benefits.

Graft Location: Skin.

Description: With the exception of your face, your skin grows small, lumpy nodules of fungus wherever it is exposed to the air. These nodules are slightly darker than your natural skin tone, and are rough and craggy.

The nodules can be broken off and consumed without dealing you damage. They taste much like fresh mushrooms and smell of dark, nourishing soil.

Activation: Breaking off a healing nodule is a move action, while consuming one is a standard action (much like drinking a potion). Only one nodule per hour carries curative abilities, because it takes time for your graft to charge a new nodule between uses. You can also use the *remove disease* effect once per day, but doing so means you cannot produce normal curative nodules for 24 hours.

Effect: The nodules that grow from your flesh have remarkable curative powers. Any creature that consumes one gains the benefit of a *cure serious wounds* spell, with a caster level equal to your character level, whichever is higher. In addition, once per day you can select a nodule to act as a *potion of remove disease*, but no curative nodules can be grown for 24 hours afterward.

Unfortunately, the energy required to power the nodules represents a drain on your physical resilience. You take a −2 penalty on Fortitude saves.

Construction: Requires Eldeen Plantgrafter, *cure serious wounds* and *remove disease* spells, 10,500 gp, 840 XP, 21 days.

Graft Donor: A piece of oak from a dryad's tree and a mushroom from a fairy ring.

Graft Sacrifice: 6 hp, −2 penalty on Fortitude saves.

Price: 21,000 gp.

Darkwood Flesh

This graft strengthens your flesh like darkwood. You can ignore blows that would cripple lesser creatures, and you can draw on the essence of darkwood to heal yourself.

Graft Location: Flesh.

Description: When the graft is implanted, your flesh tone grows significantly darker, taking on a faint barklike texture.

When a critical hit or sneak attack is negated by your darkwood flesh, your flesh grows momentarily more dense and woody, almost like the flesh of a darkwood tree. When your fast healing is active, the wound that activated the fast healing exudes a small quantity of sticky green sap.

Activation: The fortification provided by your darkwood flesh is always active once the graft is installed. Using it requires no action on your part. The fast healing effect activates automatically when a critical hit or sneak attack is scored against you.

Effect: Because your flesh is partially darkwood, you gain the ability to ignore some critical hits or sneak attacks. Whenever a successful sneak attack is made against you, or whenever a critical hit is confirmed, you have a 25% chance to ignore the extra damage dealt (though you still take the normal damage dealt by those attacks).

If you are struck by a critical hit or sneak attack that is not negated by your darkwood flesh, the graft immediately activates fast healing 3 for a number of rounds equal to one-third the damage dealt by the attack (minimum 1 round). Multiple automatic activations of this ability stack (for example, if you are struck by two critical hits, you gain fast healing 6 for the combined duration determined by the damage of the two blows).

Unfortunately, while darkwood is lighter and stronger than other types of wood, the graft still limits your agility. You take a permanent −2 penalty to your Dexterity score.

Construction: Requires Eldeen Plantgrafter, *cure serious wounds* and *plant growth* spells, 9,500 gp, 760 XP, 19 days.

Graft Donor: The heart of a living darkwood tree.

Graft Sacrifice: 4 hp, −2 Dexterity.

Price: 19,000 gp.

Fatigue Spores

A growth of spore-producing fungus is grafted to your skin. When you wish, you can cause a cloud of spores to spread from your body, causing those nearby to become fatigued.

Graft Location: Skin.

Description: Your skin, especially that of your torso, neck, and thighs, is covered in a dark green, flaky fungus. To those unfamiliar with grafts, you probably appear to be a victim of some terrible wasting disease.

You carry a faintly earthy smell, and the fungus on your body has a soft texture similar to the underside of a mushroom. However, no spores release from the fungus unless you will them to do so.

Activation: You can activate your fatigue spores once per minute as a swift action.

Effect: When you activate the graft, toxic spores spread from your body in a dark green cloud. All living creatures adjacent to you must succeed on a Fortitude save (DC 10 + 1/2 your HD + your Con modifier) or become fatigued (see page 301 of the *Dungeon Master's Guide*). A target that successfully saves against your spores cannot be affected again for 24 hours.

The effects of one individual's fatigue spores are not cumulative (so that a creature that fails to save against your spores twice does not become exhausted). However, a creature that fails a save against your spores, then fails a save against the spores of another creature does become exhausted. Immunity or resistance to poison applies against the effect of the fatigue spores.

Construction: Requires Eldeen Plantgrafter, *touch of fatigue* spell, 6,000 gp, 480 XP, 12 days.

Graft Donor: A piece of fungus grown on the body of a living treant.

Graft Sacrifice: 4 hp.

Variants: Rumors exist of other fungal spore grafts that grant their bearers all manner of effects, including those that corrode the flesh of nearby foes or send them into a deep slumber. The fatigue spores remain the most common variety among both the Wardens of the Wood and the Gatekeepers.

Price: 12,000 gp.

Grappling Vine

You can launch a thick, sticky vine from either arm, using it to ensnare your foes.

Graft Location: Arms.

Description: Your arms appear slightly swollen, especially below the elbow. Green lines reminiscent of veins are visible beneath your skin, and a puckered opening along the front of your wrist allows you to launch the living vine within you at one of your enemies.

The sticky green vine that emerges from your arm is about 2 inches in diameter. Though the vine is tough and woody, long veins run along its length, making it look more like flesh than plant.

Activation: Activating the grappling vine is a standard action that does not provoke attacks of opportunity.

Effect: You can launch a thick, sticky vine from your arm in an attempt to grapple an opponent. Doing this requires a ranged touch attack (the vine has a reach of 10 feet). If you hit, you deal no damage but can attempt to start a grapple as a free action (as if you had the improved

grab ability; see page 310 of the *Monster Manual*). The vine uses your own grapple modifier and is treated as if it had the Improved Grapple feat (+4 bonus on grapple checks). Success establishes a hold, pulls the target creature into your space, and deals constrict damage (see below). You can only grapple creatures of your size category or lower with the grappling vine.

The vine's constrict ability (see page 307 of the *Monster Manual*) allows you to deal 1d6 points of damage plus your Strength modifier each time you succeed on a grapple check during successive rounds.

If the ranged touch attack misses, or if the grapple ends, the vine automatically retracts into your arm. You can only use one vine at a time, though you can use a vine even if that hand already holds another object.

You can also use the vine to grab and reel in unattended objects within 10 feet. With a successful ranged touch attack, you latch the vine onto such an object and snap it back into your empty hand. Any object you target must be small enough to hold in one hand.

The vine isn't strong enough to support your weight, and thus you cannot hang from it or use it to help you climb.

An extended vine can be attacked as if it were a weapon. Each vine has hardness 5 and 20 hit points. A damaged vine heals entirely in 8 hours, while a severed vine regrows in one week. A *regenerate* spell regrows a severed vine immediately.

Construction: Requires Eldeen Plantgrafter, *entangle* and *plant growth* spells, 3,500 gp, 280 XP, 7 days.

Graft Donor: A living vine.

Graft Sacrifice: 4 hp.

Price: 7,000 gp.

Perception Seed

With this seed implanted in your eyes, you gain improved visual perception, and can perceive minute details even in shadowy conditions.

Graft Location: Head.

Description: This green seed is long and thin, with a tracery of faint black lines along its length. Once it has been grafted, the pupil of your eye takes on the same leaf-green hue, the color penetrating into the surrounding white like spreading plant roots.

The graft is painful to implant, but the pain is brief. When grafted, the seed binds to your optic nerve. Your vision sharpens immediately, and you can see what you couldn't before. The entire world seems more focused and acute.

Activation: The heightened senses granted by the perception seed are always active once the graft is installed. Using it requires no action on your part.

Effect: You gain low-light vision, as well as a +2 competence bonus on Spot and Search checks due to your sharpened sight. If you already have low-light vision from another source, the range of your low-light vision improves to triple normal human visual range in conditions of low light.

Construction: Requires Eldeen Plantgrafter, *owl's wisdom* spell, 2,000 gp, 160 XP, 4 days.

Graft Donor: A seed from an *awakened* tree.

Graft Sacrifice: 2 hp.

Price: 4,000 gp.

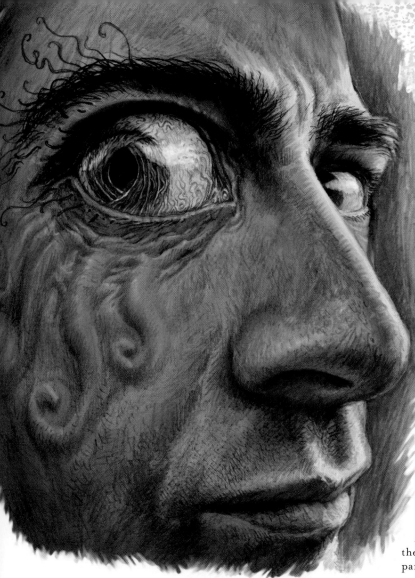

A perception seed grants superior vision and senses

Rootlegs

You can sink roots into the earth, drawing on the strength of the forest to keep yourself stable. While rooted, you can move only very slowly, but you gain the strength and hardiness of mighty old-growth trees.

Graft Location: Legs.

Description: Thick roots hide in your legs, which become swollen and dark brown once this graft is implanted. When you wish them to emerge, they do so, rooting you firmly to the earth beneath you.

While rooted, your feet seem to blend in with the ground, even if encased in boots. Your lower legs look like the massive roots of an ancient oak tree. When you take steps (which is difficult) your feet seem to have been replaced by intricate root structures that delve deep into the ground.

Activation: Activating the graft is an immediate action that does not provoke attacks of opportunity. You can use this graft a number of times per day equal to 3 + your Constitution modifier (minimum once per day). Deactivating the graft is a swift action.

Effect: When you activate this graft, thick roots grow from your feet and hold you to the ground until the end of your next turn. Your speed drops to 5 feet (and you cannot take a 5-foot step). However, you gain a +8 bonus on checks

and saves to resist being moved in any way, including bull rush, trip, or grapple attempts that would move you from your current square.

You cannot activate this graft if you aren't standing on a solid surface. If you are standing on earth (as opposed to stone or another surface) when the graft is activated, you also gain fast healing 3 for 1 round.

In addition to the physical drain on your health, the thick roots grafted to your legs render you less mobile, resulting in a permanent −2 penalty to your Dexterity score. You also have difficulty with some physical activities, taking a −2 penalty on Climb and Jump checks.

Construction: Requires Eldeen Plantgrafter, *liveoak* spell, 3,500 gp, 280 XP, 7 days.

Graft Donor: The living root of a five-hundred-year-old oak.

Graft Sacrifice: 4 hp, −2 penalty to Dexterity, −2 penalty on Climb and Jump checks.

Price: 7,000 gp.

Treebark Carapace

Your skin becomes hardened like that of a tree. The tough flesh of a living plant has been fused to key areas of your body, giving you greater protection against physical damage.

Graft Location: Skin.

Description: Your skin has a rough, barklike appearance where the graft has been applied. Its texture is rough and craggy where the graft merges seamlessly with it, and the aroma of wood faintly surrounds you.

Activation: Your treebark carapace is always active once the graft is installed. Using it requires no action on your part.

Effect: When the treebark carapace is implanted, your natural armor bonus to AC improves by 1. Creatures without natural armor have an effective natural armor bonus of +0. Because the graft improves your natural armor, effects that provide an enhancement bonus to your natural armor (such as a *barkskin* spell) stack with the treebark carapace.

This graft also grants you a limited ability to resist having your form altered. You gain a +4 bonus on saves against polymorph effects.

Construction: Requires Eldeen Plantgrafter, *barkskin* and *plant growth* spells, 1,600 gp, 128 XP, 4 days.

Graft Donor: A piece of bark from a living tree.

Graft Sacrifice: 4 hp.

Price: 3,200 gp.

ADDITIONAL GOODS AND SERVICES

To augment the standard items and services described in Chapter 7 of the *Player's Handbook* and Chapter 6 of the EBERRON *Campaign Setting*, this section introduces a number of new weapons, goods, and services specific to an EBERRON campaign.

WEAPONS

House Cannith has many interests. Though its Fabricators Guild is known for great works of craft, artifice, and magic, the guild is divided into dozens of specialties,

WEAPONS

Exotic Weapons	Cost	Dmg (S)	Dmg (M)	Critical	Increment	Range Weight[1]	Type
Light Melee Weapons							
Alchemy blade	310 gp	1d4	1d6	19–20/×2	—	2 lb.	Piercing
One-Handed Melee Weapons							
Spear spikard	200 gp	1d4[2]	1d6[2]	×2	20 ft.[3]	3 lb.	Piercing
Bolts, spikard[4] (10)	1 gp	—	—	—	—	1 lb.	—
Two-Handed Melee Weapons							
War spikard	350 gp	1d6[2]	1d8[2]	×2	—	9 lb.	Bludgeoning and piercing[2]
Bolts, spikard[4] (10)	1 gp	—	—	—	—	1 lb.	—

1 Weight figures are for Medium weapons. A Small weapon weighs half as much, and a Large weapon weighs twice as much.
2 Weapon deals additional piercing damage when loaded (see weapon description).
3 Though a spear spikard can be thrown as a shortspear, it deals its additional damage only on melee attacks.
4 Crossbow bolts and spikard bolts are functionally equivalent and can be used interchangeably.

including alchemists, architects, elemental binders, and armorers. Recently, one fabricator division branched into the forging of specialty weapons, developing a new class of spikard weapons (two of which are described below) that are quickly growing in popularity.

In addition, as part of their continued research and development of new arms technology, the Fabricators Guild has produced a few prototype weapons that have been seeing limited use in the hands of soldiers and adventurers alike. One of these is the alchemy blade, a sword that combines weaponsmithing with alchemical power for explosive results.

Alchemy Blade: An alchemy blade appears much like a normal short sword. Two slender channels form a groove on each side of the blade, and the pommel is built to accept a flask of either alchemist's fire or alchemist's frost. (It could also accept a flask of acidic fire or alchemist's spark, but a single use of either of these would render the weapon useless.)

When a flask of alchemist's fire or alchemist's frost is plugged into the pommel, the weapon is primed. When you strike a target with a primed blade and deal damage, an internal alchemical pump instantly expels the fire or frost through hollows in the hilt and out along the channels in the blade. In addition to taking any damage dealt by the blade, the target also takes damage as if it had been struck by the flask attached to the weapon. Adjacent creatures, including the wielder, are not subject to splash damage. If the blade deals critical damage, the frost or fire damage is not multiplied.

War spikard

Alchemy blade

Spear spikard

Priming an alchemy blade is a standard action that provokes attacks of opportunity. When not primed, the alchemy blade deals damage as a short sword.

Creating an alchemy blade requires a DC 20 Craft (alchemy) check in addition to the normal Craft (weaponsmithing) checks required to make a weapon. Characters who take Exotic Weapon Proficiency (alchemy blade) can treat the alchemy blade as a short sword for the purpose of any feat or ability that affects the character's ability to use a short sword (such as Weapon Focus [short sword]).

Spear Spikard: A spear spikard resembles a thicker-than-normal shortspear. In fact, it can be wielded as if it were a shortspear even by a character who is not proficient with the spear spikard, though such a character cannot access the weapon's significant added function.

A spear spikard is actually a hollow weapon capable of delivering a bolt as part of a melee strike. Along the rear third of the shaft is a miniature spring-driven firing mechanism, as well as a channel into which a bolt can be loaded.

Loading a spear spikard is equivalent to loading a light crossbow (a move action that provokes attacks of opportunity). A character with Rapid Reload (light crossbow) can reload a spear spikard as a free action, though this still provokes attacks of opportunity.

A spear spikard cannot fire bolts at range or when the weapon is thrown—instead, it discharges a bolt in conjunction with a successful melee attack. If you have the Exotic Weapon Proficiency (spear spikard) feat, any time you hit a foe in melee with a loaded spear spikard, the mechanism automatically triggers, discharging the bolt directly into the target of the attack. The target takes piercing damage equal to the base damage of the weapon (1d4 points of damage for a Small spear spikard or 1d6 points of damage for a Medium spear spikard) in addition to the damage dealt by the initial attack. No additional attack roll is required. This extra damage is not multiplied as part of a critical hit.

Creating a spear spikard requires a DC 20 Craft (weaponsmithing) check.

Characters who take Exotic Weapon Proficiency (spear spikard) can treat the spear spikard as a shortspear for the purpose of any feat or ability that affects the character's ability to use a shortspear (such as Weapon Focus [shortspear]).

War Spikard: A war spikard is similar in principle to the spear spikard, but its crossbow mechanism is melded smoothly into a weapon that resembles an oversized warhammer. The war spikard's hammerhead is a mostly solid cylinder pierced with a small channel through which the bolt is discharged. The spring-driven firing mechanism is built into the rear half of the hammerhead, and is loaded through a channel similar to the one on the striking surface of the weapon.

Loading a war spikard is the equivalent of loading a light crossbow (a move action that provokes attacks of opportunity). A character with Rapid Reload (light crossbow) can reload a war spikard as a free action, though this still provokes attacks of opportunity.

Like the spear spikard, the war spikard can't fire bolts as a ranged attack. If you have the Exotic Weapon Proficiency

(war spikard) feat, any time you hit a foe in melee with a loaded war spikard, the mechanism automatically triggers, discharging the bolt directly into the target of the attack. The target takes piercing damage equal to the base damage of the weapon (1d6 points of damage for a Small war spikard or 1d8 points of damage for a Medium war spikard) in addition to the damage dealt by the initial attack. No additional attack roll is required. This extra damage is not multiplied as part of a critical hit.

Creating a war spikard requires a DC 20 Craft (weaponsmithing) check.

Despite the similarity in appearance, the war spikard is not close enough in size and heft to a typical warhammer for a character to benefit from feats or abilities that affect the use of that weapon.

ARMOR

The dwarf crafters of the Mror Holds are capable of forging unique alchemical armor whose components and formulation are all jealously guarded secrets. Impact armor is one of these creations—armor that stiffens temporarily when struck so as to protect its wearer from harm.

Impact Armor

Impact armor appears as normal armor of its type (studded leather, chainmail, or half-plate), except that the metallic parts of the armor are composed of a special impact-sensitive alloy that has a faint lavender sheen.

Studded impact armor

Half-plate impact armor

Chain impact armor

Armor	Cost	Armor Bonus	Maximum Dex Bonus	Armor Check Penalty	—Speed— 30 ft.	20 ft.	Weight[1]
Light Armor							
Studded impact	765 gp	+3	+5	−1	30 ft.	20 ft.	20 lb.
Medium Armor							
Chain impact	1,290 gp	+5	+2	−5	30 ft.	15 ft.	40 lb.
Heavy Armor							
Half-plate impact	2,450 gp	+7	+0	−7	20 ft.[2]	15 ft.[2]	50 lb.

1 Weight figures are for armor sized to fit Medium characters. Armor fitted for Small characters weighs half as much, and armor fitted for Large characters weighs twice as much.

2 When running in heavy armor, you move only triple your speed, not quadruple.

When a wearer of studded armor is dealt any type of damage by a weapon attack, the armor instantly stiffens, then becomes pliable again a few seconds later. The wearer gains some amount of damage reduction against piercing attacks (including against the attack that triggered the effect); however, the wearer's base speed (in all categories) drops to 10 feet until the end of his next turn. Heavier types of impact armor offer more damage reduction. See the individual armor entries that follow for details.

Multiple hits in a round do not further increase the damage reduction or further decrease the character's speed.

Creating impact armor requires a DC 25 Craft (alchemy) check in addition to the normal Craft (armor-smithing) checks required to make armor.

Impact, Studded: The metallic studs of studded impact armor are composed of the special impact-sensitive alloy.

A wearer of studded impact armor gains damage reduction 1/piercing.

Impact, Chain: The metallic chain links of chain impact armor are composed of the special impact-sensitive alloy.

A wearer of chain impact armor gains damage reduction 2/piercing.

Impact, Half-Plate: The metallic strips of half-plate impact armor are composed of the special impact-sensitive alloy.

A wearer of half-plate impact armor gains damage reduction 3/piercing.

CLOTHING

In addition to the standard garb found in Chapter 7 of the *Player's Handbook* and the new types of fabric detailed in Chapter 6 of the EBERRON *Campaign Setting*, the following fabrics can enhance mundane clothing.

Chameleoweave: Chameleoweave fabric is woven from strands of the famed mimetic plants found growing along the margins of the Mournland. It is difficult to pin down the exact color and texture of the cloth, since it tends to take on the characteristics of other fabric with which it is worn. A character wearing chameleoweave clothing gains a +1 circumstance bonus on Disguise checks. Chameleoweave clothing costs 100 gp more than a normal outfit of the same sort, and weighs 1 pound less (or 1/4 pound less for Small characters).

Dolweave: Dolweave is a coarse, sickly fabric that is rumored to be woven with occasional hairs collected from dolgrims, dolgaunts, and other corruptions. The color and texture of dolweave seems to darken and pulse threateningly in time to its wearer's most violent emotions. A character wearing dolweave gains a +1 circumstance bonus on Intimidate checks. Dolweave clothing costs 150 gp more than a normal outfit of the same sort, and weighs 1 pound more (or 1/4 pound more for Small characters).

SPECIAL SUBSTANCES

The alchemists of Eberron produce a steady supple of innovations with effects derived not from magic, but from an applied philosophy of experimentation, observation, and theorization.

Bloodspike: A bloodspike somewhat resembles a thin potion vial, narrowing to a needlelike point at one end. The interior of the slender tube is filled with one of several varieties of alchemical substance (see below). To use a bloodspike, a user jabs it directly into her flesh (the fleshy part of the arm is an ideal location). Doing this deals 1 point of piercing damage (damage reduction does not apply when using a bloodspike) and causes the fluid in the narrow vial to be absorbed directly into the user's body.

Alternatively, a bloodspike can be thrown as a ranged weapon with a range increment of 5 feet. The bloodspike deals 1 point of piercing damage if used in this way, with the target subject to the effects of the bloodspike's contents on a successful hit. (Since most bloodspikes provide a beneficial effect, an adventurer will typically throw a bloodspike at an ally to grant him its benefits in a combat situation.) No proficiency is required to use a bloodspike in this way.

Regardless of the method of delivery, using a bloodspike is a standard action that provokes attacks of opportunity. The effects of multiple doses of a bloodspike's alchemical contents do not stack. Constructs, elementals, oozes, plants, and undead are unaffected by bloodspikes.

Defiling: A defiling bloodspike is filled with a degenerative alchemical mixture. Unlike other bloodspikes, defiling bloodspikes are used only against an enemy. If a defiling bloodspike deals damage to a creature, the tainted mixture is absorbed into its blood, causing the target to be nauseated for 1 round (Fortitude DC 12 negates).

Glowbug: A glowbug bloodspike interlaces your blood with an alchemical substance that reacts by emitting a luminous radiance. For 1 hour after a bloodspike is used, this radiance leaks from every inch of your skin. So long as some part of your body is exposed (hands, arms, head, and so on), the effects of the bloodspike provide bright light to a radius of 10 feet and shadowy illumination out to 20 feet.

At any time the effect is active, you can exhaust the remaining illumination as a swift action, causing your skin to flare once before guttering out. This flash dazzles all creatures within 30 feet for 1 minute (Fortitude DC 11 negates). This flash attack ends the bloodspike's effects.

Spatter: The spatter bloodspike interlaces your blood with an alchemical substance that temporarily acidifies your spittle. For 1 hour after the bloodspike is used, your bite attack deals an extra 1 point of acid damage.

At any time the effect is active, you can spit acid at a creature in an adjacent square as a free action (resolve as a ranged touch attack that does not provoke attacks of opportunity). If the acid spittle successfully strikes the target, the creature takes 1d6 points of acid damage. This spit attack ends the bloodspike's effects.

Tempo: The tempo bloodspike interlaces your blood with an alchemical substance that grants you a secret reservoir of energy. At any time in the hour after the bloodspike is used, you can draw upon this energy to take one additional move action on your turn (either before or after your other actions). If not used within 1 hour, the alchemical substance fades from your blood and is lost.

Thickener: A thickener bloodspike interlaces your blood with an alchemical substance that helps stem blood flow should you take damage. For 1 hour after the bloodspike is used, any weapon damage dealt to you is reduced by 1 point, to a minimum of 1 hp (if you take just 1 point of damage, the thickener has no effect).

DOCUMENTS

The countries of Khorvaire, especially the prosperous nations of the central region, are especially fond of documentation. From identification to credit, grants of passage and indulgences of activity, proper records can be more valuable than gold in Khorvaire.

Indulgence: If one carries identification papers that have standing in Aundair, Breland, Karrnath, Thrane, Zilargo, or the Mror Holds, then one might also qualify to purchase that most golden of documents—an indulgence. One of these documents is supposedly good for the pardon of punishment that any one of those nations might otherwise levy against the trespasser. It is not absolution from the crime, but rather a promise not to prosecute if the purchaser of the indulgence takes on some mission or other penance for the wronged nation instead. Usually, an indulgence can only be purchased within the nation in which the offense was committed, and then only by someone of high enough class and wealth to know of and be able to afford the indulgence.

For example, an indulgence might be purchased by a group that burned a warehouse, destroyed a public house, or even murdered a government official (depending on who died and under what circumstances). In return for the cost of the indulgence (a sum that always begins with at least the base amount noted on the Goods and Services table, but which can climb depending on the offense), the

Dolweave cloak

Chameleoweave outfit

MT

Bloodspikes

perpetrators are not immediately prosecuted. Instead, they are given the opportunity to clear their names through service—a mission to drive pirates from a shipping lane, an expedition to reopen a mine that has become fouled with wights, or some other necessary (and likely dangerous) undertaking determined by the state. If the service is performed adequately, then the governing body that issued the indulgence will confirm it, and no further legal remedies against the holder of the indulgence will be pursued.

Lenience: A lenience is somewhat related to an indulgence, but is much narrower in scope and must be purchased ahead of time. When a lenience is purchased, the buyer receives both the proper documentation and a dated banner that indicates how long the lenience is good for (measured in days). The banner is meant to be displayed on a carriage, ship, skyship, or other form of conveyance. Once affixed (and while the dates are good), that conveyance can proceed at any speed without regard to caution, laws of reasonable speed, rights normally accorded to those in a queue, and so on.

The banner is a sign to others that the conveyance in question is likely to make sudden turns and unsafe maneuvers, and that it is their responsibility to get out of the way. Usually only so many leniencies are granted in the same area during any particular time period, which cuts down the chance for two conveyances both traveling with leniencies to encounter each other.

GOODS AND SERVICES

Clothing

Item	Cost	Weight
Clothing, chameleoweave	+100 gp	See text
Clothing, dolweave	+150 gp	See text

Special Substances

Item	Cost	Weight
Bloodspike (defiling)	150 gp	—
Bloodspike (glowbug)	50 gp	—
Bloodspike (spatter)	50 gp	—
Bloodspike (tempo)	150 gp	—
Bloodspike (thickener)	100 gp	—

Documents

Item	Cost	Weight
Indulgence	1,000 gp	—
Lenience	250 gp	—

NEW SPECIAL MATERIALS

The secrets of earth, ore, and power are sometimes frozen into the substance of existence itself. For those with the proper lore and understanding, these secrets can become manifest in arms and armor of subtle quality and unique ability.

Calomel: Calomel is a hard white ore that is most often found and quarried in Argonnessen, at great expense and danger. Calomel was famously utilized by the famous adventurer Arthul Vernuthan prior to his single combat against the power-mad red dragon Xarkapastarthan. Secretly mined, refined, and forged into a blade of slender gray death, the ore's special attributes carried Arthul to victory, but his defeat of Xarkapastarthan embittered other dragons of the region, who decried

Arthul as an opponent of the draconic Prophecy itself. Presumably Arthul was slain, and his blade lost. However, knowledge of calomel, where to mine it, and how to refine it still persists.

Raw calomel ore is distinctive in its whiteness. It can be almost translucent, and is lustrous in bright light. It is always found adjacent to subterranean springs. When forged in the appropriate secret fashion, the resultant metal cools to a consistency and ductility like that of a standard steel alloy. Though any item can be crafted from it, calomel's particular qualities make it most suitable for weapons.

A weapon forged from calomel is pale gray, almost translucent, and water droplets constantly condense on the naked item. A calomel weapon overcomes damage reduction of creatures with the fire subtype as if it were a magic weapon, even if it does not have an enhancement bonus. For example, a mundane calomel blade wielded against a mature adult red dragon (fire subtype) would overcome that creature's damage reduction 10/magic as if it were a magic weapon.

Weapons made of calomel cost twice as much as their normal counterparts. For example, a longsword made of calomel would cost 30 gp. Items without metal parts cannot be made from calomel (so that an arrow could be made of calomel, but a quarterstaff could not). A double weapon with only one half made of calomel increases its cost by 50%. For example, a two-bladed sword with one blade of calomel and the other of steel would cost 150 gp. Calomel has hardness 10 and 30 hit points per inch of thickness.

Mournlode, Purple: Mined only in the Mournland in and under the Field of Ruins, mournlode is something of a rarity, and considered by many churches to be an ideal tool for combating undead manifestations. When mined, this iron ore has a mottled purple color, resembling some awful blight. When it is refined, it takes on a more vibrant silvery hue, streaked with veins of purple. In fact, various grades of mournlode exist, each with a slightly different appearance. To date, purple mournlode is by far the most well known (to the point where it is often referred to simply as "mournlode").

Many people (including members of a number of good-aligned organizations) are confident that mournlode is touched with a protective presence, and they use it to make armor, holy symbols, weapons, and other implements. Mournlode has the same weight and other physical characteristics as iron (hardness 10, 30 hit points per inch of thickness), but displays special qualities depending on the type of item it is forged into.

A mournlode weapon overcomes the damage reduction of undead creatures as if it were crafted of either cold iron or alchemical silver, whichever is more appropriate.

Mournlode armor grants the wearer a +1 resistance bonus on saving throws against any spells, spell-like abilities, and supernatural abilities used by undead.

A character who uses a mournlode holy symbol to turn undead deals damage equal to her turning level to undead affected by the turning attempt. For example, a 9th-level paladin (effective turning level 6th) using a mournlode holy symbol would deal 6 points of damage to any undead creature she successfully turns.

A mournlode weapon or suit of armor costs an extra 700 gp. A mournlode holy symbol costs 400 gp. Items without metal parts cannot be made from mournlode.

The psiforged and the daelkyr halfblood entered the ruins, their uneasy truce still holding despite the fact that they both sought the same ancient relic. For a moment, neither appeared to notice the shadowy figure stalking them—but then . . .

Adolghast," the halfblood warned, spinning to meet the monster's charge. "Perhaps we should continue working together until after we find Ozrin's amulet. Then, if you want, we can fight it out to see who keeps it."

A fine plan," the psiforged said, thrusting his weapon at the monster. "I look forward to our battle. . . ."

CHAPTER SIX

CREATURES

The many creatures of Eberron vary in species, bloodline, form, and culture. New breeds of monster appear on a regular basis throughout the world, often due to deliberate or accidental magical experimentation.

Among most people of the Five Nations, symbionts (if known at all) are considered the domain of the sanity-defying daelkyr. However, daelkyr half-bloods, those who dare to become impure princes, and even the occasional random adventurer might discover that symbionts can be trained to serve if caught and tamed. This chapter presents seven new symbionts to add to those introduced in the EBERRON *Campaign Setting.*

Homunculi are the servants of artificers and wizards in Eberron, created to aid their masters in their magical labors. Homunculi are extensions of their creators, sharing the same alignment and basic nature. Three new types of homunculi, all with unique characteristics and abilities, are described in this chapter.

Finally, some creatures are simply evil. Nothing more than monsters, these creatures are good only for killing, and indeed must be put down to prevent their corruption from spreading. From undead spawned in the laboratories of Karrnath to new types of quori and their Inspired vessels, this chapter presents a host of new creatures capable of challenging any party of Eberron adventurers.

MONSTERS

Creatures that run rampant in nightmare are more than mere bad dreams in Eberron—they are physical threats that embody evil, corruption, and lies told too long and believed by too many. The monsters described in this chapter bedevil the pure and seek to overturn all that is good across Khorvaire.

DOLGHAST

Medium Aberration
Hit Dice: 6d8+6 (33 hp)
Initiative: +2
Speed: 30 ft. (6 squares)
Armor Class: 17 (+2 Dex, +5 natural), touch 12, flat-footed 15
Base Attack/Grapple: +4/+8
Attack: Claw +8 melee (1d6+4)
Full Attack: 2 claws +8 melee (1d6+4) and bite +3 melee (1d6+2)
Space/Reach: 5 ft./5 ft.
Special Attacks: Dissolution, stench

Special Qualities: Darkvision 60 ft., fast healing 5, half-dead, scent
Saves: Fort +3, Ref +6, Will +5
Abilities: Str 19, Dex 14, Con 13, Int 6, Wis 11, Cha 14
Skills: Listen +2, Spot +2, Survival +9
Feats: Alertness, Lightning Reflexes, Track
Environment: Underground
Organization: Solitary, band (2–5 plus 2–5 dolgrims), or company (2–5 plus 7–12 dolgaunts and 20–50 dolgrims)
Challenge Rating: 4
Treasure: Standard
Alignment: Usually lawful evil
Advancement: By character class
Level Adjustment: —

This humanoid is messily bisected by a division of boiling flesh running from the tip of its skull down its face, chest, and groin. It is as though one creature has been formed from two halves—one living and one dead. The line where the two meet churns with liquefying flesh, as unholy life constantly fights against necrosis, giving rise to a smell too ghastly to describe. The living half is hunched and emaciated, while the dead half is partially skeletal and rotted.

Dolghasts live agonizing half-lives

When the daelkyr emerged from Xoriat to conquer Eberron, they captured and transformed many races into corruptions of their former selves. Dolgaunts and dolgrims live on as examples of this, but though the daelkyr have fallen, their corruption continues (albeit more slowly). Dolghasts are bred from various degraded outsider specimens capable of quickly healing physical wounds—a synthesis of dead and living flesh stitched into a single insane whole. Though the animated dead flesh of a dolghast resembles an undead creature in many ways, these creatures are not undead, and they are not subject to turning.

Dolghasts live pain-filled lives filled with rage and sorrow at their constantly decaying forms. That rage is typically channeled into daelkyr service in the depths of Khyber, though dolghasts are sometimes sent on missions to the surface for other higher-ranking daelkyr servants.

Dolghasts speak Common and Undercommon.

Combat

While its living side is lithe and agile, hinting at its graceful extraplanar origins, a dolghast's dead side is ungainly and shuffling, giving the creature a lurching demeanor. Dolghasts have learned to live with their deformities, though, and can use their half-dead strength to great advantage. Dolghasts rarely use weapons or armor, though they are capable of doing so.

Dissolution (Ex): If a dolghast hits with both claw attacks, a living opponent must succeed on a DC 15 Fortitude save or its flesh begins to boil away. The target takes 1d4 points of Constitution damage and is stunned for 1 round. On a successful save, the target takes only 1 point of Constitution damage and is not stunned. The save DC is Charisma-based.

Stench (Ex): The fracture line bisecting a dolghast's living half from its dead half roils with rot and putrescence, as the dead half constantly seeks to overcome the living half's healing power. The stench is overwhelming, and living creatures within 10 feet must succeed on a DC 15 Fortitude save or be sickened for 1d6+4 minutes. A creature that successfully saves cannot be affected again by the same dolghast's stench for 24 hours. A *delay poison* or *neutralize poison* spell removes the effect from a sickened creature. Creatures with immunity to poison are unaffected, and creatures resistant to poison receive their normal bonus on their saving throws. The save DC is Charisma-based.

Half-Dead (Ex): Half-dead creatures are aberrations, in that they share some of the traits of both living and undead creatures (though they cannot be turned as undead). Half-dead creatures have the following traits (in addition to the normal aberration traits):

—Immunity to fatigue, exhaustion, poison, sleep effects, paralysis, stunning, disease, and death effects.

—50% chance to ignore the extra damage dealt by a critical hit or sneak attack.

—A half-dead creature can be healed by both negative energy (such as from an *inflict* spell) and positive energy (such as from a *cure* spell), but only if it successfully saves against the spell (using the spell's normal DC). If the save fails, the spell deals damage as if the half-dead creature were living (for *inflict* spells) or undead (for *cure* spells).

INSPIRED

The Inspired are specially bred humans who have willingly surrendered their bodies to quori spirits. The EBERRON *Campaign Setting* presents one sample Inspired (host to a tsucora quori spirit). Two more sample Inspired follow, using the quori spirits presented in this book.

All Inspired share the following traits.

Dual Spirit (Ex): The dual spirit of an Inspired grants several benefits, described below.

—Ability Scores: An Inspired adopts the mental ability scores (Intelligence, Wisdom, and Charisma) of the quori spirit, if they are higher than the human vessel's.

Bereft of its quori spirit, a human vessel's skill modifiers change as indicated for each Inspired, below.

—Dual Mind: An Inspired can reroll any failed save against a mind-affecting spell or ability. If the reroll save also fails, the Inspired suffers the effects normally.

—Profane Gift: An Inspired has a +4 profane bonus to Charisma.

—Quori Abilities: An Inspired gains full use of all the quori's psi-like abilities and spell-like abilities (but not its extraordinary or supernatural abilities).

—Reduced Sleep: An Inspired only needs 4 hours of sleep per day, during which time the quori spirit returns to its body on Dal Quor.

—Resist Exorcism: The quori spirit inhabiting an Inspired is subject to a *dismissal* spell, an exorcism, or a similar effect. Use the total of the human vessel's character level and the quori's Hit Dice for the purpose of determining whether the spirit resists dismissal or exorcism. If the effect is successful, the quori spirit is temporarily driven back to Dal Quor. This effect lasts for 10 minutes per caster level of the character who cast the spell or performed the exorcism, after which point the quori spirit can return and possess the human vessel again.

If a quori spirit returns to Dal Quor for any reason (to protect its body, for example), its human vessel loses the benefits of the dual spirit and all the quori's psi-like and spell-like abilities until the quori spirit returns.

Naturally Psionic (Ex): An Inspired gains 1 extra power point per character level, regardless of whether she chooses a psionic class.

Inspired Shock Trooper

Tsoreva Quori Spirit/2nd-Level Inspired Psychic Warrior Vessel

Medium Humanoid (Human, Psionic)

Hit Dice: 2d8+10 (22 hp)

Initiative: +1

Speed: 40 ft. (8 squares)

AC: 17 (+1 Dex, +4 *inertial armor*, +2 heavy steel shield), touch 11, flat-footed 16

Base Attack/Grapple: +1/+2

Attack: Masterwork Riedran crysteel longsword +4 melee (1d8+2, 19–20)

Full Attack: Masterwork Riedran crysteel longsword +4 melee (1d8+2, 19–20)

Space/Reach: 5 ft./5 ft.

Special Attacks: Psi-like abilities, psionic powers

Special Qualities: Dual spirit, naturally psionic

Saves: Fort +5, Ref +1, Will +3

Abilities: Str 13, Dex 12, Con 14, Int 15, Wis 17, Cha 21

Skills: Autohypnosis +17, Bluff +16*, Concentration +17, Diplomacy +9*, Disguise +8 (+10 when imitating a human)*, Intimidate +14*, Jump +9, Listen +12, Knowledge (psionics) +16, Knowledge (the planes) +14, Psicraft +16, Search +7, Sense Motive +10, Spot +10

Feats: Psionic Body, Psionic Weapon, Speed of Thought, Weapon Focus (longsword)

Environment: Any

Organization: Solitary, pair, or squad (2–5 plus 1 tsucora quori spirit/Inspired psion vessel; see page 290 of the EBERRON Campaign Setting)

Challenge Rating: 3

Treasure: Standard

Alignment: Usually lawful evil

Advancement: By character class

Level Adjustment: —

A slim but muscular figure blocks your progress, easily steadying into a catlike fighting stance. A dim glow emanates from his confident eyes as he raises his glistening violet-hued longsword in a battle salute. A shimmering field of force surrounds him.

Some vessels are bred to serve as the elite foot soldiers of Riedra and the Dreaming Dark. Formidable psychic warriors in their own right, these vessels serve as hosts for tsoreva quori spirits (see page 147). These Inspired are used as shock troops, deployed wherever a quick and dreadful strike is needed.

Tsoreva quori vessels are a slightly stronger and hardier stock than a typical Inspired vessel. Like all Inspired, these vessels are tall and slender, with almond-shaped eyes, pale skin, and long, straight hair that varies from black to shades of blue, purple, or green.

Combat

Called into action when more mundane forces are not adequate, shock troopers strike quickly and strike hard. A shock trooper has *inertial armor* active whenever combat might be near.

Knowing that a devastating initial blow can end a fight before it begins, a shock trooper typically manifests *dissolving weapon* in the opening round, adding an extra 4d6 points of acid damage to his next strike, then expending his psionic focus to add another 2d6 points of damage to that attack (from his Psionic Weapon feat).

If given warning before combat begins, a shock trooper manifests *biofeedback* (giving him damage reduction 2/— for 2 minutes) and *offensive precognition* (+1 insight bonus on attack rolls for 2 minutes). He can activate this suite of powers up to three times each day thanks to his 6 power points.

Psi-Like Abilities: 3/day—*inertial armor*; 1/day—*dissolving weapon.* Manifester level 4th.

Psionic Powers: As a 2nd-level psychic warrior, the shock trooper knows two psionic powers of 1st level. The save DCs for the psychic warrior's psionic powers are Wisdom-based.

Typical Psychic Warrior Powers Known (power points 6): 1st—*biofeedback, offensive precognition.*

Dual Spirit (Ex): Bereft of its quori spirit, a shock trooper vessel has the following skill modifiers: Bluff +6, Concentration +7, Diplomacy +6, Disguise +4 (+6 when imitating a human), Intimidate +6, Jump +9, Search +7.

Skills: *An Inspired gains a +2 racial bonus on Bluff, Diplomacy, and Intimidate checks. He also gains a +2 racial bonus on Disguise checks made to impersonate a human.

Inquisitors are covert agents that can perform delicate tasks; shock troopers can strike quickly and strike hard

Urdarks take shape from the bodies of the utterly insane

T. GIORELLO

Combat

Urdarks prefer to attack from ambush. Their incorporeality makes them eminently suitable for sneaking up on any potential victims. When they attack, their opponents must immediately contend with the unsettling aura caused by the creatures' incessant and disturbing childlike laughter. Urdarks then use their incorporeal touch to deal Wisdom damage to their victims.

Create Spawn (Su): Any humanoid or monstrous humanoid reduced to Wisdom 0 by an urdark becomes an urdark within 2d4 rounds. Its body remains intact and inanimate, but its spirit is torn free of its corpse and transformed. Unlike the spawn of other undead, the spawn of urdarks are not under the control of the creature that created them.

Unsettling Aura (Su): The childlike giggling of an urdark is extremely disturbing. Any creature within 30 feet of an urdark becomes shaken for 1 minute unless it succeeds on a DC 17 Will save. Creatures that successfully save cannot be affected by the same urdark's unsettling aura for 24 hours. This is a mind-affecting sonic fear effect. The save DC is Charisma-based and includes a +2 bonus for the urdark's Ability Focus feat.

Wisdom Damage (Su): An urdark deals 1d6 points of Wisdom damage each time it hits with its incorporeal touch attack. Any creature reduced to Wisdom 0 by an urdark dies. On each successful attack, an urdark gains 5 temporary hit

points, which last for 1 hour. An urdark can only gain temporary hit points equal to its normal hit point total.

Any creature struck by an urdark's attack must succeed on a DC 15 Will save or have 1 point of Wisdom damage treated as Wisdom drain.

VOUR

Medium Undead
Hit Dice: 10d12+20 (85 hp)
Initiative: +3
Speed: 30 ft. (6 squares), fly 30 ft. (perfect)
Armor Class: 19 (+3 Dex, +6 natural), touch 13, flat-footed 16
Base Attack/Grapple: +5/+14
Attack: Tentacle +11 melee (1d6+5)
Full Attack: Four tentacles +11 melee (1d6+5) and bite +8 melee (2d6+2/19–20 plus energy drain)
Space/Reach: 5 ft./5 ft.
Special Attacks: Create spawn, energy drain, improved grab
Special Qualities: Darkvision 60 ft., fast healing 5, scent, undead traits, unholy toughness
Saves: Fort +3, Ref +6, Will +9
Abilities: Str 21, Dex 16, Con —, Int 8, Wis 14, Cha 15
Skills: Hide +10, Listen +15, Move Silently +9, Spot +15
Feats: Cleave, Improved Critical (bite), Multiattack, Power Attack, Track[B], Weapon Focus (tentacle)
Environment: Underground
Organization: Solitary, pair, or pack (3–6)
Challenge Rating: 7
Treasure: Standard
Alignment: Always neutral evil
Advancement: 11–18 HD (Medium); 19–30 HD (Large)
Level Adjustment: —

The torso of some humanoid creature floats in the air before you. Where its arms and legs should be, tentacles writhe and twist in the air. The creature's jaw is terribly distended, filled with at least three rows of broken, gnashing teeth. Its lashing tongue is cut and abraded from its awful fangs, but the creature seems unfazed. Its hairless body is drawn and withered, with purple veins throbbing just beneath the surface of its taut skin. However, the creature's most terrible feature is the remains of its face. Its eyes protrude from sockets above a hole where its nose should be, and the raw sore of its shredded flesh oozes a constant flow of foul ichor.

Vours are terrible undead spawned from the laboratories of Karrnath's chief necromancer, Count Vedim ir'Omik. One of his earliest experiments, the research that led to the first vour was intended to produce a creature that could create spawn quickly, was amenable to command (but intelligent enough to follow complex orders), and had greater mobility than Karrnathi zombies or skeletons. The first experiments were failures until Vedim tried duplicating the flotation magic of the beholders. The tentacles—a completely unexpected side effect—seemed similar enough to eyestalks that Vedim quietly surmised that perhaps the beholder's flotation and tentacles were physiologically connected in some way.

Relatively few vours have been encountered in Karrnath as yet, let alone the rest of Khorvaire. However, the creatures breed quickly, and a few of Vedim's field tests have resulted in unrecovered corpses that later spawned more of the creatures. A few have been encountered near Korth, where Vedim's main laboratory is located, with some spotted as far away as the Mournland and the Talenta Plains. Their great mobility has enabled the vours to spread much more quickly than Vedim would have liked, but no connection has yet been made between Karrnath and the appearance of these undead. So far, the count is unconcerned about the few renegade vours that have come to light, and King Kaius III remains apparently unaware of their existence.

The first vours were created from the terribly twisted bodies of captured wights. Vedim appreciated the wights' energy drain ability, as well as their ability to quickly reproduce. Vours live to feed on the flesh of the living, but some perverse accident of their creation makes them desire to eat only the faces of their fallen foes. Once a victim has succumbed to their physical attacks or energy drain, a vour carefully, almost lovingly, peels the flesh and skin from the victim's face and devours it ravenously. In fact, newly spawned vours always tear their own faces off and devour them shortly after their creation. For this reason, the creatures are also sometimes called "face eaters."

Vours can move quickly along the ground using their four tentacles as limbs, but they prefer to fly.

Combat

A vour attacks with the aid of its fellows whenever possible, so the creatures are most often encountered in small packs. They are perfectly aware of their ability to create new spawn, so fresh additions to the pack are never hard to come by should a member fall in battle. The creatures prefer to kill quickly, relying on their four-tentacle full attack and Power Attack feat to bring their foes down. They try to grapple smaller creatures first in combat and will typically attack from above, floating down from the concealment of treetops or the dark eaves of buildings to surprise their next meals. Once a victim is down, a vour—alone or one in the pack—typically scoops it up and floats away with it to devour its face in peace.

Create Spawn (Su): Any humanoid slain by a vour's energy drain attack becomes a vour in 1d4 hours. Spawn are under the command of the vour that created them and remain enslaved until its death. They do not possess any of the abilities they had in life. The transformation from corpse to vour is sudden. The victim's arms and legs are shed from its body as writhing tentacles sprout from the gaping wounds left behind (which quickly close due to the creature's fast healing ability). Its jaw grows and distends as extra teeth sprout from it, and if it still has a face, it quickly tears it off and devours it in a single gulp.

Energy Drain (Su): Living creatures hit by a vour's bite attack gain one negative level. The DC is 17 for the Fortitude save to remove a negative level. The save DC is Charisma-based. For each such negative level bestowed, a vour gains 5 temporary hit points.

Improved Grab (Ex): To use this ability, a vour must hit a Large or smaller opponent with a tentacle attack. It can then attempt to start a grapple as a free action without provoking an attack of opportunity. If it wins the grapple check, it establishes a hold and deals automatic bite damage each round. A vour has a +4 racial bonus on grapple checks due to its four prehensile tentacles, which is already factored into the statistics above.

Unholy Toughness (Ex): A vour gains bonus hit points equal to its Charisma modifier [ts] its Hit Dice.

HOMUNCULUS

The homunculi presented here represent additional variations of the companion constructs created by the artificers and wizards of Khorvaire. Like the homunculi presented in the EBERRON *Campaign Setting* and the *Monster Manual*, these new homunculi are extensions of their creators, sharing the same alignment and basic nature. They are telepathically linked to their creators. A homunculus knows what its creator knows and can convey to its creator everything it sees and hears, out to a distance of 1,500 feet. A homunculus never travels beyond this distance willingly, though it can be moved forcibly.

An attack that destroys a homunculus deals 2d10 points of damage to its master. If the master is slain, the homunculus also dies, and its body disintegrates.

Construct Traits: A homunculus has immunity to poison, sleep effects, paralysis, stunning, disease, death effects, necromancy effects, mind-affecting spells and abilities (charms, compulsions, phantasms, patterns, and morale effects), and any effect that requires a Fortitude save unless it also works on objects or is harmless. It is not subject to extra damage from critical hits, nonlethal damage, ability damage, ability drain, fatigue, exhaustion, or energy drain. It cannot heal damage, but it can be repaired. It has darkvision out to 60 feet and low-light vision.

Construction

Each kind of homunculus has a body constructed from different sorts of materials. Each individual description indicates the materials, cost, and Craft skill and DC required to make the body. The creature's master can assemble the body or hire someone else to do the job.

After the body is made, it is animated through an

Vours have a taste for face flesh

extended magical ritual that requires a specially prepared laboratory or workroom, similar to an alchemist's laboratory and costing 500 gp to establish. If the creator is personally constructing the creature's body, the building and ritual can be performed together.

ARBALESTER

Tiny Construct
Hit Dice: 1d10 (5 hp)
Initiative: +4
Speed: 10 ft. (2 squares)
AC: 16 (+2 size, +4 Dex), touch 16, flat-footed 12
Base Attack/Grapple: +0/−9
Attack: Bite +1 melee (1d4−1) or masterwork light crossbow +7 ranged (1d8/19–20)
Full Attack: Bite +1 melee (1d4−1) or masterwork light crossbow +7 ranged (1d8/19–20)
Space/Reach: 2–1/2 ft./0 ft.
Special Attacks: Receive enhancement
Special Qualities: Construct traits, darkvision 60 ft., low-light vision
Saves: Fort +0, Ref +4, Will +0
Abilities: Str 8, Dex 19, Con —, Int 12, Wis 10, Cha 7
Skills: Balance +8, Listen +4, Spot +4
Feats: Point Blank Shot
Environment: Any
Organization: Solitary
Challenge Rating: 1/2
Treasure: None
Alignment: Any (same as creator)
Advancement: 2–3 HD (Tiny)
Level Adjustment: —

What at first appeared to be a carving of arms and a face on the stock of a crossbow suddenly springs to life, the arms moving to reload the crossbow while the face looks for another target.

An arbalester is a homunculus created to assist with ranged attacks. Built around the stock of a light crossbow, the arbalester can fire and reload the crossbow using the normal rules for crossbow attacks. The arbalester includes a quiver capable of carrying 20 bolts. Bolts stored in the quiver do not count against the creature's carrying capacity. Once built, the crossbow and arbalester cannot be separated without destroying the homunculus.

Combat

An arbalester is somewhat effective at providing ranged support, shooting targets designated by its master. An arbalester is automatically proficient with the crossbow that has been built into its body.

Receive Enhancement (Ex): The crossbow built into an arbalester can be magically enhanced as if it were a normal masterwork weapon. The costs for enhancing the weapon with enhancement bonuses and other special qualities are independent of those associated with constructing or advancing the homunculus.

Construction

An arbalester is carved from green wood, threads of silver and gold, a pint of the creator's blood, and a masterwork light crossbow. The materials cost 350 gp. Creating the body requires a DC 14 Craft (sculpting) or a DC 14 Craft (carpentry) check.

An arbalester with more than 1 Hit Die can be created, but each additional Hit Die adds 2,000 gp to the cost to create.

Craft Construct, *arcane eye, mending*; Price — (never sold); Cost 1,250 gp + 93 XP.

PACKMATE

Small Construct
Hit Dice: 2d10+13 (24 hp)
Initiative: +0
Speed: 30 ft. (6 squares)
AC: 15 (+1 size, +4 natural), touch 11, flat-footed 15
Base Attack/Grapple: +1/+0
Attack: Slam +5 melee (1d3+3)
Full Attack: Slam +5 melee (1d3+3)
Space/Reach: 5 ft./5 ft.
Special Attacks: Throw flask
Special Qualities: Construct traits, darkvision 60 ft., feed potion, hold item, low-light vision, ready item
Saves: Fort +0, Ref +0, Will +1
Abilities: Str 16, Dex 11, Con —, Int 8, Wis 12, Cha 7
Skills: Climb +6, Swim +5
Feats: Toughness
Environment: Any
Organization: Solitary
Challenge Rating: 1
Treasure: None
Alignment: Any (same as creator)
Advancement: 3–6 HD (Small)
Level Adjustment: —

A chest that moments ago was resting upon the floor suddenly stands on legs of its own. As it opens a lid on its top, an arm folds out from the side of the chest and begins sifting through the contents of its internal compartments.

A packmate homunculus is designed to carry items for its master. It resembles a wood and metal chest with many compartments. Four legs support it from below while two arms, tipped with pincerlike claws, stow and store items.

The compartments on the packmate are difficult to open. Treat each as if protected by an *arcane lock* spell cast by a 3rd-level caster.

A packmate can carry up to 76 pounds as a light load, 153 pounds as a medium load, or 230 pounds as a heavy load.

Combat

A packmate homunculus's place in combat is at the side of its master, where it can retrieve items or pick up anything dropped on the ground.

Throw Flask (Ex): A packmate can be directed to make ranged attacks with vials of acid, holy water, or similar splash weapons. It can throw any such item it carries.

Feed Potion (Ex): A packmate is dexterous enough to retrieve a potion from one of its storage compartments, uncork it, and administer it to a fallen creature. A packmate is typically given instructions to use a *cure* potion on its master if he falls.

Ready Item (Ex): The telepathic connection between a packmate and its master allows the packmate to anticipate what item its master might call for next. If the homunculus and its master are adjacent, then the master can retrieve an item from the packmate as a swift action that does not provoke attacks of opportunity.

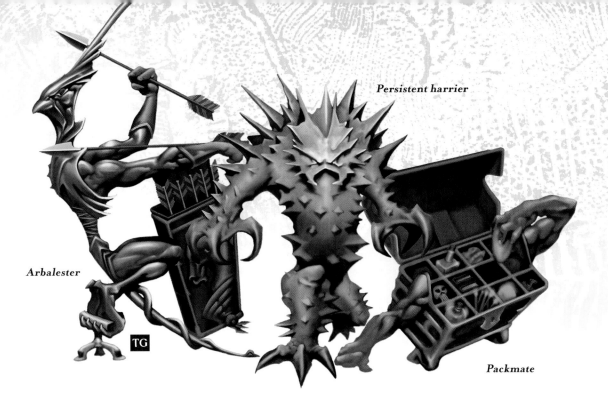

Persistent harrier

Arbalester

TG

Packmate

Construction

A packmate is crafted from wood, metal, and a pint of the creator's blood. The materials cost 50 gp. Creating the body requires a DC 14 Craft (sculpting) check.

A packmate with more than 2 Hit Dice can be created, but each additional Hit Die adds 2,000 gp to the cost to create.

Craft Construct, *arcane lock, arcane eye, mending*; Price — (never sold); Cost 1,260 gp + 93 XP.

PERSISTENT HARRIER

Small Construct
Hit Dice: 2d10+10 (21 hp)
Initiative: +3
Speed: 40 ft. (8 squares)
AC: 18 (+1 size, +3 Dex, +4 natural), touch 14, flat-footed 15
Base Attack/Grapple: +1/−2
Attack: Spike +3 melee (1d6+1)
Full Attack: Spike +3 melee (1d6+1)
Space/Reach: 5 ft./5 ft.
Special Attacks: Sneak attack +1d6
Special Qualities: Construct traits, darkvision 60 ft., low-light vision
Saves: Fort +0, Ref +3, Will +0
Abilities: Str 12, Dex 16, Con —, Int 11, Wis 10, Cha 7
Skills: Jump +14, Tumble +12
Feats: Acrobatic
Environment: Any
Organization: Solitary
Challenge Rating: 1
Treasure: None
Alignment: Any (same as creator)
Advancement: 4–6 HD (Small)
Level Adjustment: —

A small, wiry figure darts between the legs of combatants, poking dangerous-looking spikes toward its foes.

Barely 2 feet tall, a persistent harrier is designed to be in the middle of combat, distracting opponents or setting up flanking opportunities.

Combat

A persistent harrier will move around into flanking position, taking a 5-foot step or using the Tumble skill where appropriate. If it does not attack, it can be directed to use the aid another action to provide an Armor Class or attack roll boost.

Sneak Attack (Ex): A persistent harrier deals an extra 1d6 points of damage when it is flanking an opponent or at any time when the target would be denied its Dexterity bonus. See the rogue class feature, page 50 of the *Player's Handbook*.

Construction

A persistent harrier is crafted from leather, metal, clay, and a pint of the creator's blood. The materials cost 50 gp. Creating the body requires a DC 14 Craft (sculpting) check.

A persistent harrier with more than 1 Hit Die can be created, but each additional Hit Die adds 2,000 gp to the cost to create.

Craft Construct, *arcane eye, mending*; Price — (never sold); Cost 1,250 gp + 93 XP.

SYMBIONTS

As many of Khorvaire's wisest have long suspected, daelkyr magic is the original source of the symbiont creatures that now writhe and wriggle their way across (and under) Eberron. The following symbionts add to those introduced in the EBERRON Campaign Setting, See page 298 of the EBERRON Campaign Setting for more information on symbionts.

Symbiont Traits: When joined with a host, a symbiont gains a number of benefits. It acts on its host's turn each round, regardless of its own initiative modifier. It is not flat-footed unless its host is, and it is aware of any danger its host is aware of.

If a symbiont is grafted onto a visible part of the host creature's body, opponents can attack the symbiont itself instead of its host creature. Doing this works the same way as attacking an object: The symbiont gains the benefit of the host's Dexterity modifier to AC instead of its own, and gains any deflection bonus to AC the host has as well. Its own size modifier and natural armor bonus, if any, apply.

Attacking a symbiont instead of its host provokes an attack of opportunity from the host.

A symbiont never takes damage from attacks directed at the host. Like a worn magic item, a symbiont is usually unaffected by spells that damage the host, but if the host rolls a 1 on its saving throw, the symbiont is one of the "items" that can be affected by the spell (see Items Surviving after a Saving Throw, page 177 of the *Player's Handbook*). A symbiont uses its host's base saving throw bonuses if they are better than its own.

Share Spells (Su): Any spell the host creature casts on itself automatically also affects the symbiont. Additionally, the host can cast a spell with a target of "You" on its symbiont instead of on itself. Likewise, a symbiont can choose to have any spell or spell-like ability it uses on itself also affect the host creature, and can cast a spell with a target of "You" on its host instead of itself. The host and symbiont can share spells even if the spells normally do not affect creatures of the host's or symbiont's type. Spells targeted on the host by another spellcaster do not affect the symbiont, and vice versa.

BREED LEECH

Tiny Aberration (Symbiont)
Hit Dice: 1d8 (4 hp)
Initiative: +2
Speed: 20 ft. (4 squares)
Armor Class: 15 (+2 size, +2 Dex, +1 natural), touch 14, flat-footed 13
Base Attack/Grapple: +0/–10
Attack: Bite +4 melee (1d3–2)
Full Attack: Bite +4 melee (1d3–2)
Space/Reach: 2-1/2 ft./5 ft.
Special Attacks: —
Special Qualities: Symbiont traits, bolster body, blindsight 60 ft., telepathy
Saves: Fort +0, Ref +4, Will +1
Abilities: Str 6, Dex 15, Con 11, Int 5, Wis 8, Cha 10, Ego 2
Skills: Hide +12, Move Silently +4
Feats: Lightning Reflexes, Weapon Finesse^B
Environment: Underground
Organization: Solitary
Challenge Rating: 1 (singly) or host +1 (when worn)
Treasure: None
Alignment: Usually lawful evil
Advancement: None
Level Adjustment: —

An eyeless black slug pulls itself forward, its tri-mandibled mouth clacking and grasping, seeking to attach itself to living flesh.

Breed leeches are an extraordinary leap in daelkyr corruption magic. Instilled in each leech is a terrible infection that corrupts a regular pregnancy if allowed to run its course. The resulting child is born a daelkyr half-blood (see page 37). The vile purpose of a breed leech is to extend the influence of the daelkyr in the waking

SYMBIONTS AND GRAFTS AS TREASURE

Symbionts enhance a character's abilities in much the same way as magic items, but they are not as readily available. Symbionts can be found and recovered as treasure, or encountered as creatures and acquired that way. Because of their disturbing nature, the unique difficulties of stocking such creatures, and the general fear of aberrations across Eberron, symbionts are never available on the open market.

With enough searching (and a willingness to deal with many dangerous and deceptive creatures), a character might find a symbiont for sale. The work required to find and acquire a symbiont should, in most cases, equate to a short adventure or side quest.

Because symbionts affect a character's abilities like equipment does, their power level is measured in gold pieces. The numbers below do not represent a sale price, but rather serve as a means of comparing a symbiont's value to other treasure. The easiest way to use these numbers is to simply remove an equivalent amount of treasure from a different encounter whenever a symbiont is encountered on its own.

When adding a symbiont to an NPC, the Dungeon Master should count the symbiont's gp equivalent as part of the total value of the NPC's equipment. After all, the powers granted by a symbiont are directly included in the NPC's Challenge Rating just like magic items are. However, since many player characters might be loathe to use a captured symbiont, a DM might choose to augment the NPC's treasure (but not equipment) by an amount somewhere between 50% and 100% of the symbiont's gp equivalent. For example, if the PCs defeat an NPC wearing a stormstalk but

are unwilling claim it as treasure, the DM should consider adding somewhere between 2,000 and 4,000 gp of treasure to the NPC's hoard (in the form of jewelry, gems, or coins, but not additional equipment). The lower end of this range is what a party would get for selling an equivalent magic item, while the upper end is how much an equivalent magic item would cost them to buy.

Symbiont	GP Equivalent
Breed leech	2,000
Crawling gauntlet	2,000
Living breastplate*	No gp value†
Shadow sibling	8,000
Spellwurm	8,000
Stormstalk	4,000
Tentacle whip*	8,000
Tongueworm*	25,000
Throwing scarab	1,000
Winter cyst	4,000

*See page 298 of the EBERRON *Campaign Setting*.
†Artifact-level item.

When adding grafts (see page 126) to an NPC, the DM should take a similar approach. Since an NPC's grafts are almost certainly not going to be claimed as treasure, the monetary reward for defeating such an NPC is lower than it would be for an NPC with a magic item of equivalent power. If you anticipate this being a problem, consider adding treasure to the NPC's hoard (as described above) to make up for the loss.

world, creating aberrations that partake of a daelkyr's deranged power.

A breed leech does not speak any language, but it understands Undercommon.

Combat

A breed leech can attach itself only to a willing or helpless host (as a full-round action). In general, a creature either seeks out a breed leech to gain its benefits or encounters the breed leech accidentally. The breed leech attaches with its tri-mandibled mouth, usually on the back of the upper arm, the shoulder, or the lower leg. As such, it is not usually visible on creatures that wear clothing.

Attaching or removing a breed leech deals 1d3−2 points of damage and 1d3 points of Constitution damage.

Host Benefit: A creature with an attached breed leech gains the benefit of the breed leech's bolster body ability.

Bolster Body (Su): While a breed leech is attached to a creature, the host is flooded with bolstering chemicals. The supercharged host gains 5 bonus hit points per day (which replace any leftover bonus hit points granted by the breed leech on the previous day) and a +1 bonus on Fortitude saves.

Symbiont Traits: See page 299 of the EBERRON Campaign Setting.

Telepathy (Su): A breed leech can communicate telepathically with its host, if its host has a language.

CRAWLING GAUNTLET
Tiny Aberration (Symbiont)
Hit Dice: 1d8 (4 hp)
Initiative: +8

Speed: 20 ft. (4 squares)
Armor Class: 17 (+2 size, +4 Dex, +1 natural), touch 16, flat-footed 13
Base Attack/Grapple: +0/−10
Attack: Claw +6 melee (1d4−2 plus strangle)
Full Attack: Claw +6 melee (1d4−2 plus strangle)
Space/Reach: 2-1/2 ft./5 ft.
Special Attacks: —
Special Qualities: Symbiont traits, telepathy
Saves: Fort +0, Ref +4, Will +1
Abilities: Str 6, Dex 18, Con 11, Int 5, Wis 8, Cha 10, Ego 3
Skills: Hide +14, Move Silently +6
Feats: Improved Initiative, Weapon Finesse[B]
Environment: Underground
Organization: Solitary
Challenge Rating: 1 (singly) or host +1 (when worn)
Treasure: None
Alignment: Usually lawful evil
Advancement: None
Level Adjustment: —

A reddish blot spiders forward on five legs. As it scampers closer, its shape resolves into palm, fingers, and trailing forearm—the creature is a disembodied hand, grasping its way forward, eager to clutch and choke. A resinous crust covers the gauntlet, giving it an even more ominous appearance.

Crawling gauntlets are a naturally evolved symbiont that first appeared on daelkyr half-bloods. The daelkyr now commonly outfit their own aberration servants with these helpful hands.

A crawling gauntlet does not speak any language, but it understands Undercommon.

Shadow sibling

Stormstalk

Winter cyst

Crawling gauntlet

Throwing scarab

Breed leech

Spellwurm

Combat

A crawling gauntlet can attach itself only to a willing or helpless host (as a full-round action). In general, a creature either seeks out a crawling gauntlet to gain its benefits, or encounters a crawling gauntlet accidentally. A crawling gauntlet surrounds the host's hand and forearm like a real gauntlet, sending tiny tendrils into the flesh to feed itself directly from the host's blood.

Attaching or removing a crawling gauntlet deals 1d3 points of Constitution damage.

Host Benefit: A creature with an attached crawling gauntlet gains a natural claw attack. The damage dealt by this claw attack depends on the creature's size, as indicated below.

Size	Claw Damage
Small	1d3
Medium	1d4
Large	1d6
Huge	1d8
Gargantuan	2d6
Colossal	2d8

If the creature already has a better claw or slam attack, the crawling gauntlet has no effect on the creature's attack, but the other symbiont traits still apply.

Symbiont Traits: See page 299 of the EBERRON *Campaign Setting.*

Telepathy (Su): A crawling gauntlet can communicate telepathically with its host, if its host has a language.

SHADOW SIBLING

Medium Aberration (Symbiont, Incorporeal)
Hit Dice: 1d8+3 (7 hp)
Initiative: +4
Speed: 15 ft. (3 squares)
Armor Class: 15 (+4 Dex, +1 insight), touch 15, flat-footed 11
Base Attack/Grapple: +0/—
Attack: Incorporeal touch +4 melee (1d6)
Full Attack: Incorporeal touch +4 melee (1d6)
Space/Reach: 5 ft./5 ft.
Special Attacks: Corrupting touch
Special Qualities: Symbiont traits, second skin, telepathy
Saves: Fort +0, Ref +4, Will +2
Abilities: Str —, Dex 19, Con —, Int 5, Wis 12, Cha 10, Ego 2
Skills: Hide +14, Spot +4
Feats: Toughness, Weapon Finesse[B]
Environment: Underground
Organization: Solitary
Challenge Rating: 1 (singly) or host +1 (when worn)
Treasure: None
Alignment: Usually lawful evil
Advancement: None
Level Adjustment: —

A diaphanous shape undulates forward, shaped faintly like a humanoid, but hollow and faceless.

Despite their appearance, shadow siblings are not undead, just immaterial. A shadow sibling is twin to the daelkyr half-blood with which it was birthed (see page 37), or to the other character who later grows or acquires one.

A shadow sibling does not speak any language, but it understands Undercommon.

Combat

A shadow sibling can attach itself only to a willing or helpless host (as a full-round action). In general, a creature seeks out a shadow sibling (or grows one, as in the case of a half-blood) to gain its benefits. A shadow sibling completely bonds with its host, melding flesh with incorporeal substance.

Attaching or removing a shadow sibling deals 1d3 points of Wisdom damage.

Host Benefit: A shadow sibling settles around its host like a second skin, granting the host protection from some physical attacks. While wearing a shadow sibling, a creature can gain 50% concealment against any single attack as an immediate action. You must decide whether to use this benefit before you know the result of the attack roll. The creature can use this ability a number of times per day equal to its Constitution modifier (minimum once per day). This concealment has no effect against weapons or effects that ignore the miss chance of incorporeal creatures (such as force effects or weapons enhanced with the ghost touch special ability). Using this ability does not provoke attacks of opportunity.

Moreover, a shadow sibling partly blocks ambient light, giving the host creature and its equipment a shadowy appearance even in full daylight. This effect grants the host a +4 circumstance bonus on Hide checks.

While attached to the host, a shadow sibling does not make any attacks of its own.

Corrupting Touch (Ex): If a shadow sibling makes a successful touch attack, it disrupts a foe with its ability to bond flesh, dealing 1d6 points of damage.

Symbiont Traits: See page 299 of the EBERRON *Campaign Setting.*

Telepathy (Su): A shadow sibling can communicate telepathically with its host, if its host has a language.

SPELLWURM

Tiny Aberration (Symbiont)
Hit Dice: 1d8 (4 hp)
Initiative: +2
Speed: 20 ft. (4 squares)
Armor Class: 19 (+2 size, +2 Dex, +4 *mage armor*, +1 natural), touch 16, flat-footed 13
Base Attack/Grapple: +0/−10
Attack: Bite +4 melee (1d3−2)
Full Attack: Bite +4 melee (1d3−2)
Space/Reach: 2-1/2 ft./5 ft.
Special Attacks: Spells
Special Qualities: Symbiont traits, telepathy
Saves: Fort +0, Ref +2, Will +3
Abilities: Str 6, Dex 15, Con 11, Int 5, Wis 8, Cha 16, Ego 5
Skills: Hide +12, Move Silently +4
Feats: Iron Will, Weapon Finesse[B]
Environment: Underground
Organization: Solitary
Challenge Rating: 1 (singly) or host +1 (when worn)
Treasure: None
Alignment: Usually lawful evil
Advancement: None
Level Adjustment: —

A thick, purplish snake undulates forward, about as long and thick as a humanoid arm. Where a head would surmount a natural serpent you see a nest of five finger-length tentacles surrounding a horribly humanlike mouth.

The daelkyr create spellwurms for their servants, and they are most commonly found attached to beholders, dolgaunts, mind flayers, and daelkyr half-bloods.

A spellwurm does not speak any language, but it understands Undercommon.

Combat

A spellwurm can attach itself only to a willing or helpless host (as a full-round action). In general, a creature either seeks out a spellwurm to gain its benefits or encounters the spellwurm accidentally. A spellwurm attaches at its base, and can either take the place of a missing arm on a humanoid, or attach under the left or right arm to create a third tentaclelike appendage. In either case, the spellwurm can perform none of the natural functions of a real arm—it can only cast spells. It is usually hidden in the clothing of its host, only snaking out to gesticulate and cast its spells when combat beckons.

Attaching or removing a spellwurm deals 1d3 points of Constitution damage.

Host Benefit: A creature with an attached spellwurm gains increased spellcasting ability. Creatures that cast arcane spells spontaneously (such as sorcerers, bards, or warmages) gain *mage armor*, *ancient knowledge**, and *blur* as additional spells known, even if these spells are not normally on the spell list for their class. Wizards and other arcane spellcasters who prepare their spells ahead of time can prepare those same spells without the aid of a spellbook, as if they had previously known all those spell and taken the Spell Mastery feat for each.

*New spell described on page 94.

Spells: A spellwurm knows and can cast spells as a 5th-level sorcerer. When the spellwurm is attached to a host, this spellcasting ability is suppressed.

Typical Sorcerer Spells Known (6/7*/5): 0—*daze, ghost sound, mage hand, ray of frost, read magic, touch of fatigue* (DC 13); 1st—*cause fear* (DC 14), *mage armor, magic missile, sleep* (DC 14); 2nd—*ancient knowledge**, flaming sphere* (DC 15).

*The statistics block above assumes that the spellwurm has already used one 1st-level spell slot to cast *mage armor*.

**New spell described on page 94.

Symbiont Traits: See page 299 of the EBERRON *Campaign Setting*.

Telepathy (Su): A spellwurm can communicate telepathically with its host, if its host has a language.

STORMSTALK

Tiny Aberration (Symbiont)
Hit Dice: 1d8+3 (7 hp)
Initiative: +6
Speed: 10 ft. (2 squares)
Armor Class: 19 (+2 size, +6 Dex, +1 natural), touch 18, flat-footed 13
Base Attack/Grapple: +0/−4
Attack: Eye ray +8 ranged touch (3d6 electricity)
Full Attack: Eye ray +8 ranged touch (3d6 electricity)
Space/Reach: 2-1/2 ft./5 ft.
Special Attacks: Eye ray
Special Qualities: Symbiont traits, telepathy
Saves: Fort +0, Ref +6, Will +0

Abilities: Str 6, Dex 22, Con 10, Int 5, Wis 8, Cha 10, Ego 1
Skills: Hide +16, Move Silently +8
Feats: Toughness
Environment: Underground
Organization: Solitary
Challenge Rating: 1 (singly) or host +1 (when worn)
Treasure: None
Alignment: Usually lawful evil
Advancement: None
Level Adjustment: —

A wriggling snake reveals a single overly large eye dancing with static discharge. The creature has no mouth or other features, only a white eye staring at you.

Stormstalks are a daelkyr creation inspired by the eyestalks of a beholder. It is rumored that the daelkyr are working to create other beholder-inspired symbiont stalks, including charmstalks, woundstalks, sleepstalks, and a dreaded deathstalk.

A stormstalk does not speak any language, but it understands Undercommon.

Combat

A stormstalk can attach itself only to a willing or helpless host (as a full-round action). In general, a creature either seeks out a stormstalk to gain its benefits or encounters the stormstalk accidentally. The stormstalk sends rooting tendrils into the host's skull and braincase to feed itself directly from the host's blood and mind. The wriggling stalk can raise its single eye in any direction in order to bring its baleful gaze to bear.

Attaching or removing a stormstalk deals 1d3 points of Intelligence damage.

Host Benefit: As a standard action, a stormstalk's host can make a ranged touch attack with a ray of electricity emitted from the eye. This ray has a maximum range of 30 feet and deals 1d6 points of electricity damage. It also imposes a −2 penalty to Dexterity for 1 minute on the creature struck. Penalties from multiple rays (either from the same or separate stormstalks) do not stack.

While attached to the host, a stormstalk does not make any attacks of its own.

Eye Ray (Su): If not attached to a host, a stormstalk can make an eye ray attack every other round as a standard action. The eye ray has a range of 30 feet and deals 2d6 points of electricity damage. It also imposes a −4 penalty to Dexterity on the creature struck; this penalty lasts for 1 minute.

Symbiont Traits: See page 299 of the EBERRON *Campaign Setting*.

Telepathy (Su): A stormstalk can communicate telepathically with its host, if its host has a language.

THROWING SCARAB

Fine Aberration (Symbiont)
Hit Dice: 1d8 (4 hp)
Initiative: +1
Speed: 5 ft. (1 square), fly 60 ft. (perfect)
Armor Class: 19 (+8 size, +1 Dex), touch 19, flat-footed 18
Base Attack/Grapple: +0/−20
Attack: Bite +9 melee (1)
Full Attack: Bite +9 melee (1)
Space/Reach: 1/2 ft./0 ft.
Special Attacks: —

Special Qualities: Symbiont traits, darkvision 60 ft., telepathy
Saves: Fort +0, Ref +1, Will +2
Abilities: Str 3, Dex 12, Con 10, Int 5, Wis 12, Cha 6, Ego 2
Skills: Hide +17, Listen +5, Spot +5
Feats: Alertness, Weapon Finesse[B]
Environment: Underground
Organization: Solitary
Challenge Rating: 1 (singly) or host +1 (when worn)
Treasure: None
Alignment: Usually lawful evil
Advancement: None
Level Adjustment: —

This small, beautiful scarab looks like a piece of jewelry until it flutters its shimmering blue wings, which glisten in the light as if covered with a slick of oil. Also now visible is the creature's double set of wickedly sharp mandibles.

A throwing scarab is a special symbiont—vicious in its own right, but also capable of providing its host with a throwing weapon. When inactive, it is difficult to pick out (and thus makes an excellent concealed weapon).

A throwing scarab does not speak any language, but it understands Undercommon.

Combat

A throwing scarab can attach itself only to a willing or helpless host (as a full-round action). In general, a potential host either seeks out a throwing scarab (or grows one, in the case of a daelkyr half-blood) to gain its benefits. The throwing scarab prefers to attach to its host on the exterior of the hand, appearing like some strange decoration.

Attaching or removing a throwing scarab deals 1d3 points of Wisdom damage.

Host Benefit: A throwing scarab generates small shards of hard crystalline carapace. The host can grasp one of these shards as a free action and throw it as a normal ranged attack. The shard has a range increment of 20 feet, and the host is always proficient with it. When thrown in this fashion, the shard is treated as a magic weapon for the purpose of overcoming damage reduction. On a successful hit, the shard deals 1d6 points of slashing damage (critical 19–20/[ts]2) and then dissolves in its target, dealing an additional 1d6 points of acid damage.

At the beginning of the host's next action, the throwing scarab secretes another shard, allowing the host to throw one shard each round.

Shards do not last for more than 1 round once detached from the symbiont. If a shard is not used as a weapon within 1 round after being pulled from the symbiont, it dissolves harmlessly.

While attached to the host, a throwing scarab does not make any attacks of its own.

Symbiont Traits: See page 299 of the Eberron *Campaign Setting.*

Telepathy (Su): A throwing scarab can communicate telepathically with its host, if its host has a language.

WINTER CYST

Tiny Aberration (Symbiont)
Hit Dice: 1d8+3 (7 hp)
Initiative: +4
Speed: 5 ft. (1 square)
Armor Class: 17 (+2 size, +4 Dex, +1 natural), touch 16, flat-footed 13
Base Attack/Grapple: +0/−10
Attack: Eye ray +6 ranged touch (2d6 cold)
Full Attack: Eye ray +6 ranged touch (2d6 cold)
Space/Reach: 2-1/2 ft./5 ft.
Special Attacks: Eye ray
Special Qualities: Symbiont traits, telepathy
Saves: Fort +0, Ref +4, Will +1
Abilities: Str 6, Dex 19, Con 10, Int 5, Wis 8, Cha 10, Ego 1
Skills: Hide +14, Move Silently +6
Feats: Toughness
Environment: Underground
Organization: Solitary
Challenge Rating: 1 (singly) or host +1 (when worn)
Treasure: None
Alignment: Usually lawful evil
Advancement: None
Level Adjustment: —

A stubby, sluglike polyp inches forward, leaving a slime trail behind it. It heaves upright, then swivels the end of its upper portion to stare with a baleful white eye.

Winter cysts are a naturally evolved symbiont that first appeared on daelkyr half-bloods. The daelkyr now commonly outfit their own aberration servants with these helpful hands.

A winter cyst does not speak any language, but it understands Undercommon.

Combat

A winter cyst can attach itself only to a willing or helpless host (as a full-round action). In general, a creature seeks out a winter cyst to gain its benefits, or encounters the winter cyst accidentally. The winter cyst sends rooting tendrils into the host's skull and braincase to feed itself directly from the host's blood and mind. The stubby stalk raises its single eye to bring its baleful gaze to bear.

Attaching or removing a winter cyst deals 1d3 points of Intelligence damage.

Host Benefit: As a standard action, the host of a winter cyst can make a ranged touch attack with a ray of cold emitted from the eye. This ray has a maximum range of 30 feet and deals 1d6 points of cold damage. It also imposes a −2 penalty to Strength for 1 minute on the creature struck. Penalties from multiple rays (either from the same or separate winter cysts) do not stack.

While attached to the host, a winter cyst does not make any attacks of its own.

Eye Ray (Su): If not attached to a host, a winter cyst can make an eye ray attack every other round as a standard action. The eye ray has a range of 60 feet and deals 2d6 points of cold damage. It also imposes a −4 penalty to Strength for 1 minute on the creature struck.

Symbiont Traits: See page 299 of the Eberron *Campaign Setting.*

Telepathy (Su): A winter cyst can communicate telepathically with its host, if its host has a language.

INTRODUCTORY PRODUCTS

D&D® gaming is easy to learn, but can be hard to teach. With the DUNGEONS & DRAGONS® Basic Game, you can quickly bring your friends up to speed and get them ready for more adventure.

❖ DUNGEONS & DRAGONS Basic Game   0-7869-3409-3   ❏ $24.99   _____

ACCESSORIES

Keep your game moving with essential tools that put information at your fingertips. And add excitement to every session with ready-made adventures, maps, and more.

❖ EBERRON Character Sheets   0-7869-3849-8   ❏ $14.95   _____

❖ EBERRON Dungeon Master's Screen   0-7869-3850-1   ❏ $14.95   _____

❖ DUNGEONS & DRAGONS Dice   0-7869-3513-8   ❏ $9.95   _____

SUPPLEMENTS

Expand your options for developing characters, creating adventures, and building campaigns with books filled with new races, feats, equipment, spells, monsters, magic items, and more.

❖ Lords of Madness: The Book of Aberrations   0-7869-3657-6   ❏ $34.95   _____

❖ Races of the Wild   0-7869-3438-7   ❏ $29.95   _____

❖ Complete Adventurer   0-7869-2880-8   ❏ $29.95   _____

❖ Libris Mortis   0-7869-3433-6   ❏ $29.95   _____

❖ Weapons of Legacy   0-7869-3688-6   ❏ $34.95   _____

❖ Races of Eberron   0-7869-3658-4   ❏ $29.95   _____

❖ Sandstorm   0-7869-3655-X   ❏ $34.95   _____

❖ Monster Manual III   0-7869-3430-1   ❏ $34.95   _____

❖ Races of Stone   0-7869-3278-3   ❏ $29.95   _____

OTHER EBERRON® SUPPLEMENTS

Discover more action and intrigue with ready-made adventures and other books that highlight the world of EBERRON. Each supplement offers a wealth of information and inspiration that will add depth to your characters and detail to your campaign.

❖ Five Nations   0-7869-3690-8   ❏ $29.95   _____

❖ Grasp of the Emerald Claw   0-7869-3652-5   ❏ $9.95   _____

❖ Sharn: City of Towers   0-7869-3434-4   ❏ $29.95   _____

❖ Explorer's Handbook   0-7869-3691-6   ❏ $29.95   _____

Total: _____

Use this sheet to help friends and family find the books you want and when ordering from your favorite hobby shop or bookstore.

Name: _____   *Telephone:* _____

Address: _____

City: _____   *State:* _____

EXPLORE A WORLD OF EXCITEMENT

Adventure awaits around every corner in the expansive world of EBERRON®.
Throw open the covers of supplements such as *Sharn: City of Towers*™ and *Five Nations*™
to discover action, intrigue, and rich detail to add to your EBERRON campaign.

Look for them at your favorite hobby shop or bookstore.

wizards.com/eberron